RURAL DEVELOPMENT IN THE CARIBBEAN

P. I. Gomes
editor

Rural Development in the Caribbean

C. HURST & COMPANY, LONDON
ST. MARTIN'S PRESS, NEW YORK

First published in the United Kingdom by
C. Hurst & Co. (Publishers) Ltd.,
38 King Street, London WC2E 8JT,
and in the United States of America by
St. Martin's Press, Inc.,
175 Fifth Avenue, New York, NY 10010.

ISBNs
Hurst cased: 1-85065-001-2
Hurst paper: 1-85065-002-0

St. Martin's cased: 0-312-69599-3
St. Martin's paper: 0-312-69598-5

Library of Congress Cataloging-in-Publication Data

Main entry under title:

Rural development in the Caribbean.

    Bibliography: p.
    Includes index.
    1. Rural development--Caribbean area--Addresses,
essays, lectures. 2. Agriculture--Caribbean area--Ad-
dresses, essays, lectures. 3. Plantation life--Caribbean
area--Addresses, essays, lectures. 4. Villages--
Caribbean area--Addresses, essays, lectures.
5. Caribbean area--Economic conditions--Addresses,
essays, lectures. I. Gomes, P. I.
HN195.2.C6R87 1985   307.1'4'09729   85-14357
ISBN 0-312-69599-3
ISBN 0-312-69598-5 (pbk.)

Printed in Great Britain

ACKNOWLEDGMENTS

Any composite volume is fundamentally a cooperative endeavour. While it will hardly be possible to mention explicitly all those who contributed to the accomplishment of the end-product, it is incumbent on an editor not to be stinting in his gratitude where it is due.

When the initial idea of this volume was being toyed with, Robin Cohen, then Visiting Professor of Sociology at St Augustine, was extremely supportive. It was in no small way due to his encouragement over the last few years that the project has seen the light of day. Despite very demanding and anxious moments in the design and mounting of the Caribbean Agricultural Extension Project (CAEP), my two colleagues Michael Patton and Tom Henderson always saw fit to remind me that this book was not to be neglected. Their support in this and (much else) is deeply appreciated.

The kind consent of Dr Lloyd Rankine, Head of the Department of Agricultural Economics and Farm Management at St Augustine, to reproduce material from the Proceedings of the Third West Indian Agricultural Economic Conference is acknowledged with gratitude. We are also grateful for the permission of the publishers of the *IDS Bulletin* of the University of Sussex to utilize the chapter of Brian Pollitt from vol. 13, no. 4 of 1982.

The preparation of the manuscript demanded many hours of painstaking typing which was done by Miss M. Jiminez in her usual competent and inimitable manner; for her services I will always be very grateful. Mrs Karen Yorke and Mrs Anne-Marie Black gave invaluable assistance in bringing the final manuscript to completion. The other members of the team in the Department all contributed in their own various ways, and without their efforts this volume might only have been 'another good idea'. To the contributors, of course, I am profoundly indebted: their commitment and cooperation made my task rewarding, though it was heavy at times. I hope that such collaboration among colleagues will lead to other achievements for the benefit of the Caribbean people.

St Augustine, 1985   P.I. GOMES

CONTENTS

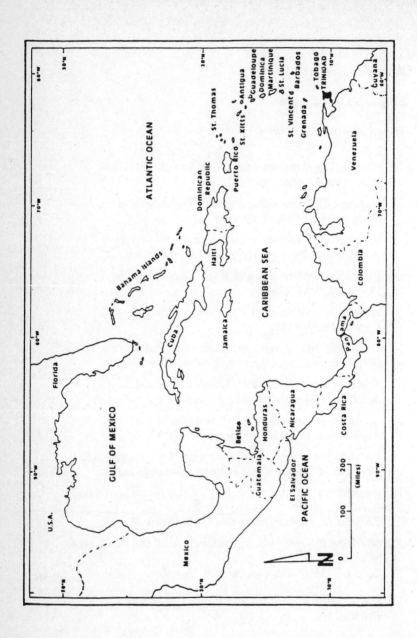

INTRODUCTION

P.I. Gomes

In these essays, we approach the subject of rural development both from the underlying structural factors by which the prevailing patterns of underdevelopment can be explained and from the direction in which strategies to overcome underdevelopment must be sought. In this sense the volume is meant to address both theoretical and practical policy measures in the rapidly expanding subject area of "rural development". It is hoped that interesting and challenging reflections will be stimulated for both scholars and practitioners.

To examine material derived from peculiar Caribbean experiences was thought necessary so as to maintain a specific geographical focus by which the "location-specific" factors in rural development can be more sharply identified from common "structural" issues. By this means fruitful comparative analyses are possible for a general understanding of development issues in relation to other geographical areas. At the same time, students and policy-makers or -implementers in the Caribbean region will also have a source-book that analyses causes of given "levels of development".

From even a cursory acquaintance with the literature of the Caribbean societies and cultures it will be clear that the essays do not equitably represent linguistic traditions, and we recognise this as a distinct limitation. The bulk of the material depicts rural situations in the English-speaking Caribbean. We have felt this limitation to be justifiable because the substantive issues treated were of such wide significance that their inclusion was considered beneficial, even though several other studies of different countries had to be excluded. To situate the studies in an appropriate historical and conceptual context, it will be helpful to provide a general overview of the theme, in the light of what we consider to be an "integrated and integral approach" to rural development.

The topic of Integrated Rural Development was the subject of a Caribbean Regional Workshop sponsored by the Caribbean Office of the United Nations Economic Commission for Latin America in Kingston, Jamaica, on 6–16 October 1969.[1] If not with the same detail, fundamental aspects of rural development were also the subject of the annual West Indies Agricultural Economics Conference for 1968, where the "bare bones" of the New World school were

---

1. See *Report of the Caribbean Regional Workshop on Integrated Rural Development*, Oct. 1969, UNECLA E/CN. 12/846.

articulated (see Best, pp. 283; Thomas' critique, pp. 339 etc.). It was then too that "rural development" — rather, the conditions of rural underdevelopment — were identified in their historical perspective of post-emancipation peasant development by Marshall and their socio-cultural context by Braithwaite. The general thrust of these analyses situated rural underdevelopment as a consequence of the structures of plantation capitalism. Of the chapters that follow, the first three by Marshall, Sleeman, and Acosta and Casimir set the historical stage in which the peasants, the plantation and the bourgeoisie played out their roles and pursued their conflicting interests. The concerns of the 1968 Conference and these brief historical portraits emphasise two important facts. The first is a reasonably *long-standing* concern of Caribbean social science with rural development/underdevelopment. It is necessary to say this because of late we have been asked to believe, and might actually be seduced into believing, that rural development is just the latest "fad" among development issues; if we were to perceive rural development in this way, our approach would, in time, seem to add up to little more than diversionary pronouncements on the so-called "rural poor" and so on. My second basic conclusion from reviewing previous literature on the topic is that to perceive the phenomenon of rural underdevelopment as historically determined through the exploitation of rural resources (human and natural) by a given socio-economic system is the only fruitful approach.

In this system the use of land and labour were such as to provide the dynamism for an on-going accumulation of wealth by those who owned capital and technology, controlled agricultural trade and marketing, and at the same time dominated the political mechanisms for decision-making in the society as a whole. To perceive rural underdevelopment as a function of the above sets of variables — namely land, labour, capital, technology, trade, marketing and political power — immediately suggests an approach to rural development that is structural and holistic; i.e. we need to define the present situation as the outcome of interconnected factors manifesting themselves through institutional forces. For instance, ownership and distribution of land in Commonwealth Caribbean societies are predominantly in the hands of the remnants of the plantocracy or foreign-based multinational corporations; hence the lack of ownership and the insecurity of tenure on the part of the large majority of the small farm population must be systematically related to the widespread rural poverty of these societies. In this way ownership of the critical resource of the countryside, the land, is seen as an underlying factor of rural poverty and rural underdevelopment. The problems of rural development are therefore traced to the need to overcome and redirect the persisting forces of underdevelopment which negate the goals and objectives of development for the great majority of rural populations.

It is important that we define an underlying perception of the problems of rural development since this will influence the form taken by attempts to overcome these problems and the kinds of strategies to be proposed. In our approach we advocate that attention should be directed to understanding the structural and causal factors of the phenomenon rather than its symptomatic and isolated aspects. To make such a distinction is not to deny or play down the need for understanding, in their entirety and by sound empirical means, the location-specific factors in the underdevelopment of a given rural community or region. These latter factors must always be investigated before programmes or projects for rural development are implemented. The chapters in this volume by Gomes, Pemberton and Durant-Gonzalez are examples of location-specific case-studies.

Our concern in this introduction is to identify the conceptual tools for a view of rural development which reveals an adequate understanding of the problem and offers appropriate strategies for its resolution.

Defining rural development

In the literature some concern has been expressed about arriving at what is meant by "rural" and the extent to which the concept can be precisely defined. But to debate what is "rural", where the demarcations between "rural" and "urban/industrial" are to be fixed, and whether these can be strictly adhered to for the purposes of development planning in a given society would be little more than an empty academic exercise. However, a general working definition to cover the *population clusters* and kinds of economic activities that can be referred to as "rural" is necessary. In a general sense, there should be no difficulty in recognising the Caribbean countryside as the geographical locale which embraces rural communities. The term "countryside" is meant to convey a demographic, economic and social entity distinct from areas such as capital cities, main towns or dormitory suburbs. The main characteristics of the rural sector of Caribbean societies will therefore include varying degrees of agriculturally-based economic activities, such as occupations on plantations/large estates as technical staff or wage-labour, small-farm subsistence cash-crop farming, fishing, and low-skilled trades and crafts. The populations employed in these activities can generally be said to live in "villages". As M.G. Smith noted some years ago, we can distinguish in the Caribbean "the flourishing country towns, fishing villages, certain isolated settlements, recently established government land settlements, the sugar areas with their plantation economies and social organization, and rural communities".[2] In this sense, *rural development can be understood as the development of the village populations of the Caribbean countryside.* The term "rural" is therefore relative. Rather than using a precise demographic connotation such as might be used in a population census — e.g. a Standard Metropolitan Statistical Area (SMSA) based on a quantified concentration of persons in a given area — we distinguish populations as rural on the basis of "participation" in agriculturally-related economic activities, and thus hope to avoid a misleading antithesis between industrial/urban and agricultural/rural development.

It is important to recognise that rural development is an integral part of the national development of Caribbean societies since the rural economy and society must be conceived as a sub-sector of the wider society. The widespread poverty of the countryside in societies dominated by the plantation system is therefore derived from structural underdevelopment. For historical reasons, this process of underdevelopment has manifested itself in a pattern associated with a "rural-urban imbalance", and as a consequence economic wealth, political power and social services are concentrated in urban centres, and the relative deprivation of the countryside results. The chain-reaction accompanying this imbalance is commonly referred to as "rural-urban drift", which has been consistently expressed in widespread labour migration of Caribbean peoples within the region and beyond.

If this process of underdevelopment is regarded as self-directing, natural or accidental, or caused by a lack of certain positive psychological attributes in rural populations, development strategies will be adopted which alleviate only the symptoms rather than the causes of underdevelopment. For this reason, as will be pointed out subsequently, it is necessary for rural development to be conceived and executed from both an integrated and integral approach.

According to Uma Lele (1976),[3] rural development may be defined as "improving living standards of the mass of low-income population residing in rural areas and making the process of their develop-

---

2.   Cf. M.G. Smith, *The Plural Society in the British West Indies*, Berkeley: University of California Press, 1965, pp. 177.
3.   See U. Lele, "Designing Rural Development Programmes: Lessons from Past Experience in Africa" in G. Hunter *et al.* (eds), *Policy and Practice in Rural Development*, London: Croom-Helm, 1976.

ment self-sustaining", for which three important measures are to be considered. The first involves "setting priorities in mobilisation and allocation of resources" which will reach a desirable balance over time between welfare and productive services available to the rural sector. Here the primary concern is *resource allocation* as an outcome of policy decisions. A second feature refers to a "choice of institutions" through which the productive and social services actually reach the target populations so that their living standards are improved. Consideration of this feature helps in the realisation of what is commonly called "integrated" development, i.e. a combination of economic wellbeing with adequate institutional services for education, health, recreation and even communications. The third aspect is making the process *self-sustaining*, and for this appropriate skills and an implementing capacity must be developed. This is a further dimension of institution-building as part of the process of rural development, and implies that education and training in the acquisition of skills must be given special consideration.

Reduced to its bare essentials, this definition helps us to see rural development in relation to resource allocation, and to institutional and training needs. However, while these may be necessary aspects of the problem, they can not suffice for an approach in which the rural sector is understood as an integral component of a wider system of social relations. Nor does this definition define precisely enough the social unit which is critical in the production, marketing and consumption process in rural areas. In other words it remains vague to speak of "the mass of low-income population residing in rural areas". Of whom does this "mass" consist? Is it an aggregate of individuals? Is it a social class with interests defined in antagonistic relations to other classes or groups whose development is necessarily at the expense of the rural poor or leads to their impoverishment? A comprehensive approach to rural development must therefore seek to answer these questions.

However, arriving at a tentative definition of rural development implies giving close attention to the empirical situation of rural underdevelopment, and here our observations and examination of the literature make us aware of two fundamental facts of Caribbean rural life: first, the all-pervasive importance of *the land tenure question*, i.e. the property relations surrounding the most basic resource of rural existence, the land; and secondly, *the centrality of the small-farm household* as the basic unit of social and economic activity. Accepting these two facts, we proceed to define rural development as "a systemic process in which the control and productive use of resources and opportunities are directed to material and qualitative improvements of standards of living by rural households". And this definition is helpful in understanding rural development in relation to:

(1) ongoing activities that have occurred over a period of time and of which various elements are recognisable patterns of behaviour;

(2) the exercise of power and authority by which decisions are made concerning resources or the means by which goods and services are produced, distributed or consumed;

(3) access to, and availability of, resources — particularly land and capital — so that they may be used in ways beneficial to defined human needs;

(4) the household as the fundamental, social, economic and cultural unit of human activity, for which the objective betterment of conditions of life remains the basic goal of development.

In the light of the above, the significance of the small-farm family or "peasant household structure" is central to both the objectives and strategies of any meaningful development. The following has been written in the context of Latin American peasant society:

The peasant household is both a unit of production and consumption. The family farm employs the husband and wife and the older children, in productive activity of producing food for its own consumption and for sale, if production and prices are satisfactory. The peasant household also provides labour, often seasonal, to larger farms and to the construction and service sectors and other non-agricultural activities of the rural economy. The income of family members is spent as a family unit. The peasant household also provides an essential social service in the care of its aged and sick, and the support of the unemployed since these benefits are often not available from the public sector. Therefore the peasant household, not the individual worker, is the planning unit in defining a rural development strategy.[4]

Acceptance of this conception of the peasant household means approaching rural development as an effort to transform the conditions to which the peasantry as a social class, organised around family units, has historically been subjected.

Objectives of rural development

We can therefore consider the principal objective of rural development as being the use of the resources of the rural economy in ways that abolish poverty, both material and non-material, among peasant families. Seen in more specific terms, three objectives can be identified:

4. United Nations FAO, World Conference on Agrarian Reform and Rural Development, *The OAS and Rural Development*, Washington DC, 1979.

(1) *Increased incomes* for rural populations, accompanied by *equitable distribution* of the goods and services available to the society as a whole. Growth and development which is "uneven", as resulted from the Green Revolution of high-yielding varieties, will not necessarily achieve this objective.

(2) To expand agricultural *production and productivity* as a means of increasing employment opportunities among the rural population, and improving food self-sufficiency and the nutritional status of the wider society. Here must be included agronomic and livestock practices, along with other agriculture-related activities, such as fishing. Also, secondary agro-based industries must be seen as constituting a significant aspect of "agricultural production".

(3) To maximise the *participation* of the rural population in the *decision-making processes* affecting the control of social services and the economic resources of the rural sector. It is particularly important that the initial designing of rural development programmes, such as land settlement schemes or land redistribution projects, should have as wide and effective participation as possible by the families and communities, or their representatives, for whom the programmes are intended and by whom they are to be carried out.

The process of successfully realising these objectives in specific circumstances of rural underdevelopment must be informed by investigations and analysis of both the structural (macro-level) factors and location-specific (micro) constraints on developments in Caribbean territories. The essays in this volume attempt to give informed and critical perspectives on both these dimensions of rural underdevelopment. So that readers can place these essays in the present-day context of the Caribbean, we should briefly outline the major features of, first, the Caribbean rural situation and, secondly, the basic needs that are felt and unfulfilled within that situation.

Overview of the rural situation

While it is difficult to generalise on the level of development in rural areas for the Commonwealth Caribbean as a whole, the social formations, derived historically from "plantation capitalism" and more recently from "import-substitution industrialisation", reveal fairly common features. These features constitute the contradictions of a rural-urban imbalance, the persistence of a plantation/peasant dichotomy, and an accompanying "wastage" of human and other resources in the rural sector.[5]

5. Useful information on these features is provided in Sergio Molina and S. Pinera,

While capital cities in Commonwealth Caribbean territories have clearly been modernised, this seems to have been accompanied by relative stagnation of rural communities. These sharp contrasts are particularly noticeable in the smaller territories of the Windward Islands. Increasing traffic congestion, and the establishment of "middle-class" suburban developments and of areas with low-income working-class housing projects indicate relatively recent modernisation of the urban-commercial sectors. City slum areas, however, also continue to show some expansion due to the absorption of rural migrants. It is clear that the limited expansion since the late 1960s of employment opportunities in the service sectors — along with tourism and, to a less extent, light (screw-driver type) manufacturing industries — close to and around capital cities have exerted a pull on rural areas.

The prospects for investment in import-substitution industrialisation have provided incentives for the movement of capital away from large-scale agricultural operations, evidence of which can be seen in the existence of semi-abandoned, unproductive large estates, often with absentee owners, while land and better wages are constantly being demanded throughout the agricultural sector. As in the Latin American situation, so in the Caribbean, one can safely conclude without the benefit of recent data that poverty is most highly concentrated in rural areas. This variation in the incidence of poverty was reported in Molina and Pinera (1979) for Latin America: although 40% of the Latin American region's population was below the poverty line (as defined specifically by the study), it varied between 20% for the urban population and 60% for the rural (cf. Beckford 1980:6). This was linked directly to the maldistribution of land under the latifundia system. As shown in the accompanying Table, uneven land distribution is a pronounced feature of the Caribbean agricultural situation.

In the context of an alienated land ownership, increasingly dominated by transnational corporations (in tourism, for example) or by a few wealthy families, the response of the smallholding peasantry has resulted in increasing fragmentation of units of land which were already "uneconomic". Recent investigations have revealed the deep-seated tendency of small farmers in St Vincent, St Lucia and Dominica to divide land equally among their offspring. Since land is seen as a source of security, this parental attitude is perceived as a

---

Poverty in Latin America: Situation, Evolution and Policy Guidelines, UNECLA, Santiago, 1979, discussed in G. Beckford, "Plantation Capitalism and Critical Poverty", mimeo, Un. of the West Indies, Mona, 1980.

PERCENTAGE DISTRIBUTION OF LAND AREA BY FARM SIZE CATEGORY*

Farm size category	Barbados (1971) % of farms	Barbados (1971) % of area	Dominica (1972) % of farms	Dominica (1972) % of area	St Lucia (1973) % of farms	St Lucia (1973) % of area	St Vincent (1972/3) % of farms	St Vincent (1972/3) % of area	Montserrat (1972) % of farms	Montserrat (1972) % of area	St Kitts Nevis (1975) % of farms	St Kitts Nevis (1975) % of area
0.01– 0.99	72.1	4.4	25.6	1.2	45.3	2.4	42.8	3.8	47.5	3.7	60.2	8.2
1.00– 4.99	24.6	7.2	47.4	11.4	36.7	11.8	44.7	19.7	42.8	16.1	35.0	31.8
5.00– 9.99	1.3	1.4	15.6	10.2	10.4	9.8	9.3	11.8	5.7	7.5	3.3	8.1
10.00– 24.99	0.5	1.3	8.0	11.4	4.5	8.9	2.3	6.0	2.4	7.3	0.7	3.2
25.00– 49.99	0.2	1.1	1.2	4.9	1.9	8.7	0.4	3.0	0.5	3.2	0.1	0.4
50.00– 99.99	0.1	1.7	0.8	5.4	0.6	6.0	0.1	2.1†	0.3	3.6	0.2	6.1
100.00–199.99	0.2	6.4	0.5	7.1	0.2	3.7	0.1	2.8	0.3	6.2	0.2	12.6
200.00–499.99	0.6	33.5	0.6	17.8	0.2	11.3	0.2	10.4	0.3	17.5	0.2	23.1
500.00 and over	0.4	43.0	0.3	30.6	0.2	37.4	0.1	40.4	0.2	34.9	0.1	6.5
Total	100.0	100.0	100.0	100.0	100.0	100.0	100.0	100.0	100.0	100.0	100.0	100.0

* Excludes farmers with no land.
† Complete data on land distribution were not available in Grenada. It is reported, however, that 56% of the farm land is held by 1% of the farmers, while at the other extreme 89% of the farmers hold 24% of the land.

Source: Agricultural censuses of the respective countries, adapted from Zuvekas (1978).

rational means of contributing to the security of the next generation. However, this makes the land more constrained as an economic means of livelihood.[6]

In addition to labour displacement of the peasantry and culturally-induced land fragmentation, modernisation offers opportunities for land use in real estate developments. In a chain reaction of factors, land speculation leads to inflation of land prices, one consequence of which is that production of food, when land is used for it, becomes more expensive. Increasing food imports and rising food prices are a common feature throughout the Region, with the contradictory result that basically agrarian societies become high importers of food.

It must therefore be acknowledged that since the structural factors underlying the stagnation of rural areas are interrelated, the overall situation will not be changed beneficially if the problems of the rural-urban imbalance are tackled separately. While there is clearly wastage in the use of the land, it is striking that this affects the human resources of the rural areas as labour power not primarily in chronic unemployment but in "seasonal *under-employment*". Employment is available only at set periods of each year, but even when it is available, the incomes earned are too low to provide adequately for the basic food, clothing, shelter, health and education needs of the families of the agrarian proletariat and the peasantry.

Thus the rural situation in its entirety needs, as a prerequisite to development, agrarian reform in which land can be redistributed for productive agricultural purposes. At the same time as these measures, land use policies are necessary to reduce fragmentation, control speculation and maximise capabilities for scientifically appropriate purposes. The chapter by Pollitt addresses these issues in the case of Cuba.

While agrarian reform remains the basic prerequisite for rural development, and effective policy mechanisms in support of it from international and regional development agencies are to be encouraged as a priority, there should be other levels of activity and phased programmes of action to achieve short-term benefits. For this the needs of the rural environment must be identified.

6. T.H. Henderson and P.I. Gomes, *A Profile of Small Farming in St Vincent, Dominica and St Lucia* (for CARDI/USAID Multiple Cropping Systems Research Project 538-0015), Un. of the West Indies, St Augustine, 1980.

Basic felt needs

Rural populations that are structurally at a disadvantage compared to the urban sector face critical economic, social, cultural and political needs. As we can see from the preceding discussion, the most basic economic need is for *meaningful employment*. The 15–25 age group is that among which the need is most urgent, for it is that which steadily migrates away from the land. Increasingly disillusioned with society's disregard of their needs, these younger people swell the *"lumpenproletariat"* which circumstances force to adopt a "hustling" existence.[7]

In the Caribbean generally, the agrarian proletariat, who survive by the sale of its labour on the plantations or are peasant producers operating small portions of land, forms a sizeable part of the population. They are an oppressed class, with low socio-economic status and living in communities where the social amenities are of relatively poor standard. As a result, improved or functioning social services for adult literacy, primary health care, and adequate housing accompanied by water supply and sanitation are desperately needed. A wide range of social needs continue to go unfulfilled, and this gives rise to increasing resentment, since the rural inhabitants no longer accept an image of themselves as "backward" second-class citizens. An additional basic need is that of improving and then transferring technologies for increasing peasant production. The chapters by Pemberton and by Henderson and Patton respectively address the response of peasant producers to new technology and a project explicitly designed for transferring improved technologies. The essay by McIntosh and Manchew argues that production has to be improved not merely for better incomes but also to satisfy the nutritional needs of the community and the household.

Since levels of education tend to be lower in the rural areas than in urban centres, rural educational standards have to be improved and skills imparted to make rural youth employable. It is in this general area of education and training that cultural needs of rural populations can be identified.

Culturally oppressed by the imposed dominant culture patterns which are integral to the process of colonisation, the masses of rural poor have as their most important cultural need the realisation of their creativity.[8] In his article in this volume, Marshall cites the

---

7. The "hustlers" of the capital cities are a fertile breeding ground for links with international crime, particularly in the "hard" drug trade. This is now common in all Caribbean territories.
8. P. Freire's *Pedagogy of the Oppressed* (1970) discusses the growth of a critical

historical evidence in support of the creative innovations shown by the newly-emancipated slaves in the nineteenth century in building their village communities. The penetration of these communities by various forms of mass media propagating consumption patterns and attitudes inimical to self-emancipation and self-reliance is now a major instrument of transnational capital in creating "needs" for metropolitan goods and American consumerism. The overall impact is the creation of behaviour patterns that are wasteful, helping to reinforce tastes and life-styles characterising "progress" whose price is little less than social and psychological decay.

Recognition of the need for so-called self-help programmes has tended to be realised by governmental community development policies in ways that are manipulative of rural populations and encourage dependence on new forms of patronage. Some major insights and the implications of such patronage are conveyed in the chapter by Susan Craig. As a counter–balance to cultural domination, the pervasive appeal of the music of popular protest, including that of Rastafarianism, of which the late Bob Marley was such an able exponent, suggests a growth in cultural awareness. The full implications of this are still to be revealed. Denied cultural fulfilment, there are distinct efforts by the people to find means of satisfying their needs. Innovative manifestations by Caribbean rural populations have a long history and they display a deep cultural creativity which can be directed to realisation in the economic form of development with more humane qualities than are now apparent.

Once we accept the implications of the prevailing structures of underdevelopment, we readily recognise the need for power and control by rural communities. The control of resources, particularly of the land, is directly related to political power; but there is virtually no participation by the Caribbean rural communities in decision-making on policies affecting allocation of resources and services for their benefit. In the political culture dominated by colonialism, with only recent experience of adult suffrage, the practice of democratic control and widespread community participation in rural villages has been negligible — to the detriment of the local people's political rights and responsibilities. Julius Nyerere has written: "If the people are to be able to develop they must have power. They must be able to control their own activities within the framework of their village communities. And they must be able to mount effective pressure

---

self-consciousness by which peasants break out of "the culture of silence". See also G. Huizer, *The Revolutionary Potential of Peasants in Latin America* (1972).

nationally also. The people must participate not just in physical labour involved in economic development but also in the planning of it and the determination of priorities.''[9] It is only to be expected that when political participation is denied or not effectively encouraged, political disenchantment results and with it a withdrawal of commitment. Hence goals — whether at national, regional or local community levels are not attained.

So to the extent that opportunities for the satisfaction of economic, social, cultural or political needs are lacking, national development will be impaired or, more precisely, the pattern of development will be ''uneven'', giving rise to semblances of modernisation accompanied by rural stagnation. The following articles proceed from the conceptual issues highlighted by the case studies to outline the measures which are needed, and are being attempted, so that there may be rural development as ''an integrated and integral process'' in the interest of rural communities and their constituent households.

9. J. Nyerere, "On Rural Development", *Ideas and Action*, FAO Rome, 1979.

1

PEASANT DEVELOPMENT IN THE WEST INDIES SINCE 1838

Woodville K. Marshall

Modern West Indian history begins without peasantry, and [this] is of particular interest because in tracing it, we trace the birth and development of an entirely new class which has profoundly affected the foundations of West Indian society.[1]

Introduction

The West Indian peasant (in this paper "West Indies" refers to the former British West Indies), because of the circumstances of his origin, cannot be fitted neatly into conventional definitions of the peasant. He has no long-established "ties of tradition and sentiment" to the land which he controls. He cannot be seen as the "rural dimension of old civilisations".[2] The West Indian community is relatively young, and moreover no peasantry survived the establishment of the plantation and slave labour-based sugar industry during the seventeenth century. Whatever elements of a peasantry existed then — the yeoman farmers — quickly disappeared. The small settlers sought new opportunities in North America as the plantation swallowed their holdings; and the Negroes who escaped the estates and established settlements in the bush and the mountains were always in danger of extermination by those who controlled the plantation.[3]

The only tenuous link that can be established between the present-day peasantry and the pre-1838 period is in the activity of the slaves as producers of most of their own food, and even of surpluses, on land granted them by their owners.[4] In this role the slaves were partly

---

1. W.A. Lewis, *The Evolution of the Peasantry in the British West Indies*, Colonial Office Pamphlet 656, 1936. p. 1.
2. R. Redfield, *Peasant Society and Culture*, Chicago, 1956, pp. 27–9.
3. See V.T. Harlow, *Barbados, 1624–1685*, Oxford, 1926; H. Merivale, *Lectures on Colonies and Colonization*, London, 1841, pp. 75–6; S. Mintz, "The Question of Caribbean Peasantries: A Comment", *Caribbean Studies*, vol. 1, no. 3, pp. 32–4.
4. See S. Mintz and D.G. Hall, "The Origins of the Jamaican Internal Marketing Systems", in *Papers in Caribbean Anthropology*, New Haven, 1960.

peasant cultivators or, as Mintz calls them, proto-peasants.[5] But of course they controlled neither the land nor their own time and labour. Our peasantry then starts at emancipation in 1838. It comprises the ex-slaves who after 1838 started small farms "on the peripheries of plantation areas",[6] wherever they could find land — on abandoned plantations and in the mountainous interiors of the various territories. "They represented a reaction to the plantation economy, a negative reflex to enslavement, mass production, monocrop dependence, and metropolitan control. Although these peasants often continued to work part-time on plantations for wages, to eke out their cash needs, their orientation was in fact antagonistic to the plantation rationale."[7]

To summarize, then, the West Indian peasantry exhibits certain special characteristics. It is recent in origin; its growth — in numbers and in acreage controlled — was consistent during the first 50–60 years of its existence; it exists alongside and in conflict with the plantation; and it did not depend exclusively on cultivation of the soil for its income and subsistence. The early peasants, and many of the later ones as well, often combined the cultivation of their land with activities like fishing or shopkeeping and casual estate work. So, for the purposes of our discussion, we shall use the term "peasant" to refer to all those variously called peasant farmers, small farmers and small cultivators. They are the individuals who, as Lewis points out, devote "the major part" of their time to cultivating land on their own account "with the help of little or no outside labour".[8] The size of holding which this requires varies with fertility of the soil and with the type of farm enterprise; but a minimum of 2 acres is probably what was (and is) required. Finally, these peasants are the founders and residents of the new village communities which sprouted near the estates and occasionally in the mountains immediately after emancipation.[9]

Available statistics do not allow us to estimate the size of the peasantry or the average size of its holdings with any precision. It is therefore probable that many of those we shall call peasants were

5. Mintz, "The Question of Caribbean Peasantries", *op. cit.*, p. 34.
6. S. Mintz, foreword to R. Guerra and Y. Sanchez, *Sugar and Society in the Caribbean*, New Haven, 1964, p. xx.
7. *Ibid.*, pp. xx–xxi.
8. Lewis, *op. cit.*, p. 3. See, in particular, F.L. Engledow's Report on Agriculture, Fisheries, Forestry and Veterinary Matters (Supplement to *West India Royal Commission Report 1945*) Cmd. 6608, 1945, pp. 41–5.
9. See H. Paget and R. Farley, "The Growth of Villages in Jamaica and British Guiana", *Caribbean Quarterly*, vol. 10, no. 1, pp. 38–61.

those in possession of a "house-spot" and a garden. These individuals are perhaps more accurately described as smallholders, but their desertion of the sugar estates and their participation in the development of the new village communities place them near, if not inside, the peasant sector.

The growth of the peasantry

Three stages of growth can be identified. First, there is the *period of establishment* marked by the rapid acquisition of land holdings and by a continuous increase in the number of peasants. This stage lasted from 1838 to around 1850-60. Secondly, there is the *period of consolidation* during which there was continuing expansion of the number of peasants and, more important, a marked shift by the peasants to export crop production. This stage lasted to about 1900. Thirdly, there is the *period of saturation* during which the peasantry did not expand and might even have been contracting. This is the period from 1900 to the present, when the peasantry reached the limits of possible expansion inside the plantation-dominated society and economy.

The period of establishment. A combination of factors explains the ex-slaves' desire to leave the estates at emancipation and to establish themselves as independent cultivators. Emancipation had widened the range of their expectations, and these, in many cases, could not be satisfied in plantation labour and residence. Moreover, the planters, over-anxious to safeguard their entire labour supply, attempted by various means to keep all the ex-slaves on the estates in relationships closely approximating to their earlier servile condition. In particular, they devised a system of tenancy which compelled the ex-slave to labour "steadily and continuously" on the estates in return for secure residence in the house and ground which he had occupied as a slave.[10] Consequently, insecurity of tenure, as well as relatively low wages for plantation labour, sometimes high rents, and long contracts reinforced many ex-slaves' determination to seek new and better opportunities away from their estates. Some indulged in a measure of occupational differentiation; and there was a marked increase after emancipation in the number of artisans, porters, fishermen, seamstresses etc. But most of those in flight from

10. See W.G. Sewell, *The Ordeal of Free Labour in the British West Indies*, New York, 1861; W.K. Marshall, "Social Economic Problems in the Windward Islands, 1838-1865" in Andic and Mathews (eds), *The Caribbean in Transition*, Rio Piedras, 1965, pp. 247-52.

the estate attempted to acquire land. The reason for this was obvious. Cultivation of the soil was the one skill the ex-slaves possessed; moreover, in many of the territories enough land seemed to be available to furnish the would-be cultivator with at least the elements of subsistence.

Opportunities for land acquisition did not exist to the same extent in all the territories. In Barbados, St Kitts and Antigua — three of the older colonies — small size, a large population and a long-established sugar industry left few, if any, opportunities for land acquisition. Consequently, it was difficult for a peasantry to emerge in these islands; those ex-slaves who wanted to "better" themselves away from the estates had to think of emigration. On the other hand, Jamaica and the Windward Islands, Trinidad and British Guiana (now Guyana) offered opportunities for land acquisition. In Jamaica and the Windwards the sugar industry had left undeveloped much of the mountainous interior; in Trinidad and British Guiana a small population and a young sugar industry created many opportunities for land acquisition.[11] It must be noted, however, that in both of these latter territories, relatively high wages and, in British Guiana, the high cost of drainage might have moderated the desire for land acquisition. The point remains, however, that Jamaica, the Windwards, Trinidad and British Guiana provided the best opportunities for land acquisition by ex-slaves.

These opportunities were eagerly grasped, but they were not won without opposition. The ex-slaves' land hunger was enormous and evident. Observers said that the "great and universal object" of the ex-slaves was the acquisition of land "however limited in extent".[12] One St Vincent planter said as early as 1842 that the labourers were always "on the look-out" for land on which they could settle and allow their wives "to sit down" and "take charge of the children".[13] Throughout the period immediately after emancipation there is overwhelming evidence of a desire to acquire portions of the surplus land — estate land not in cultivation and Crown land.[14] But this desire brought the ex-slaves into direct conflict with the plantation.

11. In 1838 Barbados had as many slaves as British Guiana, and Antigua had more than Trinidad. The figures for Barbados and British Guiana were 82,807 and 84,915; for Antigua and Trinidad they were 29,537 and 22,359.
12. These were typical comments by stipendiary magistrates in the Windward Islands and in Jamaica.
13. H.M. Grant's evidence before the 1842 Select Committee on West India Colonies.
14. See Paget and Farley, *op. cit.*, also R. Farley, "The Rise of the Peasantry in British Guiana", *Social and Economic Studies*, vol. 2, no. 4, pp. 87–103; D.G. Hall, *Free Jamaica 1838–1865*, New Haven, 1959.

Planters feared the effect on the labour market and on the sugar industry of widespread independent land settlement. Consequently, they placed obstacles in the way of its development. The planter-dominated legislatures refused to initiate surveys of Crown land as a preliminary to smallholder settlement, and they adopted strict legislation against squatting on Crown land. The planters either refused to sell surplus and marginal estate land, or they charged high, even exorbitant, prices for small portions of it. Moreover, the legislatures instituted costly licences for the sale of small quantities of manufactured sugar and coffee and for the production of charcoal and firewood. They also levied land taxes which discriminated against the owners of smallholdings.

Small-scale land acquisition became possible, however, because of the determination of the would-be peasants and because of the failure of the planters to maintain a united opposition. Some planters were anxious to win advantage in the labour market, and these sold land to the ex-slaves in the hope that this would secure them a portion of the ex-slaves' labour. In addition, many planters were chronically in debt and therefore welcomed the cash returns they could get from the disposal of small portions of their marginal land. This particular advantage was often exploited during and after the depression of 1847. But most important was the action of the ex-slaves. They practised thrift and industry, and, as a result, laboriously accumulated the purchase money for land. Some put their savings from wages and provision cultivation in the Friendly and Benefit Societies; some, as in British Guiana, started informal co-operatives and joint stock companies. Others, as in Jamaica, got the assistance of Baptist ministers in their attempts to bargain with landowners. Generally, they paid high prices for the land. Prices ranging from £20 per acre were common, and prices of £100, £150 and even £200 per acre were often reported.[15] The land itself was of variable quality — more often than not marginal land which was barely accessible, not surveyed and even uncleared. The lots, too, ranged in size from about ½ acre to 5 and sometimes 10 and 15 acres.[16]

So successful were the efforts of the ex-slaves that within four years of emancipation officials were reporting an "almost daily" increase in the number of freeholders and an obvious extension of cultivation in territories like Jamaica, British Guiana, the Windwards and Trinidad. Eisner shows that Jamaica possessed 2,114 persons owning holdings under 40 acres in extent in 1838. By 1841,

15. See Hall, *op. cit.*, and Farley, *op. cit.*
16. See Lewis, *op. cit.*, p. 7.

however, that number had reached 7,919, and by 1845 there were 19,397 persons with holdings under 10 acres in extent. She estimates that by 1842 nearly 200 free villages with a total extent of 100,000 acres had been established, and about £70,000 had been paid by the settlers for land.[17] Farley has described a similar pattern of development in British Guiana. By 1842 there were in Demerara and Berbice over 4,000 freehold properties with an extent of about 22,000 acres which had been purchased at a cost of about £70,000.[18]

This rapid development continued throughout the rest of this first period. The profits of provision cultivation provided more labourers with the means to desert the estates for the new villages and for independent small-scale cultivation. And the perennial difficulties of the planters afforded labourers many more opportunities to acquire land at lower costs. By 1852 in British Guiana there were more than 11,000 new freehold properties with an estimated value of £1 million.[19] By 1860 in Jamaica the number of holdings under 50 acres in extent had reached 50,000.[20] By 1861 the Windward Islands of St Lucia, St Vincent, Grenada and Tobago possessed more than 10,000 freeholders, while the number of residents of villages built since emancipation totalled about 20,000 in Grenada and St Vincent.[21]

The period of consolidation. The rapid increase in the number of peasants continued during the second phase of development. In Jamaica, the only territory for which we have almost complete figures for the period, the number of small landholdings (i.e. those under 50 acres) increased spectacularly between 1860 and 1900 and up to 1930. Eisner's figures show that these holdings more than doubled between 1860 and 1902. The total figure for the later date was 133,169. Also important was the increase in the number of substantial peasants or small farmers. The number of holdings of between 5 and 49 acres increased from 13,189 in 1880 to 24,226 in 1902 and to 31,038 in 1930.[22] Moreover, as a share of the total population, the ratio of peasants rose from 11% in 1860 to 17.5% in 1890 and 18% in 1930.[23] Similar developments occurred in Grenada where the number of smallholders increased from about 3,600 in 1860 to

17. G. Eisner, *Jamaica 1830-1930*, Manchester, 1961, pp. 210–11.
18. Farley, "The Rise of the Peasantry in British Guiana", *op. cit.*, pp. 100–1.
19. *Ibid.*, pp. 101–2. According to Farley, the recovery of the sugar industry in British Guiana led to a slump in peasant development after the 1850s.
20. Eisner, *op. cit.*, p. 220.
21. Marshall, *op. cit.*, p. 252.
22. Eisner, *op. cit.*, p. 220.
23. *Ibid.*, p. 221.

more than 8,000 in 1911. By the latter date there were more than 2,000 proprietors of lots varying in size between 2½ and 10 acres.[24]

But the most important feature of this phase of development was the emergence of what Eisner calls a "new peasantry". The presence of this new group is partly indicated by the increase in the number of farms of more than 5 acres; but it is mainly indicated by a "dramatic" change in the peasant's pattern of production. Eisner's national income estimates for Jamaica for 1850 and 1890 reveal a shift from mainly provision production to a mixed provision and export crop production by the peasants. The value of export crops (sugar, coffee, rum, pimento, ginger) in 1850 is estimated by Eisner at £1,089,300, of which "small settlers" contributed £113,500 or just over 10%. In 1890 the value of cash crops (to which had been added logwood, bananas, oranges, coconuts, cocoa and lime juice) was estimated at £2,028,300; and the small settlers' share had risen to £798,800 or about 39%.[25] At the same time, the peasants had increased the value of ground provisions from £854,000 in 1850 to about £2,601,200 in 1890.[26] This meant that whereas in 1850, 83% of the peasant output consisted of ground provisions and only 11% of exports, in 1890 the share of ground provisions had dropped to 74% and that of exports had risen to 23%. It meant also a remarkable increase in the peasants' share was about half but by 1890 it had risen to about three-quarters.[27]

This change in the pattern of peasant production was also apparent in the Windward Islands. There, increased peasant activity after the 1850s in the production of arrowroot, cotton, spices, cocoa, citrus, bananas, logwood and sugar resulted in increased exports of most of those commodities. Indeed, arrowroot and cotton in St Vincent and cocoa and spices in Grenada were regarded as peasant crops from the 1850s onwards, while sugar in Tobago was produced exclusively by peasants and sharecroppers by 1898 and was already in the process of disappearance as a major cash crop in that island as well as in Grenada.

The period of saturation. In general, the shortage of land for continued peasant expansion imposed a limit on this type of development. The characteristic of the most recent stage of peasant development is the failure of the peasantry to expand at its earlier pace. Moreover, there is increasing evidence that the peasantry in some

24. The *Grenada Handbook 1946*, p. 70.
25. Eisner, *op. cit.*, pp. 53, 80.
26. *Ibid.*, p. 9.
27. *Ibid.*, pp. 221, 234. It fell to about 68% in 1930.

territories has been declining in numbers during the last 20 years. Table 1 provides some of the evidence for Jamaica.

Table 1. PEASANT HOLDINGS IN JAMAICA, 1902–1961

	Under 5 acres	1–5 acres	5–25 acres	25–100 acres
1902	108,943	—	24,226[a]	—
1930	153,406	—	31,038[a]	—
1954	138,761	95,851	53,237	5,572
1961	113,239	—	40,769	3,803

[a] Returns for holdings of 5–50 acres.

Sources: G. Eisner, *op. cit.*; Department of Statistics, *Survey of Agriculture 1961–2*; Federal Statistical Office, *Agricultural Statistics*, series 2, no. 1, 1960.

The striking feature of these figures is the evidence they provide of the dramatic decline in the numbers of *smaller* holdings in the period 1930–61. So sharp was this decrease that the total number of these holdings in 1961 barely exceeded the number recorded for 1902. There is also clear evidence that the number of *larger* holdings increased throughout the entire period. These almost doubled in number in 1902–61 despite a sharp decrease in the period 1954–61.

This pattern was not uniform throughout the West Indies. Table 2 supplies some evidence of the size of the peasantry in the other islands and of its growth during the period 1946–61. In all the Windward Islands there has been a continuing and substantial increase especially in the number of smaller holdings. In Barbados and in all the Leewards there has been a decrease in the number of smaller holdings, and only a small increase in the number of larger holdings in Antigua and Montserrat. In Trinidad there has been a slight increase in the number of smaller holdings, but a marked increase in the number of larger holdings.

This suggests that the peasants' shift to cash crop production has operated in conjunction with other factors to exhaust the opportunities for peasant landholding in the larger territories of Jamaica and Trinidad as well as in the longer-settled islands of Barbados and the Leewards. These opportunities had always been limited in the latter islands where the plantation was well established and has remained dominant.[28] A relatively small peasantry did come into evidence in

28. This is confirmed by statistics on the amount of farms with a size of more than 100 acres. In Barbados (1961) these farms occupied 81.7% of the total area; in Antigua (1961) 59.1%; in St Kitts (1946) 78.8%; in Montserrat (1957) 68.4%. (See *A Digest of West Indian Agricultural Statistics*, p. 14.)

Table 2. PEASANT HOLDINGS IN SELECTED WEST INDIAN
ISLANDS, 1946 AND 1956-61[a]

	1-5 acres		5-50 acres	
	1946	*1956-61*	*1946*	*1956-61*
Trinidad and Tobago	18,120	19,200	11,563	14,400
Barbados	4,208	2,400[b]	454[c]	292[c]
Dominica	2,760	3,781	1,934	1,748
Grenada	4,991	6,773	1,361	1,615
St Lucia	857[d]	4,887	1,976	2,361
St Vincent	3,271	4,636	1,230	1,229
Antigua	2,926	2,800[b]	344[c]	476[c]
Montserrat	1,317	1,302	142	194
St Kitts-Nevis-Anguilla	2,237	n.a.	351	n.a.

Notes

a   The dates of the second set of data for the several islands are: Trinidad and
Tobago 1957, Barbados 1961, Dominica 1956-9, Grenada 1956-9, Montserrat
1957, St Lucia 1958, St Vincent 1958.

b   Estimates based on the returns of total number of holdings under 5 acres for the
date 1956-61.

c   Holdings of 5-100 acres.

d   This low figure reflects incompleteness of the Census (see *West Indian Census
1946*, Part A, para. 43, p. 51).

Sources: West Indian Census 1946, Parts A and B; Agricultural Statistics, Series 2,
no. 1; *A Digest of West Indian Agricultural Statistics*, Dept. of Agriculture Economics and Farm Management, Un. of the West Indies, St Augustine, 1965.

these islands, but the increasing pressure of numbers on the land as
well as non-availability of land for expansion of peasant cash-crop
production seems to have resulted in both the amalgamation of some
of the smaller holdings into larger ones and a drift of peasants away
from the land. Since there are few alternative means of employment
available inside these islands, most of the ex-peasants must have
emigrated.

In Trinidad and Jamaica a combination of other factors are
involved. The expansion and consolidation of the plantation ever
since emancipation has been one limiting factor. In addition, various
types of non-agricultural economic activities during the last 40 years
have competed with agriculture both for land and labour. For
example, industries like bauxite and tourism in Jamaica and oil in
Trinidad have not only attracted the peasant away from cultivation
on his own account but have also imposed limitations on the growth
of the peasantry by occupying land which was either peasant agricul-

tural land or land which might have become available for peasant expansion. At the same time, the opening up and exploitation of migration opportunities, particularly after 1945, might well have made the peasantry more conscious of its neglected and depressed condition and more determined to improve it. It is suggested that these simultaneous pressures, added to the familiar ones of increasing population, shortage of fertile land for expansion, and demands for improved living standards, explain the "crisis" of the peasantry in territories like Jamaica and Trinidad.

The situation has been somewhat different in the Windward Islands. In these islands the peasantry has continued its expansion. The reason for this is partly historical. Mainly because of late settlement, a sparse population and mountainous terrain, these islands have never possessed a plantation system which exercised full dominance over the economy and the landscape. As a result, the plantation system was (and is) less well equipped than in other islands to withstand long depression in the sugar industry (or in other staple production). This created perennial opportunities for peasant acquisition of land. Moreover, there has been no alternative economic development in these islands to compete with agriculture or to attract the peasant away from the land. The peasantry has thus been able to sustain a competition with the plantation for land and labour in conditions more favourable to it than in any other territory. This has ensured its continuous growth. These islands, then, are more nearly peasant communities than any of the other islands in the West Indies.[29]

The role of the peasantry

Peasant activity modified the character of the original pure plantation economy and society. The peasants were the innovators in the economic life of the community. Besides producing a great quantity

---

29. This is confirmed to some extent by statistics on the percentage distribution on the area occupied by farms of different sizes:

	Under 5 acres	5-100 acres	100 + acres
Dominica	12.7	32.0	55.3
Grenada	22.9	29.9	47.2
St Lucia	14.9	37.5	47.6
St Vincent	22.5	28.0	49.5
Jamaica	11.8	32.2	56.0
Trinidad and Tobago	12.5	40.1	47.4

Source: *A Digest of West Indian Agricultural Statistics*, p. 14.

and variety of subsistence food and livestock they introduced new crops and/or re-introduced old ones. This diversified the basically monocultural pattern. Bananas, coffee, citrus, coconuts, cocoa and logwood in Jamaica; cocoa, arrowroot, spices, bananas and log-wood in the Windward Islands: these were the main export crops introduced or re-introduced by the peasantry after the 1850s. All of these were subsequently adopted by the planters and became important elements in the export trade by the 1870s. Not all of these crops succeeded; peasant coffee in Jamaica, for example, was seldom of good quality. In addition, the success of the peasants in combating attacks of disease on crops like cocoa and bananas was always severely limited by their shortage of resources of capital and know-ledge. However, this many-sided activity of the peasants represented not only "a great new area of peasant advance"[30] but also served as a vehicle for expanding the production possibilities of the region. The plantation-staple economy was being mixed with elements of a peasant-subsistence economy; and it seemed probable that a peasant economy could replace the plantation economy without any serious economic loss to the community. Peasants were producing cash crops as well as food. It was the availability of much peasant-produced food which might have cancelled out the advantages of large-scale production for export markets by introducing important elements of self-sufficiency into the economy.[31]

The alternative foreshadowed by the presence and activity of the peasants had great social significance as well. The peasants initiated the conversion of these plantation territories into modern societies. In a variety of ways they attempted to build local self-generating communities. They founded villages and markets; they built churches and schools; they clamoured for extension of educational facilities, for improvement in communications and markets; they started the local co-operative movement.

Informal co-operatives made their appearance immediately after emancipation; groups of ex-slaves pooled their resources to buy land, to lay down drainage systems, to build churches and schools. Participation in more formal organisations came later. This could be seen in peasant activity in the Friendly and Benefit Societies, in the Jamaica Agricultural Society and particularly in the People's Co-operative Loan Bank of Jamaica.[32] These banks, first established in 1905, represented a considerable initiative in the area of self-help. They were located in peasant communities and were intended "to

30. Lewis, *op. cit.*, p. 14.
31. *Ibid.*, pp. 36-8.
32. See Eisner, *op. cit.*, pp. 227-30.

encourage thrift and to provide the small farmer with loans on reasonable terms and at the lowest possible rates of interest".[33] The importance of these banks in rendering vital financial assistance to the peasants, particularly in times of natural disaster, can be judged from the fact that by 1949, 119 branches of the bank with 72,700 members had been established, and the bank had made advances and loans of nearly £2 million.[34]

So the peasantry, because of the extent of its social investment and self-conscious community-building, was a persisting factor both for stability and change inside the West Indian community. As "a nucleus of importance", which could constitute "the stability of the country",[35] the peasants' presence and activity combined to soften the rigid divisions of race and class which were a feature of the plantation society.[36] At the same time, their increasing numbers and their economic importance made a cogent case for the adoption of broader-based institutions. In this respect peasant development was emancipation in action.

Government policy towards the peasantry

The potential of peasant development was never fully realized because government had tended, most of the time, to ignore the existence of the class. The peasants, as Eisner says, "were left to themselves to experiment with different crops and techniques".[37] This helps to explain why wasteful practices like "firestick agriculture" (clearing virgin land with fire and then working it without rotation or artificial aids) still persist with their terrible consequences of soil exhaustion and soil erosion.[38] It also helps to explain the general backwardness in agricultural knowledge, the inadequate credit and marketing facilities and the shortage of fertile land for peasant expansion.

This neglect can be explained by the dominance of the estate-based

33. R. Colon-Torres, "Agricultural Credit in the Caribbean", *Caribbean Economic Review*, vol. IV, nos. 1 and 2, p. 95.
34. See "Rural Welfare Organizations" and "Credit Facilities for Small Farmers", in "Land Tenure in the Caribbean", *Caribbean Economic Review*, vol. II, no. 2, pp. 90–2, 107–11. The actual figure was £1,793,658.13.7, of which £856, 541.3.8 was still outstanding.
35. This opinion was expressed in 1850 by Drysdale, a stipendiary magistrate in St Lucia.
36. Lewis, *op. cit.*, p. 37.
37. Eisner, *op. cit.*, p. 225.
38. See Mintz and Hall, "The Origins of the Jamaican Internal Marketing System", *op. cit.*, pp. 6–7; Eisner, *op. cit.*, p. 225.

sugar industry over influential opinion both at home and in the metropolis. Planters feared that peasant expansion would ruin the sugar industry by creating labour shortages. They convinced official opinion in England that both the prosperity and civilisation of the West Indies were dependent on the survival of the estate-based industry. Metropolitan official opinion, though sometimes sceptical about the economic argument, seemed to accept (for no very good reason) the cultural argument. Both sides, therefore, co-operated for a long time in maintaining the traditional industry and in protecting the ex-slaves against "a relapse into barbarism and the savage state".[39] Both these ends could be served by ensuring that the ex-slaves continued to work for wages on the estates "not uncertainly or capriciously, but steadily and continuously".[40] Consequently, neither the Colonial Office nor the local legislature exerted themselves at first to assist peasant development, which nonetheless thrived in spite of this official indifference and, occasionally, open hostility.

Government attitude was modified only when discontent and restlessness among peasants and labourers combined with prolonged depression in the sugar industry during the 1890s and again in the 1930s to create a situation of crisis. The wisdom of the traditional policy was then questioned by those who had initiated it. The establishment of the Jamaica Agricultural Society and the appointment of a travelling agricultural instructor in the 1890s hinted at a new policy, and the Report of the Royal West India Commission in 1897 seemed to point in a new direction. The Commission recognized that the peasantry was "a source of both economic and political strength". Accordingly, it recommended land settlement and diversification of agriculture, "no other reform affording so good a prospect for the permanent welfare in the future of the West Indies as the settlement of the labouring population on the land as small peasant proprietors". The ironic point is that these sentiments had to be repeated by the Sugar Commission of 1929 and by the Moyne Commission in 1939.[41] Fundamental reform had been stillborn.

The "agricultural revolution", proclaimed as official policy in Jamaica since 1902 and hinted at in these Reports, has still not occurred. New government policy has consisted principally of the

39. Merivale, *op. cit.*, pp. 312–13; Earl Grey, *The Colonial Policy of Lord John Russell's Administration*, London, 1853, pp. 54ff.
40. This was the advice, contained in the Queen's Letter, which the Colonial Office offered to Jamaican petitioners for relief in 1865.
41. W.A. Lewis, "Issues in Land Settlement Policy", *Caribbean Economic Review*, vol. 3, nos 1 and 2, pp. 58–9.

provision of agricultural credit facilities and the institution of land settlement schemes. The first is a new departure, beginning in the 1940s,[42] and for that reason it is open to question whether it is not too little and has not come too late to ease the crisis among the peasantry. Land settlement schemes have a longer history. They were started in Jamaica in 1896, and have been used in most of the territories ever since. The schemes have not been pursued as consistent and coherent policy; rather they have been used as expedients whenever a general crisis seems to have threatened the existence of the community, as in the 1920s and again in the 1930s and 1940s. Consequently, little attention has been paid to the choice for settlers for the land or to the problem of the small farmer's deficiencies in knowledge, capital and organisation. Moreover, much of the land distributed was not particularly fertile; half of the settlements in Jamaica between 1929 and 1949 possessed soil of the "red dirt" variety which is notorious for its incapacity to retain water and plant nutrients.[43] Government has concerned itself only with distributing the smallholdings, but if land settlement is to involve reform rather than a palliative, government must commit far more resources to this type of project.[44] The amount of land distributed in many of the territories suggests that only the surface of the problem has been scratched. The peasants require access to a large quantity of "fertile" land (i.e. estate land) in order to improve their living standards and also to increase their numbers. Land settlement, which in Trinidad between 1933 and 1948, for example, involved the disposal of 4,120 acres to 2,940 settlers, will neither halt the drift from the land nor encourage permanent settlement.[45]

A more determined assault on the problem is necessary if the position of the peasants is to be strengthened and if the potential of the peasantry is to be realised. This would seem to involve a re-consideration of the role of the plantation in this community and, ultimately, a basic re-arrangement of priorities in agrarian policy.

42. R. Colon-Torres, *op. cit.*, pp. 85ff. See also "Credit Facilities for Small Farmers" in "Land Tenure in the Caribbean", *Caribbean Economic Review*, vol. II, no. 2, pp. 101–16.
43. P. Redwood, *Statistical Survey of Government Land Settlement in Jamaica, BWI, 1929–1949*, pp. 18–21. Only 4% of the settlements possessed soil of the best (alluvia) variety.
44. Lewis, "Issues in Land Settlement Policy", *op. cit.*, pp. 77ff. See also LeRoy Taylor's "A Review of Land Policy in Jamaica", mimeo., 1965, ISER, Un. of the West Indies, pp. 7ff.
45. Figures provided by Lewis for the period 1916–49 show that 5,300 acres were settled in the Leeward Islands; 14,400 acres in the Windward Islands; and 106,100 acres in Jamaica. In British Guiana 8,500 acres were settled between 1944 and 1949.

2

THE AGRI-BUSINESS BOURGEOISIE OF BARBADOS AND MARTINIQUE

Michael Sleeman

Introduction

This chapter discusses the ascendancy of a new social class in Barbados and Martinique in the second half of the nineteenth century, in a process which was co-terminous with the birth of monopoly capitalism and was local rather than international. In each island the concentration of mercantile and planter interests in the same hands produced something of a social hybrid, which I have chosen to designate as an "agri-business bourgeoisie". By the early twentieth century these new colonial élites had usurped the traditional commercial and productive functions of a northern metropolitan merchant house and indigenous plantocracy, emerging phoenix-like out of the ashes of the depression of the 1880s and '90s. The social origins of the new élite were different in each case. In Barbados the nucleus of the agri-business bourgeoisie was a locally based commercial class, which forged financial and familial ties with the surviving remnants of an older established planter class. In Martinique, the origins of the group were somewhat different, having developed out of the oldest white creole planter families who had played a central role in the foundation of the island's first "central" sugar factories.

Set within the context of nineteenth-century imperialism, West Indian plantation economies, like those of most other colonial possessions throughout the world, were fully integrated into the capitalist system via the emergence and development of international monopoly corporations. The reorganization of the plantation system along corporate lines in the Caribbean by the introduction of metropolitan finance capital has therefore to be seen within a global context. This process — which took place in nearly all the sugar islands of the Caribbean, and was to be observed contemporaneously in the tea and rubber plantations of Asia and in the banana and sugar industry in Jamaica, Trinidad, British Guiana, Guadeloupe and the smaller British colonies of the Leeward and Windward Islands — had passed out of the hands of private resident and absentee proprietors to a metropolitan corporate sector. In Cuba and Puerto Rico local control was maintained

15

slightly longer by the *hacendados*, but the same process took place quite rapidly after 1899 with the invasion of the United States and the penetration of American finance capital between 1900 and 1920. In the twentieth century Tate and Lyle came to monopolise the sugar production of Jamaica, Trinidad and British Honduras. Booker McConnell became the successor to a total of seven smaller West Indian merchant houses which had acquired a monopoly over sugar production in British Guiana by the early 1850s, and within a space of 70 years came to account for 90% of that colony's output. By the early 1900s, two-thirds of Guadeloupe's sugar production was controlled by three metropolitan joint stock corporations: the Société Industrielle et Agricole de Pointe-à-Pitre, the Société Anonyme des Usines de Beauport, and the Société Marseillaise des Sucreries Coloniales.

Viewed against the background of this near-universal phenomenon, the cases of Barbados and Martinique must be considered unique in so far as they successfully avoided the penetration of metropolitan corporate interests and kept the sugar industry in local hands. This is particularly remarkable when we consider that the phenomenon occurred against a background of successive crises in the sugar industry between 1884 and 1905, fuelled primarily by the competition from subsidised European beet sugar which sent world prices plummeting after 1884. The reason why economic power remained in local hands can be analysed in terms of the *internal* structure of these two colonial societies, which gave rise to the formation in the late nineteenth century of new élites, who were the only groups financially powerful enough to keep the sugar industry afloat during the depression.

The Barbados variant: the rise of the Bridgetown commercial class

In the case of Barbados one can point to two main factors which provided conditions favourable to the maintenance of local interests after the Abolition of Slavery (1834). First, the existence of a relatively large resident planter class and the retention of the Old Representative System, which in all other British West Indian islands gave way to direct rule by Crown Colony government, gave the white oligarchy in Barbados a degree of internal control which was unrivalled elsewhere in the Caribbean. Vested with the power to make its own laws, the Barbados planter class adopted a number of measures in the second half of the nineteenth century which had the effect of retaining estate ownership in local hands, though these measures did not have the longterm effect of keeping estates in the same hands. The most important of these measures was the refusal of the local legislature to accept the Encumbered Estates Act of 1854, through which estates in other British West Indian islands were sold on the London market mostly to merchant consignees, aided in this process by the acceptance by the English Chancery Court of the principle of consignee priority of lien. Barbados by contrast adopted its own version of the English Chancery Court system,[1] which ensured that indebted estates were re-sold to local buyers. During a thirteen-year period between 1854 and 1867, when ten colonies accepted the Encumbered Estates Act and over half the estates sold through the Court were purchased by merchant houses,[2] a total of forty-one estates in Barbados entered the Chancery Court and the majority were subsequently purchased by resident buyers. Another important measure adopted by the local legislature at the lowest point of the depression in 1887 was the enactment of the Agricultural Aids Act, which helped to prop up an ailing sugar industry and thereby prevent its total collapse. Under this Act the legislature voted for funds to be advanced out of the colony's budget for continuing the cultivation of estates in financial difficulty, both in and out of Chancery. But in 1897 roughly one-third of the sugar estates in Barbados were supported in this way.[3]

A second factor which favoured the maintenance of local interests was the way in which the sugar industry was traditionally financed by local capital. Before 1838 the most common source of credit to plantations in the British West Indies was via the "consignee system".[4] In the years following Abolition this source of credit was

1. Unlike the English system, mortgagees did not have the power to bring an encumbered estate to sale in the open market. Property under the Barbadian law could only be disposed of by the Chancery Court. An encumbered sugar estate had to be given the chance to work off its debts before disposal was resorted to, the sale of any estate in Chancery being regarded as a final measure. An accurate description of the way in which the system worked is to be found in the evidence of the Master-in-Chancery given to the *West India Royal Commission of 1897*, Appendix C, Vol. II, c.8657.
2. The Act was initially adopted by St Vincent and Tobago in 1854, and over the next thirteen years was accepted by the following: Virgin Islands and St Kitts (1860), Jamaica (1861), Antigua (1864), Montserrat (1865), Grenada (1866), and Dominica and Nevis (1867).
3. *Source*: Barbados Archives, *Index of Estates in Chancery*.
4. Under the "consignee system" planters acquired the necessary supplies for the running of a plantation on credit from an English merchant. A planter's crop would then be automatically consigned to the same merchant who would arrange for its sale on the English market. After the sale of the crop, the consignee made deductions on the planter's account for supplies shipped to the estate on credit and duly charged his commission. Finally the balance was credited, or sometimes even debited, to the planter's account.

available only to the most financially secure plantations.[5] Since land
was considered a first-rate security in Barbados, and because mortgages were one of the few avenues for investment in the island, it
seems to have been the established practice for most planters to
obtain credit locally rather than from English merchants. Confidence in this form of investment, which provided a steady income for
mortgages, is reflected in the way mortgages were commonly kept on
properties over a long period with no attempt being made to realise
the principal, so that sales of property often included their encum-
brances. Referring to the financial independence of the Barbadian
planter community in the second half of the eighteenth century,
Richard Pares noted that "Barbadians had owed money not so much
to Englishmen as to other Barbadians . . ." Anthony Trollope's
observations in the mid-nineteenth century on the financial independence of Barbados, as an island that "owes no man anything" and
"pays its own way", reinforces the impression that the financing of
the sugar industry was primarily a local affair. An analysis of
Chancery Court records turns this impression into fact, since they
clearly show that the plaintiffs represented in bills of complaint, in a
majority of cases, were other planters and *local* merchants. Between
1840 and 1920, out of a sample of 600 cases of debt foreclosure, in
only eighteen cases was the plaintiff an English merchant.[6]

The foundation of the Barbados Mutual Life Assurance Society
(BMLA) by a group of prominent Bridgetown merchants in 1840
occurred within the same decade as the collapse of a number of local
banks, such as the West India Bank of Barbados, the Jamaica
Planters' Bank and the Bank of British Guiana. This was the direct
result of a commercial crisis in the home country, which led to the
liquidation of eighteen West India merchant houses and the subsequent failure of those local banks which acted as their agents.
Almost the only form of local investment was upon mortgages
secured on sugar estates, and the Colonial Bank under its Charter of
1836 was restricted to advancing only short-term loans to meet the
working expenses. In cultivating an estate (which in effect meant the
expenses incurred on the next crop, the produce itself being considered a security against the loan), the BMLA, together with the
Barbados Savings Bank, became the major financial institution supplying credit to the sugar industry in the mid-nineteenth century. The
importance of this move by local commercial interests was threefold.
First, the inauguration of an institution of finance capital provided a

---

5. According to the evidence of one planter before the *Royal Commission of 1848*,
   credit was lacking because "investors preferred India and Mauritius".
6. *Source*: Barbados Archives, *Index of Estate in Chancery*.

means of local capital accumulation, which gave the sugar industry in Barbados far more stability than in most other British West Indian islands in the years after Abolition. Secondly, its foundation and capitalisation by local merchants ensured the retention of local ownership. Thirdly, the returns made by the BMLA from substantial investments in the sugar industry provided for further capital accumulation, which was subsequently re-invested in commerce and used to purchase sugar estates out of Chancery in the early years of the twentieth century, and to capitalise the construction of the first central sugar factories.[7]

The collapse of eighteen West India merchant houses in 1846, and the shift of trading operations by the survivors into other parts of the British empire created a vacuum which was soon filled by local commercial houses. The origins of some of the largest firms and the backgrounds of their founders are of particular interest, and should not be passed over without comment. *Gardiner Austin and Co. Ltd.*, the island's largest sugar and molasses exporter by the 1930s, can be traced back to the London merchant house of *Michael Cavan and Co.*, founded in 1797. The Barbadian branch of Cavan's separated from the parent company in the 1830s on the death of one of its partners, Michael Cavan, and became a local Barbadian concern run by Cavan's nephew, James McChlery. In 1872 John Gardiner Austin became a senior partner of Michael Cavan and Co.; he had been born in Demerara, of a long-established West Indian colonial family which had been associated with Barbados and British Guiana for 200 years. When he died in 1902 the firm of Cavan's went into bankruptcy, and the old business was revived by his two sons under the name of Gardiner Austin and Co.

Alister Cameron, the founder of *A. Cameron and Co.*, one of the foremost commission houses of the early twentieth century, originally came to Barbados from England as an estate attorney to administer the holdings of the West India merchant house, Thomas Daniels and Sons. When the company's Barbadian assets were liquidated in 1891, Cameron bought its largest sugar estates out of Chancery and subsequently purchased other estates to form

7. The importance of the BMLA as a source of credit to the Barbadian sugar industry in the nineteenth century is indicated by the fact that by 1877 the Society had already over £150,000 invested in the form of loans to planters. The importance of these investments is reflected in the rate of interest paid to policyholders, indicating a direct relationship between the bonus paid and the state of the international sugar market at any given time. From an average of 2¼% between 1845 and 1885 the bonus dropped to ¼% in 1902, rising to 2% in 1910, dropping again to 1½% during the brief depression of the early 1920s and rising again to 2¾% at the end of the decade. *Source: BMLA Records.*

Sunbury Estates Ltd. Another prominent commission agent, Arthur Sydney Bryden, came to Barbados from England as an agent for Lloyds Marine Insurance. He founded the firm *A.S. Bryden and Sons* in the 1890s, and henceforth operated as a commission agent, wholesaler and retail distributor. John Hadley Wilkinson, the son of a partner in the London West India merchant house of Wilkinson and Gaviller (formally Maxwell and Lascelles), came to Barbados in 1908 to take charge of the local branch of the firm. In 1920 the Barbados branch detached itself from the parent company and went into partnership with an old-established planter family, to form the commercial house of *Wilkinson and Haynes Co. Ltd.* A final example in this series of organisational transformations is afforded by the case of *Da Costa and Co. Ltd.*, a firm of general merchants founded in 1868 by David Campbell Da Costa, a trader of Portuguese Jewish extraction from St Vincent, out of the eighteenth-century Barbadian commercial house of Barrow and Dummet.[8]

From these examples it is evident that the Bridgetown commercial houses did not develop entirely out of a total vacuum created by the failure or departure of English firms. Several local firms in fact grew out of established metropolitan merchant houses. It must also be noted that the acquisition of sugar estates during the depression (1846–7) by mercantile interests was not novel in Barbados's history. Leading English firms in the past, like Maxwell and Lascelles, Higginson and Stott, Thomas Daniels and Sons and the Colonial Company, have all been landed proprietors at one time or another. What need to be explained are the factors responsible for the complete exclusion of metropolitan mercantile interests at this period, in favour of a local trading sector which between 1880 and 1920 succeeded in achieving a virtual monopoly over all three sectors of the colonial economy.

The development of a strong local trading sector is linked with the abandonment of protectionist principles in trade. The repeal of the Navigation Acts in 1849, which came as a logical sequel to the equalisation of duties on foreign and British colonial sugar products under the Sugar Duties Act of 1846, enabled the British West Indies to reach new markets, particularly Canada and the United States. Access to the North American market was particularly vital to Barbados in the second half of the nineteenth century, since the

8. *Sources*: Barbados Chancery Court, *Chancery Sales Ledgers: 1885–1893, 1894–1901*; Barbados House of Assembly, *Record of Members of the General Assembly* (compiled by E.W. Shilstone); Peter Campbell, *Commercial Hall*; interview material.

maintenance of an outmoded technology[9] resulted in a low-grade sugar which could not compete with more refined products in demand on the European market. With the introduction of a lower scale of duties for muscovado, the American market grew rapidly after 1872. It quickly became a more attractive proposition than the British one, particularly after the complete abolition of all sugar duties in the United Kingdom in 1874, which set "bounty-fed" refined beet sugar in open competition with unrefined muscovado. The extent to which the pattern of Barbados's trade shifted from Britain to the United States in the last quarter of the nineteenth century is indicated by the growth of sugar exports to the US market from 7,383 hogsheads in 1874 to 43,807 in 1896. During the same period exports to the United Kingdom dwindled from 36,760 hogsheads to 1,101. Commercial houses like Musson's, Da Costa's and Cavan's (reconstituted as Gardiner Austin in 1902) were the largest commission agents of the period which built up trade connections with the North American market.[10] With this shift in trade away from the European market, greater proximity and hence lower freight charges resulted in lower overheads for both merchant and planter. The Bridgetown commission houses benefited doubly from the American market: lower freight charges in particular encouraged the importation of cheaper foodstuffs and estate supplies as return cargoes. In this way the Bridgetown merchants did not restrict their commercial activities to the export of sugar and molasses; they also actively engaged in food importation and wholesaling, dealt in dry goods, and acted as manufacturers' agents and shipping agents.

With the expansion of their commercial activities, the new mercantile class became increasingly differentiated into several strata. At the apex of the hierarchy were to be found the commission agents, manufacturers' representatives and steamship agents. These included such well-known names as Da Costa and Co., S.P. Musson and Co., Wilkinson and Co., R. and G. Challenor Ltd. and J.A. Lynch and Co. At a lower level in the hierarchy were firms which operated as wholesalers. Some of the most prominent in this category were J.R. Bancroft and Co., Evelyn, Roach and Co., A.S. Bryden and Sons, Manning and Co., Collymore and Wright, and

9. Most sugar mills continued to be powered by wind at the end of the nineteenth century. Less than one-quarter had been converted to steam. The most important technological advance in the sugar industry in the second half of the nineteenth century, the vacuum pan, was to be found in operation in only nine mills in the island, representing a very small quantity of sugar produced by the new method.
10. Evidence of the extensive role played by these individual firms as sugar brokers and exporters to the USA can be found in their sugar export ledgers which are housed in the library of the Barbados Museum and Historical Society.

James H. Inniss and Co. At the same time, a number of the largest firms in the first group also acted as wholesalers. Situated at the lowest rung of the ladder were those firms operating solely as retail distributors, supplying dry goods, provisions and hardware. The retail sector is the most difficult to characterise, since it included a wide range of both large and very small businesses situated in the main commercial area of the city. Within this category were also numerous small entrepreneurs: black Barbadians who operated rum shops and small provision stores in the capital itself and scattered across the length and breadth of the island, as well as an army of almost 3,000 hawkers and pedlars, purchasing goods in Bridgetown and selling on credit to the rural proletariat located in the tenantries and free villages.

As early as the 1880s we can see the emergence of a process of horizontal integration, in which the most powerful commercial houses begin to monopolise all three strata of commercial activity in Bridgetown. The last two decades of the nineteenth century saw intense cut-throat competition in which wholesalers and retailers were at the mercy of the commission agents, who controlled the supply of goods, fixed prices and decided to whom they would sell. The power of the major commercial houses was far-reaching. As well as controlling the granting of credit to merchants and traders, which they manipulated through the Commission Merchants' Association,[11] they also wielded great influence in the estates sector which was dependent on them for extending credit, either as individuals or through the BMLA as policyholders. Their control over the credit system was an important mechanism, giving them the power to make or break a business, or to force a planter into bankruptcy. The formation of the trading conglomerate Barbados Shipping and Trading in 1920 was the logical culmination of the developments in the commercial world in the preceding three decades which saw the full-flowering of monopoly capitalism in Barbados. Barbados Shipping and Trading was formed with the express purpose of bringing together the various interests of the six largest commercial houses: Manning's, Gardiner Austin, Da Costa's, Musson's, Challenor's and Wilkinson and Haynes. From its inception, the heads of the subsidiaries which formed the "Big Six" have been majority shareholders, and throughout its history have provided the board of management with directors.

In retrospect, the last two decades of the nineteenth century can be

---

11. To protect their monopoly, one of the rules of the Association stated that "no direct importation of supplies shall be made by local dealers from firms which are not represented in Barbados."

regarded as a crucial period in which the white oligarchy maintained its economic power through the Chancery Court system, which enabled it to monitor the crisis in the sugar industry and to ensure that Barbadian estates remained in hands that were both *local* and *white*.[12] However, it was also a period in which the membership of the oligarchy was transformed. From the onset of the crisis something like two-thirds of the island's sugar estates went into receivership, and most of the casualities were old-established resident and absentee proprietors.[13] As a result, in the words of one surviving representative of the older planter class, "the plantocracy was no more; shopkeepers from the nineties were henceforth the new masters of the island." The first two decades of the twentieth century were a formative period for today's white élite, just as the last two decades of the nineteenth were a period of decline for the plantocracy, when the Bridgetown merchants consolidated the gains of the previous two decades and fully emerged as an agri-business bourgeoisie.

The Martiniquan variant: the ascendancy of the Grands Békés

Like Barbados one can isolate two main factors which contributed to the maintenance of local interests after Abolition in 1848. The first was the continuing stability of an indigenous plantocracy untouched by the political consequences of the French Revolution, which effectively destroyed the economic power of the *Grands Blancs* of Guadeloupe. The second was the existence of readily available local sources of capital to finance the sugar industry. Planters in Martinique were traditionally used to obtaining credit locally to meet the working expenses of cultivating their estates. However, the Martinique planters were dependent for their sources of credit not so much on *other* planters as on the *commissionnaires* of Saint-Pierre, who from the early eighteenth century had operated as factors handling sugar,

12. It is difficult to ascertain precisely in what way the white oligarchy conspired to keep the sales of estates in Chancery within a tight, inner circle. None of the records of the Chancery Court nor any of my discussions with older informants has produced any ·evidence conclusively to prove a "conspiracy theory". However, from the documentary evidence there appear to be a remarkably large number of sales in which only single individuals made successful bids. This would seem to suggest the operation of "ringing".
13. The demise of absentee proprietorship was particularly swift and dramatic. In 1860 about 50% of the total land resources was absentee-owned. By the late 1880s their share had declined to one-third. By 1921 their share had further declined to one-sixth of the total land resources of the period. In 1929 only 7.4% of estate land in Barbados was absentee-owned.

slaves and plantation supplies — for the planters of Martinique as well as the other French islands. Although members of this commercial class continued to be referred to as *commissionnaires* well into the nineteenth century, many in fact also operated as merchants on their own account. Saint-Pierre's development as a traditional and commercial centre was due to its being the terminus of all shipping convoys between metropolitan France and the Antilles, and this meant that at a very early stage the commission earned on both sugar and slaves throughout the French Caribbean made for rapid capital accumulation, which in turn was invested as loans to sugar planters. Thus it can be argued that the pierrotine *commissionnaires* played an active role in preventing the transfer of estates into the hands of outside interests. As a source of credit to the sugar proprietors of Martinique, the *commissionnaires* acted as intermediaries within a similar kind of consignee system to that which operated in the British West Indies. As factors with no overheads their earnings were substantial, and those who operated as wholesalers and retailers fixed a high mark-up on the sale of imported goods, which was usually as much as 40%.

Who were the *commissionnaires* of Saint-Pierre? Did *commissionnaire* and planter belong to two quite different social strata in white creole society? Moreover, did the nucleus of the agri-business bourgeoisie which emerged in the twentieth century develop out of this local trading sector in the same way that it did in Barbados out of the Bridgetown mercantile class? The evidence suggests that on the whole they did not belong to different social strata. An hypothesis was initially formulated that a substantial proportion of today's landed families were originally *commissionnaires*, and that the progression from merchant to planter represented an improved social status for those individuals who made this transition. However, from the evidence available such a regular pattern of upward social mobility is not discernible. Only two *Grand Béké* families appear to have been engaged in commerce during the eighteenth century and up to 1902 (*Béké* is a patois word meaning white and refers to the upper-class white people). A number of pierrotine commission houses were the local branches of metropolitan merchant houses located in such metropolitan ports as Nantes, Bordeaux and Le Hâvre. A very high proportion of the white pierrotine population was in constant flux as a result of the close commercial and trading ties with metropolitan France. Of Saint-Pierre's white population of 4,000 before 1902, one contemporary observer remarked that "amongst the white population many were from Bordeaux, this port being the one which maintained the most important commercial links with Martinique . . . The ports of Marseilles, Nantes and Brest were also in constant communication with the town, and numerous families living in these towns had some of their members in our colony.''[14] By the end of the nineteenth century, however, a number of immigrants who had arrived earlier in the century had permanently settled in Martinique as pierrotine commission agents and traders. Among these arrivals who entered commerce and became incorporated into Béké society were the Bordaz, the Berté, the Lasserre brothers and MacHugh. One notable individual who was later to play a central role in the transformation of the sugar industry in the second half of the nineteenth century was Eugène Eustache, who came to Martinique as an employee of a metropolitan merchant house in the 1820s. Very soon he acquired his own commission house, which he operated until 1853. The returns he accumulated from commerce in the 1840s provided the capital for purchasing a number of sugar estates in the 1850s and 1860s and for forming one of the largest and most profitable of the central factories built in the second half of the nineteenth century, Le Galion.[15]

However, with the notable exception of Eugène Eustache, the *commissionnaires* did not come to play a central role in the sugar industry in the twentieth century in the same way that the merchants of Bridgetown did. The eruption of Mont Pelée on 8 May 1902 resulted in the complete destruction of Saint-Pierre and annihilation of its population, and when commercial life was re-established in Fort-de-France, traditionally the seat of administration and government, it was the newly-created class of *usiniers* who founded the new commercial houses and replaced the now extinct *commissionnaire*.

The specific nature of the Martiniquan situation is exemplified by the active role of the French state in the economic transformation of the colony, and the alliance between metropolitan and local capital with the foundation of the Crédit Colonial. In 1861 the passing of legislation to found the Crédit Colonial was of momentous importance to the future of the sugar industry in the French Antilles. The prime objective of this government initiative was "to lend . . . either to sugar proprietors individually or to syndicates of proprietors, the sums necessary to construct sugar factories in the French colonies or to renew and to improve the equipment of factories in existence at

---

14. *Source*: De Croze, *La Martinique: Catastrophe de Saint-Pierre* (1903:190).
15. It was actually in the role of mortgagee that Eustache acquired his first two estates, Galion (277 ha.) and Grands Fonds (146 ha.). He took over the debts of the aforesaid plantations from their owners in 1843, and managed them himself as a condition of the loan. When the planters were unable to continue payment of interest after 1848, Eustache seized their properties. Galion and Grands Fonds subsequently formed the nucleus of the *centre agricole* of Galion.

the present time.''[16] Another government initiative taken a decade earlier had ensured that a portion of the compensation received by planters and merchants after Abolition was put to good use, with the setting up of colonial banks in both Martinique and Guadeloupe capitalised by one-eighth of the total compensation accorded by the French government.[17] However, the Banques Coloniales like the pierrotine *commissionaires* gave only short-term credit of 9 months on average. The importance of the 1861 legislation lay in its provisions for long-term credit (between 5 and 30 years) which made the undertaking of capital projects possible, resulting in the construction of a modern central factory system in the French Antilles nearly half a century before its introduction in Barbados.

An examination of documentary sources reveals that the prime movers to set up the Crédit Colonial represented an alliance of *Béké* planter interests (along with planters from Guadeloupe and Réunion) and French commercial and industrial interests. Prominent names which figure in official sources are those of Eugène Eustache; Baron de Lareinty, an absentee proprietor and former senator of Martinique; Jean-François Cail, one of France's wealthiest industrialists of the period, whose iron foundry at Lille specialised in the manufacture of equipment for the sugar industry in the Antilles and the sugar beet industry in northern France; and several prominent French food wholesalers and import/export houses. The benefits accruing to the *Békés* as a result of this alliance with the industrial and commercial bourgeoisie of metropolitan France were enormous. With the introduction of central factories in the 1860s, production figures for sugar make a distinction between *sucre d'usine* and *sucre brut* or *sucre d'habitant*, the latter being the moist muscovado produced by using the same time-honoured methods advocated by Père Labat a century and a half earlier. In 1883, 22,800 metric tons of *sucre d'usine* valued at 12⅓ million francs were exported to France, and 19,200 tons of *sucre d'habitant* valued at 8 million francs were exported to the United States.[18] Translated into modern values sugar exports in 1883 would have been valued at over 220 million NF. During the boom years of the 1870s earnings on capital invested in the new factories were unusually high; an official source[19] in the early 1880s quotes rates

16. *Source*: Letter dated 8 September 1860, sent by the Minister for Colonial Affairs to the Minister of Agriculture, Commerce and Public Works, Archives d'Outre-Mer, Paris (Ref. *Général C32 D265*).
17. *Ibid.*
18. *Source*: Jourjon, *Chemins de Fer à Voie Etroite de la Martinique*, Archives d'Outre Mer, Paris (Ref. *Martinique C20 D180*).
19. *Ibid.*

of between 15% and 30% being earned on investments by shareholders. Documentary analysis carried out on accounts books and private papers of several factories in the north-east and south of the island for the 1870s and early 1880s indicated that net profits were as high as 25% in most years.

When reviewing the period from the year the Crédit Colonial started operating in 1861 to the onset of the crisis in 1884, what is striking is the speed with which the new factory system was inaugurated. As early as 1872 a total of eleven factories had been erected at a cost of 14 million francs, 80% of this sum having been advanced by the Crédit Foncier Colonial.[20] By 1884 seventeen *usines centrales* had been erected at a total cost of 28 million francs. Before 1884 the sugar industries had been profitable for both *usinier* and ordinary *habitant sucrier*. Unlike the situation in Guadeloupe and Réunion, no factories or estates had been expropriated by the Crédit Foncier Colonial for bad debts.[21] After 1884 this situation changed rapidly, and this is reflected in the numerous sales and expropriations of properties which were announced in the colony's official gazette, *Le Moniteur*. The speed and efficiency with which a revolution had occurred in the sugar industry, and the astonishingly high rewards reaped by some *Békés* during the boom of the 1870s, makes the tone of righteous indignation underlying the following statement made by the President of the Chamber of Commerce in Saint-Pierre, in response to an official enquiry into the causes of the crisis in the sugar industry, understandable, even though the independent role attributed to local capital is quite erroneous: "All our large *centres agricoles* are endowed with modernised factories, our agriculture has got itself known for its unremitting progress. . . . And this great industrial revolution so quickly and so peacefully accomplished is, we proudly proclaim, our own work. It is we, we alone who have accomplished this with our own hands and our own money.[. . .] The twenty-eight million that our factories cost has been borrowed from our savings and the savings of our families."[22]

The introduction of a central factory system resulted in the creation of a new social class of *usiniers*, in whose hands were concentrated both land and productive processes. The combination of large

20. The Crédit Colonial was re-named the Crédit Foncier Colonial in 1863, and its capital was increased from 3 million to 12 million francs.
21. By the end of 1879 a total of 43 plantations had been expropriated by the Crédit Foncier Colonial: 35 in Réunion and 8 in Guadeloupe. *Source*: Minutes of the Ordinary General Meeting of the Crédit Foncier Colonial, 29th May 1880 (Reported in *Le Moniteur: Journal Official de la Martinique*, 6, 9 and 13 July 1880).
22. *Source*: *Le Moniteur* (16 May 1885).

modern factories and adjacently owned estates formed the nucleus of the new units of production: the *centres agricoles*. By the mid-1930s the eighteen *usines* of the period supplied 60% of their grinding requirements from their own plantations.[23] The emergence of a tiny minority in white creole society monopolising both land resources and production is linked with the creation of these *usines centrales* and the social ascendancy of a small, restricted group of *Grands Békés* who owned them. The most prominent names among this group are Hayot, Despointes, de Reynal, Laguarigue de Survilliers, Clerc, Asselin, de Gentile and Assier de Pompignan. By the turn of the century this powerful group of families, said to have both "name and fortune", owned sugar estates and factories throughout the major sugar–growing areas of Martinique.

Factors of class consolidation

In analysing the strategies by which both merchants and *usiniers* consolidated their newly-won position of power, it is possible to isolate three main factors of class consolidation:
— economic and financial coercive power,
— degree and nature of status boundary maintenance, and
— control of central political mechanisms.

Coercive power. In charting the new élite's consolidation of its economic power in the early twentieth century, we are witness first and foremost to a process in which merchants became planters in one island and planters became merchants in the other. In the case of Barbados, the Chancery Court records are a rich mine of information indicating a swift and dramatic shift in estate ownership. They clearly show that the Bridgetown merchants in a great number of cases had liens on sugar estates, and that many of the plaintiffs who filed bills of complaint against proprietors were merchants. The BMLA for its part was plaintiff in a total of 33 cases in the late nineteenth century. Even more pertinent, many of the purchases of estates out of Chancery were made by merchants, who in the early twentieth century acquired groups of contiguous estates which formed the holdings of the first Central Factories, aided in this process by the Plantations-in-Aid Acts, which granted Barbados £80,000 for modernising the sugar industry. This sum was subsequently put to good use by the merchants who used it to capitalize the Sugar Industry Agricultural Bank in 1907, from which

23. *Source*: Service de L'Agriculture de la Martinique, *Rapport sur l'Industrie de la Canne à la Martinique* (1935:70).

loans were made to planters and merchants at interest. The structural transformation of estate ownership became particularly rapid after 1902, when the merchants decided to suspend loans to planters in view of the latter's inability to extricate themselves from the quagmire of increasing debt.

In Martinique the *Grands Békés* consolidated their sugar interests even further during the depression by extending their domains at the expense of the ordinary planter. Individual *habitations sucreries* had continued to play an important part in sugar production throughout the 1860s and 1870s, as a result of the abolition of duties by the Conseil Général in 1866, which ended the restriction of duties by the 200-year-old *Pacte Colonial*. The abandonment of protectionist principles in trade opened up the United States to the French islands, which created vitally important markets for the several hundred owners of small *habitations sucreries* which survived for a long time beside the *usines centrales*. Those *Békés* who continued to produce muscovado on small family estates after the introduction of central factories ceased grinding in the 1880s as the crisis deepened. Other *Békés* who had closed their mills became totally dependent on the *usine* as suppliers under contract. Ultimately the *usine* came to exert an economic stranglehold over these independent planters. All risks were taken by the planters whereas the *usine* was relatively unencumbered, since payment under contract was determined by a fluctuating market price and the profitability of the *usine* in any given year. This relationship of dependence was reinforced by the *usine* extending credit to its suppliers during inter-crop periods. An inability to repay these loans in periods of falling prices, particularly after 1883/4, resulted in their plantations being seized by the *usine* and incorporated into its domain.[24]

When commercial life was restored again after 1902, it was the returns from sugar realised by the *usiniers* in the last quarter of the nineteenth century which capitalised the new commercial houses in Fort-de-France, giving the *Grands Békés* a virtual monopoly in the tertiary sector as commission agents, wholesalers and exporters. Like their counterparts in Barbados, a restricted group of about ten families owning land, factories and commercial houses came to exert

24. Other proprietors indebted to the Crédit Foncier Colonial also had their *habitations* expropriated. As at 31 December 1900, the Colony had purchased a total of 31 estates for a programme of land reform. It is interesting to note that the subdivision of estates which took place at the beginning of the twentieth century, actually underwent a reversal in the 1920s and '30s. In comparing the Agricultural Censuses for 1911 and 1936, Revert (1949:268-70) shows that the area covered by larger estates increased by one-third between these two dates. This was accounted for by an increase in the size of the domains owned by the *usiniers*.

a tight control over every aspect of the colonial economy. By the early 1920s the *Grands Békés* had established an 85% share of the export trade and held a similar percentage of all shareholders in the town's business houses. Legislation passed by the French government in 1922 and 1935, fixing quotas respectively on rum and sugar exports, effectively strengthened the monopolistic power of the *Grands Békés*, since under this system quotas were accorded to each *usinier* on the basis of productive capacity. The *bourgeois de couleur* were effectively excluded from the most lucrative commercial activities, being principally confined to entertainment, publishing and the smaller retail distributive trades. Through a process of "secondary colonisation", the *Grands Békés* also gained a foothold in Guadeloupe, where they became the owners of between one-fifth and one-quarter of the island's land resources, as well as setting up commission houses, sugar factories and distilleries.

Of paramount importance in this process was the control that the agri-business bourgeoisie exerted over access to credit. In Barbados this was through such institutions as the Colonial Bank, the local branches of several Canadian banks, the BMLA, the Barbados Savings Bank and the Sugar Industry Agricultural Bank. In Martinique this control was exerted through the Banque de la Martinique, the Banque de France and the Crédit Foncier Colonial. Since the agri-business bourgeoisie in both islands controlled access to finance capital through their extensive shareholdings and directorships in these institutions, it had the power to decide *who* could raise the necessary capital to purchase estates, set up central factories and open commercial houses. In Barbados, where a system of patronage and sponsorship existed, the agri-business bourgeoisie was able to control the entry of personnel into its ranks. In Martinique, where the ranks of the *Grands Békés* were closed to outsiders, credit was usually only granted to other *Grands Békés*. Professional and trading associations also played a "watchdog" role. In Barbados, for example, the all-powerful Commission Merchants Association dominated by the "Big Six" operated a credit system which controlled the necessary supplies of credit to the Bridgetown traders for purchasing goods wholesale. Thus a combine of the major commercial houses was able to decide *who* they would advance credit to at their own discretion. This inevitably meant that no businesses owned by black Barbadians grew to any appreciable size in the twentieth century, whereas a number owned by urbanised "redlegs" in the first decade or two of the century prospered considerably.

Status boundary maintenance. While the new élite in both islands continued to maintain the established status boundary of race and ethnicity, the mechanisms of social reproduction differed considerably. In Barbados at a very early stage the ascendant commercial class forged financial and familial links with the surviving remnants of the nineteenth-century plantocracy, linking the names of planter families like Haynes, Sealy, Pile and Chandler to those of Manning, Bryden, Wilkinson and Da Costa. The extent to which intermarriage took place between members of the indigenous plantocracy and the Bridgetown commercial class points to an *incorporative* strategy of class consolidation. The extent to which the social structure of the new élite was open is also indicated by the process of upward social mobility for poor white and plantation supervisory staff which existed in the twentieth century, through a system of patronage and sponsorship. One particularly striking phenomenon in the early twentieth century was the rise of the self-made "redleg" businessman who, having migrated from the Scotland district (the traditional preserve of marginality for the poorer white rural populace subsisting outside the plantation system), in Sheppard's words "led his one cow into Bridgetown" and within a generation became the owner of a business empire, a sugar planter and a member of the most prestigious white social and sporting clubs of the island. This pattern of upward social mobility has been repeated many times over during the twentieth century, as families of "redleg" origin like the Goddards, the Dowdings, the Emtages and the Seales rose rapidly in the social hierarchy and became incorporated into the ranks of the agri-business bourgeoisie.

Conversely, in Martinique the extent to which the *Grands Békés* not only upheld the solidarity of "caste" but also maintained a rigid internal hierarchy in white society is indicative of a strategy of *exclusivity*. The stratification of *Béké* society into three major sectors or classes — *Grands Békés*, *Békés Moyens* and *Petits Blancs* — produced a segmentation into patronymial groups which have tended to remain distinct and separate through the practice of intra-group endogamy. By the early twentieth century, the socioeconomic differences between the *Grands Békés* and the *Békés Moyens* had already become institutionalized. Many of the *Békés Moyens*, having lost their estates during the depression, had become a middle-class administrative and supervisory cadre employed in the commercial houses, sugar factories and on the plantations owned by the *Grands Békés*. Others who had continued to operate as owner-managers on their *habitations* had been forced to abandon sugar production and to transform their ancient mills into distilleries, producing *rhum agricole* for local consumption. Unlike their poor white counterparts in Barbados, the situation of the *Petits Blancs* in the social hierarchy changed little in the twentieth century. Those *Békés*

Goyaves who abandoned smallholding in the countryside and came to Fort de France found clerical posts and unskilled manual work in the businesses owned by other white creoles, and some managed to establish themselves as small shopkeepers. However, there was no equivalent phenomenon in Martinique white creole society to the successful "redleg" businessmen in Barbados.

Political control. In the sphere of politics, the Bridgetown merchants acceded to a direct political role in a way that the *usiniers* of Martinique were unable to do. Every major commercial house had members who sat on statutory boards, served as vestry members, and were members of the House of Assembly, the Legislative Council and the Executive Committee. In the case of the elected house, commercial interests were established very early in the City of Bridgetown and the urban parishes of St Michael and Christ Church. The members of the House of Assembly for the City of Bridgetown, for example, were regarded by Commercial Hall (the local Chamber of Commerce) as representatives of business interests, and therefore of the Hall itself. The Hall usually "requisitioned" (a term it used itself) a candidate to fill a vacancy in the City, and the selected candidate was virtually assured of success at the polls. It also had the ear of the Governor which gave it a direct line of communication with the Colonial Office at home, and it did not hesitate to avail itself of this privilege. Referring to its political influence, Peter Campbell states: "The Hall usually had the Governor and the Government, as well as the West India Committee, on its side. Time and time again memoranda submitted by the Hall were forwarded by the Governor to the Colonial Office with his blessing and endorsement."

In Martinique, the *Békés* lost their direct political role after 1871, when the government of the Third Republic accorded universal suffrage. After that date it was a rising coloured political élite which filled the offices of the Conseil Général and the Conseil Privé. By 1901 only four out of the 36 members of the elected house were *Békés*. During the 1870s and 1880s the political aspirations of the white creole community and the middle-class *gens de couleur* became increasingly polarized, as the coloured political élite, imbued with the social democratic ideals of the Third Republic, sought to counteract the aristocratic pretensions of the *Grands Békés*, who continued to believe in their divine right to rule. No longer able to impose their political will by force, or through the ballot box, the *Grands Békés* retreated from political life and in the twentieth century adopted indirect forms of political influence, which at some periods have proved extremely pervasive.

Conclusion

In both islands it is evident that the conditions conducive to the maintenance of local interests at the high noon of imperialism were similar in two respects, namely the presence of stable indigenous plantocracies, and the existence of plentiful local sources of capital for cultivation and production. However, in the modern world the paths by which forms of monopoly capitalism were developed from *within* colonial society by local élites were different. Whereas in Barbados a relatively independent role was played by the Bridgetown merchants in this process, in Martinique the same outcome was predicated upon the alliance of local planter interests with the industrial and commercial bourgeoisie of metropolitan France, via the intervention of the French state as acting intermediary.

With varying success, the agri-business bourgeoisie in each island succeeded in manning all the strategic posts of the colonial economy, administration, finance and banking. However, in having consolidated its newly-won position of power, the new agri-business bourgeoisie has not had an entirely immutable composition. This is particularly true of the Barbadian case, in which the existence of avenues of social mobility for the poorer classes of white creole society has resulted in the boundaries of what constitutes the agri-business bourgeoisie being fairly fluid. Moreover the development of a second monopoly corporation, Plantations Ltd., founded by a group of planters in 1917 and originally conceived as a means of counteracting the monopoly wielded by the merchants in the handling of estate supplies, later diversified its activities into the sphere of commerce. Changes in the composition of the agri-business bourgeoisie in Martinique, via the incorporation of other groups into the ranks of the *Grands Békés*, have been a more recent phenomenon. A number of *Békés Moyens*, having profited from the commercialisation of banana production and the growth of the retail distributive trade sector during the last two decades, now have wealth and influence equal to that of the *usiniers* of old.

3

SOCIAL ORIGINS OF THE COUNTER-PLANTATION SYSTEM IN ST LUCIA

Yvonne Acosta and Jean Casimir

Background

The fabric of St Lucian society has not been patterned by a close relationship with the outer world. Political interferences of colonial powers had a scant impact on the content of locally created economic and social organizations. Initially, the parameters of the island's strategic location largely determined the history of agricultural development. This development was initiated by French settlers in a similar way to that of the majority of Caribbean colonies — with the typical unit of production being the small farm with the tendency towards self-sufficiency. Subsequently, the establishment of plantations was retarded during the "golden age" of plantation economy in the Caribbean.

Attempts were made to develop a plantation economy on the island in the last few decades of the eighteenth century. Nevertheless, in this period and later St Lucia never matured as a plantation colony; this was mainly the result of a lack of metropolitan sponsorship but also because of the limited physical capacity of the island. Physical expansion of plantations was restricted by soil conditions, since the island is mountainous with the only available areas of suitable undulating and fertile land being the few valleys and coastal areas.

Retardation of the plantation economy in its early stages was inevitable as a consequence of a number of events, both internal and external. Of great impact was the actual abandonment of estates by the enslaved African labour force, in what can be referred to as the first emancipation (1793), during the period of the French Revolution. St Lucia subsequently suffered, as a disputed territory, in the international warfare that followed. An initially impoverished plantocracy found it impossible to survive in the early nineteenth century and declared bankruptcy by the 1830s.

In the period following St Lucia's second, metropolitan-sponsored emancipation (1834), the renewed plantocracy managed to survive by the introduction of the *métayage* system as a compromise system of production between itself and the peasantry. This system, as well as the endeavours of the ex-enslaved to establish

34

some measure of self-sufficiency in agriculture, ensured that the dual systems of plantation and peasant economies would coexist during the rest of the nineteenth century and the twentieth century — with further decline of the former and minor progress by the latter.

There is evidence of diversified agricultural output in early decades of the twentieth century,[1] followed by a brief return to the monoproduction of sugar at the beginning of the second half of the century, the sugar industry becoming the main employer and money earner. Banana production replaced sugar cane by the 1960s. With the predominance of banana production, the economic organization of plantations underwent important modifications, and consequently transformed the relations between the plantation owners and the peasantry.

Early development of a counter-plantation system

A major hypothesis emerges from an in-depth study of the historiography of St Lucia: that within the society there emerged a system in opposition to, but dependent upon, the plantation. This counter-plantation system represented a number of stages towards the development of a peasantry, or what could preferably be referred to as a quasi-peasantry.[2] The plantation system, being severely constrained, allowed avenues for minor progress in the establishment of a peasant movement. The typical reaction by the dominant class in the society was the imposition of controls in the embryonic stages. These constraints were economic, political and social on the part of the plantocracy and its political machinery, and obviously inhibited the full deployment of a peasant system.

In St Lucia, the transition from a slavery-based economy to some type of market economy took place during the whole of the nineteenth century. Within this context three actors took part: the metropolitan country whose only interest was the island's ability to contribute to its own (Britain's) progress towards industrial

1. Sugar remained the predominant crop, but citrus and other fruits and vegetables were responsible for a sizeable part of total imports.
2. One could apply to St Lucia, Marshall's definition of West Indian peasantry: "The West Indian peasantry exhibits certain special characteristics. It is recent in origin; its growth — in numbers and in acreage controlled — was consistent during the first forty or sixty years of its existence; it exists alongside and in conflict with the plantation; and it did not depend exclusively on the soil for its income and subsistence". (W.K. Marshall, "Notes on Peasant Development in the West Indies since 1838", *Social and Economic Studies*, University of the West Indies, vol. 17, no. 3, Sept. 1969, p. 253.)

capitalism; the colony itself, which had to rely on a given organization of its resources and to produce a surplus of merchandise to be exchanged for metropolitan goods and services; and the would-be wage-earners. The last of these had their own ideas about life and only a small number of the labour force actually became wage-earners, or rather a small part of their time was actually exchanged for a wage which was continually held at depressed levels.

Emancipation in 1838 unleashed the tendency of the population to be independent of the plantation, i.e. to secure some part of the available resources. Despite tremendous odds, there was a gradual movement away from the estates. Labourers resisted participation in wage relations under prevailing conditions. The planters, anxious to safeguard their entire labour force, attempted by various means to keep all the ex-slaves on the estates in relationships which closely approximated to their earlier servile condition. Insecurity or lack of tenure, as well as relatively low wages for plantation labour, and sometimes high rent and long contracts, reinforced the determination of the ex-enslaved to seek new and better opportunities away from the estates.[3] They attempted to buy land, even at prohibitive prices. By the 1840s the changing trends of land tenure were already apparent. For example, the estimated numbers of freeholders between 1845 and 1861 indicate the trend: 1845, 1,345; 1846, 1,390; 1849, 1,920; 1853, 2,343; 1857, 2,045; 1861, 2,185.[4]

The limits to more rapid freehold land acquisition were numerous and consequently, renting and leasing of land from planters became a feature of the peasantry's development. Thus early peasant movement was restricted to lands on the periphery of the estates. Marshall, for example, refers to the rapid transformation of Micoud and Dennery, main plantation areas. Planters opposed freehold settlement and encouraged leaseholding and renting, in order to accommodate yet still control. Where access to land was prohibited, squatting became an important avenue for establishing an independent existence. During the 1850s and 1860s this quasi-peasant system was able to expand,[5] as the plantation system became subject to the vicissitudes of the international market. (After 1846–8 many estates were abandoned.)

The fact that St Lucia was then a Crown colony meant that

3. *Ibid.*, p. 254
4. W.K. Marshall, 'The Social and Economic Development of the Windward Islands, 1836–65', Ph.D. thesis, Cambridge University, 1963.
5. As early as 1845, mention is made of a new village in the heights of Soufriere which is considered the first inland settlement " . . . Lieutenant Governor Power of St Lucia observed in 1845 that cultivation might be seen creeping up the mountain in every direction." *ibid.*, pp. 313 and 317.

extensive areas of land were monopolised by the government, and prohibitions to its use and discriminatory land taxes were introduced to "deter labourers from obtaining possession either by purchase or lease of detached or remote plots of ground and becoming what in these islands are usually denominated squatters . . ."[6] In 1849, a tax of 4 shillings was imposed on cultivated land and was designed to operate, as in Tobago, against all smallholders while favouring labourers on the estates and cultivating land as "provision grounds".[7] The imposition of this tax was the cause of a major uprising in the island in the same year.

The expansion of this quasi-peasant system continued during the second half of the nineteenth century, after a brief respite in the contraction of the sugar industry. Moreover, there was another sugar depression in the 1880s and as a result more land was available for peasant acquisition. Lewis,[8] Marshall[9] and others refer to this period as one of "expansion of the peasantry" in the Windward Islands generally. Peasants took the opportunity to participate in the export-oriented economy via their production of new staple crops, particularly after the 1870s. By the end of the 1880s government policy towards peasants was ostensibly modified. There was even a token of Crown lands for sale in 1890, but the conditions of sale and settlement were not attractive to labourers, since by this time squatting on Crown lands had greatly increased.[10]

In general, the limited access to land and the destitution of the plantation system made the circumstances ripe for the introduction and acceptance of a compromise solution. The *métayage* system was a solution to the existence of plantation and counter-plantation alike — the need to contribute to the imperial economy and the need to secure some degree of self-sufficiency. The system of land tenure and labour organization fostered an even greater increase in smallholdings and at the same time increased the production of export-oriented crops (sugar) as well as peasant crops of cocoa and provisions (as early as 1857). The system competed with wage labour and existed for approximately three decades (but was reverted to at later points in time). Thereafter sharecropping in various forms established itself as a definite feature of rural St Lucia.

6. *Ibid.*, p. 352.
7. *Ibid.*, p. 354.
8. W.A. Lewis, *The Evolution of the Peasantry in the British West Indies*, Colonial Office pamphlet, no. 656, 1936.
9. W.K. Marshall, *op. cit.*, p. 253.
10. R.A. Foreman, *Land Settlement Scheme in St Lucia*, based on a survey of the Agricultural and Social Conditions of the Island, p. 15.

Sharecropping or *métayage*[11] represents an economic institution, a compromise between agriculture for self-subsistence linked to the plantation system and self-propelled inward-oriented ventures. From the planter's viewpoint, one of the reasons for its failure was the importance which the *métayer* attached to his own provision crops, hence the neglect of export crops.

Labourers, on the one hand, were able to establish a semi-independent existence within the plantation system, which in principle allowed their income to exceed the expected output of their own subsistence plots. On the other hand, *métayage* created tenant employees in preference to wage labour, and a milieu propitious to forms of exploitation which sidestepped imported labour legislation. *Métayage* contracts, mostly unwritten, left the *métayers* unprotected from the whims of the landlords even though there was an Ordinance in 1850 to protect them. Nonetheless, in practice and particularly during the second half of the century, difficulties faced by the planters seemed to indicate that the *métayers* were not devoid of bargaining power.

The extensive use of the *métayage* system in St Lucia is understandable in view of the predominance of small planters. In this context, it was particularly amenable to periods of crisis since it produced a higher yield per acre with lower production costs and reduced recurrent expenditure.[12]

A temporary solution to economic problems did not however ensure the evolution of a separate system. St Lucian society appeared as a dual structure: a colonial one, imposed by the political authorities through public administration, import-export trade and plantation activities, and a local one emerging around inward-oriented agriculture, family and community life. At no time had the bearers of the local structure been able to develop fully the model which can be designed on the basis of their practices, nor had they been able to isolate themselves from the dominant plantation system, to create a distinct peasant economy.

11. Under the system both planter and *métayer* were interdependent. The planter supplied the land for cultivation of sugar, by the *métayer*. By a share system, the *métayer* paid the cost of manufacturing the sugar out of his half share of all the sugar produced which he received in compensation for his labour. The planter received the other half portion of the sugar and all the incidental products of sugar manufacture. *ibid.*, pp. 227–8.
12. "Circumstances forced the system on planters who lacked capital for wages and immigration . . . This was clearly seen on the small estates. On these, because only small outlays of capital are necessary, *métayage* was highly successful, provided that the . . . planters had some stock and a good mill". (*Ibid.*, pp. 247–8.)

To surmount the numerous obstacles to their development, the peasantry of St Lucia developed at least two social instruments which made it unique. These local innovations, linked to counter-plantation activities, have been obviously viewed as the very source of backwardness. It is important nonetheless to find out their rationales.

During the nineteenth century (and up to the present)[13], when St Lucians were solving their problems with their own resources, the negotiations would be carried out in patois. In this case, the basic concepts used in the course of discussions were laid down by the natives. This fact ruled out any external influence which was not accommodated by or adapted to the local circumstances. The colonial authorities could limit the range of relations carried out in patois, but they had no mechanisms to interfere in these relations let alone to arbitrate conflicts developing from them, unless invited by the St Lucians and to the extent permitted by them.

In conflicts in which the French Creoles and the British administration were opposed, as they were throughout most of the nineteenth century, the problem of patois as an obstacle to law enforcement and consequently to "economic progress" as designed by the dominant classes was never raised. According to one interpretation,[14] the perpetuation of patois is integral to an understanding of the political conflicts between the Roman Catholic Church and the administration. The use of patois as a main means of communication was the most important bond between St Lucians and the Church, and undoubtedly excluded the British. The bilingualism (English versus patois) gives the first indication of cultural dualism in the society.

As they developed a parallel language, so too the St Lucian peasantry, realising that there is no peasantry without land, found a means of extracting their land from control other than their own. The small amount of land on which their survival was based was removed from colonial interference. To avoid any possibility of repossession by the planters or the Crown, the decisions on alienation of property (land) were taken away from individuals and deposited in the hands of the community.

The "Community Property System" emerged as an institution

---

13. At Public Hearings of the St Lucian Land Reform Commission 1980, the very first sentence directed to the Chairman, Dr Beckford, was the following: "Excuse me, Sir, but I cannot speak English so much, I prefer to speak Patois instead". The second sentence explains that: "I do not want to start in English and I cannot complete". (St Lucia Land Reform Commission, Transcript of Second Session, 25 February 1980.)
14. Insight gained from interviews conducted in St Lucia during 1980.

under which the legacy of land is the common prerogative of the entire family, "even generations of the same family" having descended from the original owner-occupier. Rights to plots of land so controlled — and commonly known and described as "family land" — and produce derived therefrom are shared. Those who inherit such lands are not allowed to sell or dispose of them at will, unless perhaps by agreement of the entire family.

In publications discussing the peasantry, the Community Property System is seen as a main barrier to development and progress.[15] In St Lucia, multiple ownership is supposed to restrain individual initiative and to prevent the peasant from utilising credit facilities while one would think of it as the only avenue for individual initiative to evolve away from metropolitan influences. The irrationality of the St Lucia peasant is mentioned by most observers, among whom the more benign would speak of ignorance and low levels of instruction. It is remarkably difficult to find a study which will see "the inability of existing Agricultural and Credit Institutions to devise a workable relationship with the institution. . . ."[16]

Multiple ownership of land is widespread in terms of the numbers of people involved, and it seems that rather large areas of land can be categorised as "family land".[17] The St Lucia Five Year Development Plan 1966–70 estimates that a total acreage of approximately 20,000 acres may be involved. This may even be an understatement, since the system by nature defies official records.

The Community Property System, as an institution of the Caribbean peasantry, recognises the right of all descendants to a given inheritance, i.e. land, since it is such a scarce resource. Hence the most specific feature of the system is the inalienability of the right to dispose of the land. This inherent feature was intended to extricate the system from the bourgeois capitalist conception of the world. What is denied in the Community Property System is precisely one of the pillars of Western thought, the *jus uti et abuti*, the right to use and abuse one's property.

The creation of these totally new and innovative institutions was a

15. Of. R.A. Foreman, *op.cit.*, and J.J. Finkel, "Patterns of land tenure in the Leeward and Windward Islands and their relevance to the problems of agricultural development in the West Indies" in Horowitz (ed.) *Peoples and Cultures of the Caribbean*, p. 299.
16. Weirs Consulting Services Ltd., *Small Farming Study in the Lesser Developed Member Territories of the Caribbean*, vol. 1(a) Country Reports. Prepared for the Caribbean Development Bank, 1976, p. 9
17. In detailed discussions we have contested the arguments which posit that the origin of the institution is Napoleonic, on the basis of the logic of the system and on the basis of comparisons with similar institutions in Haiti and Jamaica.

response to the monopoly of the dominant strata over land resources and the attempt to keep those of African descent in a state of inarticulacy and disaggregation. These descendants organized their communal life and introduced forms of economic organization which resulted in quasi-full employment, forcing the planters to turn to indentured labour, which they could ill afford. Above all this, they created and preserved their language distinct from both French and English. Finally, they completely removed the small proportion of land on which they achieved control from the influence of the dominant classes and from the state.

While the local initiatives were being created by the pseudo peasant society, all avenues to and social intercourse with the outside world were monopolised by the tiny sector of the population in control of the unviable plantation system. The dominance and perpetuation of the plantation system were ensured by political factors determined by the interplay of international politics within the British empire. These political factors, channelled through the dominant class, strangled local initiatives and local social intercourse and ensured that the peasant society was totally excluded from participation in the political process. Social intercourse seemed aimed at safeguarding what had been achieved by each social subsystem. More specifically, the differences in economic interests of planters and non-planters acquired a fundamental political character in spite of their visible economic overtones. Class formations were observed at the level of this structural twist of the St Lucian society.

Hence the dual structure one perceives in nineteenth-century social developments was basically of a political nature, although the two social groups are clearly visible through the differences in their economic interests — with the superimposed political structure strongly determining the basis of local intercourse.

Further analysis reveals that St Lucia's dual society ought to be visualised as a single binary system of processes arranged in a way which would reproduce each of its components in their distinctiveness unless the space in which this dualism originated were modified. Rearrangements or modification of the economic practices meant adjustments in the social relations in the process of producing and sharing the bulk of the local wealth.

In the twentieth century, international politics continued to influence the social structural arrangements of colonial territories, like St Lucia. The prevailing ideology of the "imperial political economy" helped to prolong the existence of West Indian plantocracy, but only briefly. According to Lord Olivier, "I have no desire to avoid or dissemble the basal issue which is — do we prefer to have cheaper sugar or to preserve our oldest colonies, which regard themselves as part of our community?"[18] By the first quarter of the century the political interest in keeping the doomed plantation sector afloat had been substantially eroded. The extension of its buoyancy depended on the International Sugar Agreement of 1937, which established specific quotas. Some viability for the sugar plantations was then assured, but paradoxically it buried once and for all the sugar plantocracy (of proprietors and managers) by preventing its specific interests from playing any leading role in the development of the country as its bargaining power diminished. Instead of economic competition, groups of interests involved in sugar production, i.e. factory and estate owners, cane farmers and agricultural workers, were driven in a political game to secure the trickling down of the preference-cum-quota system.

Sugar producers were compelled to invest in other economic areas. On the demise of sugar, banana production was introduced. The switch to this particular staple resulted in fundamental changes in the island's social structure. All strata of the society then competed for a share in the economic wealth of bananas. This competition was played out in the political milieu since decisions on wages, profits or prices were made without recourse to the market situation.

Background to the development of agriculture in the twentieth century

In the late 1920s Lord Olivier's Sugar Commission reported on the diversity of production in St Lucia. Apart from sugar and sugar products, which accounted for 45% of the exports, lime, lime products, cocoa, copra, fruits and vegetables were also exported. It is apparent that food production was fairly high.[19] The versatility of the local productive system was reiterated by the West India Royal Commission in 1938, although it identified sugar as "the main crop in St Lucia", but grown on a small scale.[20] In 1951, the industry still played a vital part in the economy of the Colony "and the workers in the industry constituted the largest group of employees in the

18. "The Sugar Crisis as a menace to the West Indies", speech by the Rt. Hon. Lord Olivier, London, Roy. Empire Soc., April 1930, p. 8.
19. Report of the West Indian Sugar Commission, London: HM Stationery Office, 1930, pp. 85-9.
20. West India Royal Commission Report, London: H.M. Stationery Office, 1945, pp. 409-10. This Report is hereafter referred to as the Moyne Commission Report.

island."[21] In 1953, however, St Lucia Banana Growers Association Ltd. was being created as banana production began to expand in competition with sugar. By 1964, banana cultivation expanded throughout the island. Sugar was no longer produced.

The shift to banana cultivation meant a shift in emphasis by peasants away from inward-oriented crops to the production of the export crop as their main activity. Banana growing became predominantly a small farm crop by the 1960s. From the point of view of the rural population, the opportunity to gain the more steady income that banana could provide was apparently the greatest impetus to the adoption of the crop, to the neglect of others. The development of marketing and other arrangements which favoured production also facilitated the shift. It was estimated that farms of less than 10 acres were responsible for at least 56% of the banana crop produced,[22] though extensive mixed cultivation was still relevant.

The diversity of agricultural produce, and the flexibility with which productive factors were re-allocated to ensure the switch from one staple to another, makes it apparent that the economy of the country is characterised by an articulation of production for export and for local consumption. One is under the impression that the scale of both sectors would in itself and *inter alia* demand this arrangement.[23] Hence the conclusion of the West Indian Sugar Commission with respect to St Lucia: "There is no reason why, with intelligent handling . . . the island should not be made self-sufficient."[24]

What appears economically feasible faces the same sociological and political hurdles that made it impossible for a self-sufficient society to evolve during the previous century. The involvement of large numbers of producers in small-scale agriculture, whereby the basic food production is ensured, reproduces at the same time several forms of isolation and deprivation, very functional to the maintenance of a flexible export-oriented sector.

The complete picture on the expansion of access to land resources

21. Report of the Commission of Enquiry into the Stoppage of Work at the Sugar Factories in St Lucia in March 1952, and into the Adequacy of existing wage-fixing machinery in that Colony. pp. 71 and 77. This Report is hereafter referred to as The Malone Commission Report.
22. *Small Farming Study* (1976), *op.cit.*, p. 46.
23. "The organisation of local food supply . . . even if affected will leave the labouring population largely devoid of means to buy clothing and other imported necessaries of life." Lord Olivier, *The West Indian Sugar Crisis: a Basal Issue for the Empire*, London: Roy. Empire Soc., 1930, p. 6.
24. West Indian Sugar Commission Report, *op.cit.*, para 302, p. 89.

on the part of the peasantry remains blurred. One has had to rely on studies carried out at certain points in time to assess the situation. In this study on *Social Structure of the British Caribbean*, published in 1946, G. Cumper gave the first global appraisal; estates in St Lucia, he said, held 40% of the farm acreage and were less important than the combined shares of middle and large peasant holdings.[25] Data available for the period 1946 and 1958 reveal a tendency towards land acquisition and/or fragmentation of existing holdings as well as an increase in the number of peasants.[26] Peasant holdings remained scattered in very small acreages (under 5 acres).

In 1976, less than twenty years later, peasants with 0–5 acres accounted for 82% of the total number of holdings and occupied only 14.2% of total farming land. Farmers in the 200-acre category represented 0.6% of the farming population, yet held 52.7% of the total acreage in holdings.[27] Ownership of extensive estate acreages employing wage labour is controlled by a multinational company and a few individuals. Large numbers of the labour force involved in small-scale agricultural production on their miniscule acreages are also wage earners.

Peasant holdings were, according to a 1958 report,[28] held by a variety of tenurial arrangements — freeholding, leaseholding, renting, squatting and sharecropping — thus presaging an intricate knot of social relations between modern companies, traditional estate owners, salaried workers, *métayers* and independent farmers. One is tempted to conclude that the nineteenth-century linkages of plantation and counter-plantation economies remain the underlying structural arrangements of St Lucian agriculture — or at least did to up to 1958. It will be seen that the demise of the planters as a social class set in motion other forms of social articulation.

Economic practices of the employers in the sugar and banana industries

Relatively detailed description of economic practices in St Lucia has been found in the Commissions of Enquiry Reports of 1952 (Malone Commission), 1957 (Jackson Commission) and 1980 (Interim report of the Commission of Enquiry into the Banana Industry and Interim Report of the Beckford Land Reform Commission together with the

25. G. Cumper, *Social Structure of the British Caribbean* (excluding Jamaica), part III, Un. of the West Indies, p. 14.
26. W.K. Marshall, *op.cit.*, p. 258.
27. *Small Farming Study*, (CDB), *op.cit.*, p. 47.
28. R.A. Foreman, *op.cit.*, p. 6.

Transcripts of its Public Hearings). The first two reports deal with the production of sugar cane, the third with banana production and the last one with the general infrastructural question of land tenure.[29] These data cover the economic activities which are responsible for the bulk of St Lucia's wealth at a given time, and their scrutiny assists in clarifying the mechanisms through which the population makes a living.

As Lord Olivier puts it, "Some colonies depend for money earnings wholly upon one industry."[30] The case of St Lucia is not as extreme, but sugar represented in 1951 47% of its total value of exports[31] and had the largest single impact on the utilisation of its labour force.[32]

When the quota system was introduced, it set prearranged quantities to be supplied. Sugar production could not be expanded on the initiative of the sugar companies, but was based on the expected demand situation within the metropole. The price was arrived at year after year, before initiating the cycle of production, and one could infer *ex-ante* the revenue for the year's production.

A memorandum by the chairman of the St Lucia Sugar Association in January 1952 presented the mechanics of the industry in a systematic form, through a breakdown of the total revenue under four heads: 1). payments for supplies; 2). wages; 3). overhead expenses; and 4). depreciation and profits.[33] When the total price of the end-product was known, the St Lucia Sugar Association discussed a wage agreement with workers' representatives, the basis of which was "the price variation and not the selling price in relation to production costs."[34] Hence the rate of profit is never revealed and is never considered in wage negotiations. In these circumstances wages showed little or no variation or adjustment and could indeed be compared with those of the previous century.[35] The practice of the

29. Report of the Commission of Enquiry into the Banana Industry not consulted due to its unavailability.
30. *The West Indian Sugar Crisis*, Lord Olivier, *op.cit.*, p. 13.
31. Malone Commission Report, para. 7, p. 3.
32. "The sugar industry is of considerable importance to St Lucia as a whole. Not only does it provide employment directly for a large number of workers, but a proportion, by no means small, of those not actually engaged in the cultivating and reaping of sugar canes, and in the manufacture of sugar, derive employment indirectly from the prosperity of this industry." (*Ibid.*, para. 9, p. 4.)
33. *Ibid.*, p. 43.
34. *Ibid.*
35. "In some parts of the West Indies notably the smaller and poorer islands, rates for agricultural labourers have advanced little beyond the shilling-a-day introduced after emancipation. Examples are the ls 2d a day in St Kitts [. . .], the statutory minimum of ls 3d (ls for women) in Grenada and St Lucia, ls ld and 10d

industry in the 1950s of non-disclosure of profits was heavily criticised by the Malone Commission,[36] and in fact what was true then could be viewed as characteristic of industrial relations in the island. The argumentation presented was valid as to the effect of the system of wage negotiation on the worker's attitude and on the perceptions of the whole society, then and subsequently: "It is realised that [the necessity for revealing profits made] will be repugnant to the sugar companies and perhaps to other employers, but it must be pointed out that this secrecy about profits has been a weighty factor in breeding profound and deep-seated distrust of the employers among the sugar industry workers [and other citizens of St Lucia too]."[37]

What is referred to as entrepreneurship in this economic context was of a specific character. The point is that when risks and uncertainty are eliminated from an economic undertaking and returns can be determined with accuracy before a cycle of production is initiated, such undertaking is not managed by an entrepreneur, nor can the returns obtained be considered as profits. This undertaker receives contractual payments since he knows in advance, like other factors of production, what he is to receive for his services. The term profit is used in such context by analogy and quite improperly.

The system under which the sugar companies operated was also unfair to contributors of sugar cane production. Companies were in an advantageous position in that they were more or less self-sufficient units. They depended on external supplies of sugar cane for less than 20% of the total input to their mills. This average varied between more than a third at the Dennery Factory Company and 12% at the Roseau Company. The additional supply of raw materials would come from the production of *métayers* and contributors which was sold to the factory under unfavourable terms.[38]

---

in St Vincent". (Moyne Commission Report, *op.cit.*, chapter III, para. 7, p. 32.)
36. "It has been the policy of the sugar companies not to disclose their profits".
     Malone Commission Report, para 13, p. 5. "In any event the undisclosure of the
     individual profits of each company puts those negotiating with the representa-
     tives of labour in the advantageous position of having a monopoly of the
     information on which the negotiations should be based." *ibid.*, para 14, p. 5.
     "We cannot see how they (sugar employers) can adopt a position that the wages
     paid are fair according to the price of sugar and production costs and refuse to
     support it except with vague figures, and expect to be believed." *ibid.*, para. 58,
     p. 17.
37. *Ibid.* para. 97, p. 26.
38. "In addition to the canes grown by the three Sugar Companies, canes are
     supplied to the factories by contributors and *métayers*. Contributors are small
     farmers who own lands which they plant in sugar canes, and sell the canes to the

The Commissioners' perception of *métayers* and contributors in the 1950s was one of "ignorance" and lack of interest in the industry. Yet the report conceded that the group was insecure and powerless[39] in the face of the monopoly position held by the sugar companies. However the Commission failed to realise that in the case of the *métayer* and the contributor — already inserted into the counter-plantation system — the profit motive was not of paramount importance, even though profit would have been welcome. The interest was simply the procurement of cash. The selling of canes, even at a loss, was "structurally necessary" in terms of the degree of openness required by the counter-plantation system. This is why and how both plantation and counter-plantation articulate themselves as a "single binary system of processes".

In conclusion, up to the 1950s, social intercourse as regards the distribution of economic wealth in the society — more exactly of marketable economic wealth — was devoid of any economic rationale. The profit motive of the controllers of the sugar industry was satisfied through political discussions surrounding the fixing of the quota and the preferential price of sugar. Economic bargaining on behalf of the other groups, viz. wage-earners, *métayers* and contributors, was non-existent if focussed in terms of the market. But as regards the survival and eventual expansion of the counter-plantation system, i.e. owner-operated multicrop agriculture, the various types of worker entertained a global set of negotiations oriented towards obtaining at least the minimum of cash necessary for the acquisition of capital goods and manufactured items for the owner-operated sector of the economy.

Economic practices in the banana industry. The facts observed in 1952 led the Malone Commission to endorse the views of the St Lucia Sugar Association and to state in several passages of the report that

---

Companies at a price per ton fixed by the Companies; the canes are weighed at the factory on the Company's scales. *Métayers* are usually workers on the sugar estates who are permitted [. . .] to plant small areas of the Companies' lands in sugar canes, and in lieu of rent deliver to the Companies one-fifth of the canes supplied by the *métayer* to the factory. The canes are weighed at the factory, and the *métayer* is paid at the same rate per ton as the contributor, for four-fifths of the cane weighed". (*Ibid.*, para. 43, pp. 12–13.)

39. "Another matter which has given rise to considerable distrust has been the method of fixing the price of sugar canes. It is based on a formula evolved by the employers and imposed on the suppliers of canes — it must be appreciated that so far as buying of cane is concerned the St Lucia Companies have a monopoly". (*Ibid.*, para. 49, p. 14.)

the sugar industry is "vital to St Lucia's economic life". History soon proved that to be an exaggeration of the importance of the industry. Some ten years later, sugar represented barely 1.3% of the total domestic exports, of which bananas represented 78.5%. How vital banana is to the economy cannot be determined at the present time since its share has declined steadily from 1972 onwards, in spite of the constant increase in value and volume. But it is unnecessary to point out the continuing development of multicrop agriculture which served as a background to the changes from sugar cane to banana, within the market sector of the economy.

Banana Growers' Associations were started in the Windward Islands in the 1930s, but were allowed to lapse during the Second World War, to be revived in the post-war period with the boom in banana production. The Banana Growers' Association of St Lucia, like the associations in the other Windward Islands, was granted a local banana trade monopoly, It "established and operated buying stations; and negotiated purchasing agreements with Geest, a shipper with his own refrigerated ships as well as the sole buyer; and administered various schemes for wind insurance, spraying and fertiliser."[40]

Relations between the banana growers, the local merchants and the transnational ones differ from those entertained by the sugar producers. The Windward Islands' Banana Association (WINBAN), through Geest, abides by the price quoted in the London market. The situation has severe disadvantages, but at least it relies on economic factors at the international level with regard to the value of the produce. Moreover, local political parameters play a determinant role in relation to the remuneration of the factors of production.

The predominance of bananas introduced another relevant particularity to St Lucia's economic practices. The main issue of these practices, in contrast to sugar plantations, in the case of banana production, revolved primarily around bargaining the price of the product;[41] fixing of rural wages became secondary. Vital to an understanding of such aspects of the industry is an insight into the

40. Carleen O'Loughlin, *Economic and Political Change in the Leeward and Windward Islands*, London: Oxford University Press, 1968, pp. 109-10.
41. As noted, "The price received by the grower is arrived at only after Geest has deducted from the green market price per ton, 40% for freight charges, variable costs, fixed costs, and a shrinkage and wastage charge, and after the Banana Association has made a further deduction of 35% for operating expenses and current debt. The Association also deducts charges for leaf spot, spraying, diothene, fertiliser and weedicide purchased on credit". (*Small Farming Study*, Caribbean Development Bank, *op.cit.*, pp. 42-3.)

structure of the Banana Growers' Association. This was created in 1953 by five planters, a merchant and an accountant as a private company limited by shares. The membership consisted of share-holders and registered growers, i.e. any owner-occupier of land with at least thirty banana trees. The original company was dissolved in 1967. There were claims of discriminatory treatment of small growers during its early period. Also in 1967, the House of Assembly of St Lucia (under the St Lucia Corporation Act)[42] re-established the Association as a Statutory Corporation on which powers were conferred for the marketing of bananas. This act ensured govern-ment participation in the policies formulated by the merchants to whom large growers gave a supervisory role over the Board's finances, as well as making provision for accountability.[43] Government's participation did not lessen the level of disenchantment and dissatisfaction expressed by the majority of the growers and related population.

The estimated number of members in the Association in 1967 was 17,000, but in 1977/8 a membership of less than 6,400 was counted.[44] This remarkable decrease is not explained. However, the growers are divided into four categories: "grower", "small grower", "medium grower" and "large grower".[45]

The data of banana production by category of grower suggest that the institutionalisation contained in the 1967 Act appears to be oriented towards granting protection to those who produce more, but not necessarily towards maximising production as such. In effect, the principles enacted by the House of Assembly granted two representatives to the large growers, 0.1% of the total number of members. They were five persons in 1977, and six in 1978. Two representatives were allocated to the medium growers (0.5% of the membership, i.e. thirty-one persons), and two to the small growers with slightly less than 10.0% of the total membership. Hence 90% of the Association was kept away from the decision-making bodies, this percentage numbering more than 5,500 persons.[46] The Board of

42. Preamble of the St Lucia Banana Growers' Association Act, 1967
43. In 1980, Commission of Enquiry into the Banana Industry was appointed as a result of the expressed dissatisfaction and disenchantment of the growers and related population with the functioning of the Association.
44. Inquiry into the Banana Industry, Interim Report, June 1980, ch. III, pp. 11–12.
45. Before 1971, the criteria for categorisation was annual production of stems of bananas, ranging from under 1,000 stems to over 25,000 stems. Post 1971, the categories were arrived at on the basis of weight and average weekly production — ranging from under 500 lb. to over 12,000 lb. *ibid.*
46. These growers — 99.4% of the membership — were responsible for approximately 65% of the total production of bananas (1978). *ibid.*, p. 14

Directors dominated by the 'large' and 'medium' growers — transformed by their accession to the directorship position into merchants — would have needed an exceptional degree of altruism to dedicate itself to the promotion of measures favouring the development of the excluded 90% of the membership.

It is apparent that the Directorate of the Association, as established by the 1967 Act, did not address itself to the expansion of productive activities. Over the thirty-year period the most vital questions raised by the growers were dealt with in a flippant way by the Board. These referred to such concerns as fertiliser cost, assistance, supply and distribution; communication between management and growers; establishment, repair and maintenance of feeder roads; management cost and efficiency; qualification for Delegate status; and aerial spraying cost and value.

In general, the Directors seemed to show a lack of any economic rationale in conducting the internal affairs of the Association. Gross irregularities were discovered by the Commission of Enquiry. Specific reference was made to the misuse and unauthorised use of the funds.[47] Recommendations to redress this state of affairs and above all to assist in placing the decision-making processes in the hands of the large majority of growers are still under consideration.[48] It can nonetheless be concluded that many changes have already been initiated and that the present structure of social negotiations is substantially different from what it was in the 1950s. In fact, the substitution of bananas for sugar as the country's main export crop introduced profound modifications in its whole social organisation. While cultivation of cane and its transformation into sugar involved relatively limited agricultural areas, located within the reach of the sugar mills, cultivation of banana spread all over the country and embraced most of the rural population in one single set of social and economic practices.

Expansion of banana cultivation seems to have taken place without any conflict arising with the production of sugar canes;[49] gradually most cultivable lands and important portions of marginal ones were encompassed in the banana venture. However, the original asymmetric relations in the banana industry between

47. *Ibid.*, p. 41.
48. It would seem, for instance, that the Board presently comprises 13 directors, 7 government appointees and 6 elected ones. (*Trinidad Guardian*, 6 Feb. 1981, p. 5.)
49. In 1959, Geest bought the Sugar Manufacturers Ltd., which in turn was a merger of Cul de Sac Company Ltd, and Roseau Company Ltd. Sugar Manufacturers Ltd. was created in 1953.

planters, *métayers* and contributors has changed completely; this is because planters and estate owners were producing altogether less bananas than the aggregated output of the growers, and were not enjoying a distinct bargaining position.

With banana cultivation local knowledge necessary to grow the crop was given an opportunity to guide new practices in production and marketing and give open access to diffusion and application of related science and technology.

Another consequence of the present predominance of banana over the previous cash crop consists in the destruction of traditional linkages between the small-scale farming and estate farming. The plantocracy lost its privileged economic position whereby it used to control the only avenue open to the small producers — contributors and *métayers* — on the world market. Estate owners became a simple social stratum in a universe of farmers. Only farmers who entered commercial ventures could maintain a distinct position *vis-à-vis* other producers, in fact as merchants and not actually as planters. In effect, both large and small growers of bananas had access to, or a conflict of interests with, the same commercial concern: the Banana Growers' Association. In times of sugar cane predominance, it was not conceivable — and no evidence had been gathered in that sense — that proprietors of sugar cane estates could share the same interests as *métayers* and contributors.

With the demise of the sugar planters as a group, domination of the large group of small farmers now shifted to the group of large farmers/merchants who now controlled the organization which established the rules of the agricultural export sector. All growers, large and small, now shared the same interests, but small farmers were disproportionately represented in the Association and were therefore excluded from participation in the process of economic bargaining.

Accommodation of employers and employees in the rural economy

This study of social structural changes in St Lucia has addressed itself primarily to the original components of the population and has searched for the principles of its differentiation and its ramification. However, the existence of sub-groups and minority groups are not denied, but they are not of major importance in this study. It is necessary to understand the economic practices of the dominated group in terms of its participation in the agricultural sector[50] of the

50. Specifically workers on sugar and banana estates as they existed this century.

twentieth century. This sector of the population, consisting of the descendants of the enslaved, has managed some limited access to land and has introduced itself to the production of export crops. It was completely excluded from international trade, where monopoly was held by Europeans and their descendants.

The series of social changes whereby conflicts between plantation and peasant (or pseudo-peasant) economies tend to fade out — allowing for the survival of ideological prejudices and conflicts — and to yield to clashes of interests between producers and merchants cannot be appreciated without an appraisal of the evolution of landless persons working in the agricultural sector, and from whom the peasants and the *métayers* have emerged, and are still apparently emerging.

The negotiations into which the working class entered in the course of its evolution are geared towards the modification of working conditions on estates producing "valuable export crops". These practices were strongly affected by the continual threat of intervention from external repressive forces[51] altering the course of social negotiations and deterring the advances of nation-building processes. In spite of their constant opposition to the local conditions of plantation development, they remained at the same time an integral part of it. In practical terms freeholders, squatters and *métayers* have largely detached themselves from the plantations, but freeholding, squatting and *métayage* are, under the conditions observed, nonetheless inescapably related to plantation economy.

In spite of the difference in participation in the rural economy, one need not distinguish two lines of evolution of the original class of negro workers, which have never become fully separated. For "the negroes [who] had one function only — the provision of cheap labour",[52] the retreat or "escape" to the counter-plantation system by some of them does not introduce a breaking point with those who remained imprisoned in the dominant form of organization. This is self-evident for the *métayage* system, which in a way prolonged the span of life of "provision grounds".[53]

The same can be said for any agricultural exploitation of an uneconomical size, be it of freehold or squatting tenure. The striving of the labourers towards independent agriculture is certainly not

51. For instance, British warships circled St Lucia during the strike of sugar workers in 1957. Additional police forces were brought in from Barbados and Grenada. (Interview with ex-trade unionist, February 1980.)
52. Moyne Commission Report, *op.cit.*, ch. III, para. 2 p. 29.
53. "Only the prevalence of 'food gardens' even among estate labourers mitigates the severity of conditions in rural areas". *ibid.*, ch. III, para. II, p. 33.

denied. However, it is being proposed that in the original conditions in which such efforts were made, there was no possibility for the emergence of a class of small farmers, independent from the landless workers.

Hence, the majority of rural St Lucians had few alternatives. These included an attempt at self-sufficiency or plantation wage labour, or, as occurred in many instances, a combination of the two. The adoption of banana resulted in a change of emphasis. It allowed a step forward in social organization by promoting the operation of food gardens together with the production of the staple crop, stimulating a higher degree of participation of the labour force in the main industry.

In the rural sector, wage labour continued to exist in the poorest circumstances as referred to by the Commission.[54] In spite of this, the estates are still an important avenue for wage labour. In 1963 the sugar industry accounted for employment of 900 persons during the crop season. Up to 1967, it was recorded that large estates occupied 53% of the farm acreage, which made them relatively dominant; and they continue to employ manual labourers. Estimates from the St Lucia Agricultural Statistics (1974) numbered paid agricultural workers at 5,402 (3,525 male and 1,877 female).

In St Lucia, as elsewhere in the Caribbean, the system of labour on the plantations did not facilitate or encourage any attachment to the place of work. The Moyne Commission drew attention to the system on the plantations, then and earlier:

The exact form of employment in agriculture varies from Colony to Colony, but everywhere task work is characteristic. Task work is the West Indian terms for what is described in Great Britain as "piece work" or "payment by results". By far the greater proportion of agricultural workers in the West Indies are paid for the amount of work they actually perform and not according to the length of time they take to do it. Payment by the day and not by the task is the rare exception for field work in West Indian agriculture and the rates, though varying greatly from one Colony to another, are extremely low. [. . .] Thus, generally, when sums paid to labourers are quoted, these are usually *earnings* and not *wages*. This is an important consideration and it cannot too often be repeated that most West Indian labourers employed on agricultural work are paid for what they actually do.

54. "To say that the West Indian labourer is placed at a disadvantage in bargaining with his employer, who in all probability owns the range in which he lives, and could evict him at short notice, is to understate the case. Devoid of any effective protection by means of trade unionism, the labourer is helpless and, if he wishes to live, must accept the rate of pay offered to him. In the light of this it is not surprising to find that earnings have remained extremely low, even in periods when planters were making good profits". (*Ibid.*, ch. 10, para. 11, p. 193.)

This system of task work has certain consequences. The rate of pay for particular tasks are not fixed by any general agreement or collective bargaining, but are usually decided on the spot.[55]

More important than its impact on the homogenisation of pay, the prevalence of "task work" indicates a peculiar form of integration — one is tempted to say "marginalisation" — in the enterprise. On the one hand, such relations with the labour force grant to the employers an extreme flexibility which allows rather quick adaptation to changes in schedules of production and in the arrangement of productive factors. On the other hand, in this form of absorption of the labour force, the employees can never initiate a lifelong endeavour, what is commonly called a career, an occupation or a trade. Their practices remain a succession of unrelated and unarticulated *jobs*. Hence, *earnings* in agriculture can assist in making a living, but this form of insertion in the sector is not a way of living. The output of the rural worker is aggregated to an articulated set of material goods, but he himself is not trapped in a complex set of industrial relations. He does not form part of the enterprise. There is no possibility for him to increase his qualification nor is there for the employer a self-propelled motive for promoting new dexterities or absorbing new technologies, because of pressures coming from within the enterprise.

"Task work" is functional to cyclical and seasonal variations in the demand for labour force. Seasonal intermittency is particularly relevant to the present discussion. The Moyne Commission underlines that:

The actual wages paid may or may not be reasonably satisfactory for persons in full employment — we consider that in many cases they are not — but at the present time the question does not arise for a tragically large proportion of the labouring population: full employment and regular wages are not available for them.[56]

In St Lucia, around 1950, "most field work including the cutting, heading and loading of canes, is paid for on a piece work basis."[57] There seem to have existed, cases in which the workers assembled a fair amount of money for a day, a week or a month's work. According to the Malone Commission this would have been quite common:

55. Moyne Commission Report, *op.cit.*, ch. 10, paras 7–8 pp. 192–3: May it be remembered that the *quid pro quo* between *earnings* and *wages*, parallels the one between *profits* and *contractual payments*.
56. *Ibid*, ch. III, para. 9, pp. 32–3.
57. Malone Commission Report, *op.cit.* para. 41, p. 12.

Any idea that the willing and able-bodied canecutter or header of canes employed at Roseau or Cul de Sac is existing on a bread-line wage . . . is quite incorrect. No doubt the aged and infirm will have difficulty in living, and so will the children without proper [*sic*] parental care, or a family with an exceptionally large number of young children, but these conditions are primarily social problems which exist everywhere.[58]

The fundamental and most hidden characteristic of piece work is to be found in analysing this statement. This form of hiring labour, as its name should make readily apparent, does not impinge on the time dimension. When a job is completed, the employer has no obligation to offer another one to the employee nor has the latter an obligation to supply his labour for the next job, in case he were offered it. The unpredictability of the demand for labour is usually conceived as an apparent unpredictability of the supply. "Men and women, living and working together or apart, with or without vegetable gardens or growing canes, small farmers (contributors) and employees as *métayers*, are so intermixed and there is so much freedom to work or not to work at particular times, with estate labour demands rising or falling, dovetailing or not with private production labour requirements . . ."[59] The idea that there is always something that an "able-bodied person" can do obscures the structural relations between employers and employees in St Lucia's agriculture. Both systems of practices are closely interdeterminate, the "liberty" of the employer to demand or not to demand labour corresponding to the "liberty" of the employee to supply or not to supply. As far as the employer is concerned, it is taken for granted that he is free to contract Mr X or Mr Z. This is true for any labour market, but in classical market economies the employee is contracted for a given time, even though he may be paid for the tasks performed. In agricultural piece work one is hired and paid for the job.

This form of encounter of supply and demand for labour has two consequences on community life in relation to levels of living and cultural development. First of all, intermittent earnings for piece work are not geared to cover the life span of the worker, much less the whole issue of raising a family or of taking care of the "non-able-bodied" components. Piece work in agriculture has to be viewed as a sub-contract passed to an independent or self-employed producer who will forever remain independent and self-employed. His wellbeing and his survival is of no concern to his employer. In fact, if the employer does not pay "wages" to his employee, he cannot be

58. *Ibid.*, para. 40, p. 11.
59. *Ibid.*, para. 42, p. 12.

concerned with his needs or level of living, since such a level of living does not directly affect the productivity of the enterprise.

Secondly, the prevalence of piece work makes it impossible for employers and employees to evolve a joint outlook of their society and shared institutions for ruling the life of the island community. Each one of them may live in his separate cultural world for as long as this arrangement persists. "It has been found in other countries, like St Lucia, where employers are separated from workers by wide cultural gaps, that there is a tendency to regard workers as little more than machines that have to eat. We are convinced that the Directorates of the Sugar Companies in St. Lucia . . . have been inclined to pay little, if any, regard to encouraging improved standards of living among the workers . . ."[60]

When alternative forms of employment other than task work exist, either a *métayage* contract or what can be coupled with self-employment on freehold or squatted land, the worker is forced to have recourse to a set of marginal activities giving rise to what has been termed occupational multiplicity.[61] The original and fundamental lack of integration to the agricultural enterprise is strengthened by a process of circular causation which tends to make economic bargaining and industrial relations geared towards a betterment of working conditions even more difficult, and hence the global productivity of the economic system. In short, piece work as a form of labour contract isolates the workers from each other, alienates them in relation to the enterprise in which they make a living, and keeps them apart from what is occurring in the larger world. No ground is left for industrial relations between employers and employees. The community becomes the basic place for social cohesion, and the conflicts emerging between the "people" and the employers have to be solved outside the economic domain.[62] Thus the aggregation of a multitude of "task works", even under a very wise management, creates a context where confrontation is unavoidable. Strike actions become the only tolerable instrument of negotiations. "We consider the evidence put before us shows that the employers failed in the field of labour management and that that failure was partly responsible (not wholly) for bringing about a position where a strike was possible, perhaps inevitable."[63]

60. *Ibid.*, para. 15, p. 6.
61. L. Comitas, "Occupational Multiplicity in Rural Jamaica (1964)" in Comitas and D. Lowenthal (eds), *Work and Family Life: West Indian Perspectives*, New York: Doubleday, 1973, pp. 163–4.
62. Malone Commission Report, *op.cit.*, para. 42, p. 12.
63. *Ibid.*, para. 58, p. 16.

Hence, by the very nature of their participation in the industry, the workers did not constitute an articulated whole in their relations with their employers. As a result the strike actions sprang from the community and, instead of being fostered by "genuine labour leaders", were led by politicians whom the officialdom conceived of as agitators. This point must be seen as the specific trait of social relations in the St Lucia economy and deserves further elaboration. Employers feared the leadership potential of the so-called "agitators", and expressed the wish that workers should be left to themselves. They perceived the labour force as ignorant and uneducated, and if left to itself, no threat to the established order. Task work kept the labour force disaggregated, hence the fear of the leadership potential of politicians and "agitators" who would take up the cause of the worker in the wider political arena. This fear of employers, of labour force leadership, can be seen as intrinsic to social relations in the island.

However, the creation of trade unions did not ensure that economic bargaining strictly on behalf of workers was carried out, since where wages are actually not paid, and where labour relations do not evolve as an articulated set of internal relations of an undertaking, there cannot be a trade union "in the universally recognised sense of the word".[64] At the beginning, the St Lucia Workers' Co-operative Union tried hard to stay clear from "politics" and to function within this "universally recognised sense of the word". In fact, the unions existing at the time of the Enquiry had proved themselves unable to organize the workers. Hence, while employers and Trade Union leaders seemed to agree that the 1952 stoppage was due to the action of political activists, the Commission had to raise certain questions which clearly led to the answer that what appeared to be industrial relations was straightforward political bargaining in St Lucia.

Since other principles of trade unionism could not be attained in the St Lucian context, no more could collective bargaining: "Collective bargaining is by no means repudiated, but it is our view that adequate machinery does not exist at present to carry this out."[65] Hence the creation of a Wages Council was recommended by the Malone Commission; this mechanism had to be resorted to so as to fill the gap of trade unionism. The Recommendation stated "that a Wages Council be established for the sugar industry of the Colony under the provisions of the Wages Council Ordinance, 1952 (no. 1 of 1952) of St Lucia for the purpose of regulating the amount of the

64. Malone Commission Report, para. 18, p. 7.
65. *Ibid*. para. 105, p. 27.

remuneration and, as far as possible, the conditions of employment of workers in the industry".[66]

The mix of politics and trade unions continued to be unavoidable. Organised trade unionism continued to elude St Lucian workers.[67] The strike of 1952 revealed a separation of interests between workers and leadership. In 1980, the Interim Report of the Commission of Inquiry into the Banana Industry further substantiated the possibility of the trade unionists, in their capacity of political leaders, departing from the function on behalf of the workers and enacting a set of practices with their own interests as a middle-class stratum. Before that, however, the political power of trade unions had diminished with the introduction and expansion of banana cultivation.[68] The main sources of social conflict ceased to be located between employers and employees and switched to conflict between growers and merchants, as referred to earlier.

The discussion here regarding the rural wage earners reveals that this group can safely be classified as a continuation of the original dominated class of St Lucian society, i.e. the enslaved, which was not able to develop its full potential as a working class and so be in the forefront of social change

The Inquiry into the Banana Industry acknowledged the central position of the "growers"; the enhanced visibility of the farmers has eclipsed the rural "wage" earners. This is particularly clear in the evidence gathered at the same date by the Beckford Land Reform Commission which operated with the concept of development which considers plantation-like activities as one among many other alternatives. The importance of wage earners is not challenged, but self-employment, particularly in agriculture, is seen as definite progress *vis-à-vis* what seems to be salaried employment. Many wage earners in the agricultural sector look towards ownership of land and becoming farmers.

Social evolution, as perceived, appears to be the unfolding of an original group of farmers. The basic trunk of the society is, in the words of the Moyne Commission, that "solidest and most enterprising section of the negro population" — today's farmers, yesterday's runaways, maroons or brigands. The other social group-

66　Malone Commission Report, *ibid*., para. 101, p. 27.
67. Jackson Commission Report, *ibid*., para. 27, p. 12.
68. In 1963, "the predominantly trade union backed Labour Government was over-thrown and elections led to the return of a party in which more business and pro-fessional men figured. The banana industry, with its emphasis on the self-employed peasant farmers has contributed much to the weakening of the political power of the trade unions in all the Windwards not least in St Lucia". (Carleen O'Loughlin, *op.cit*., p. 45.)

ings appear whenever their roots are alluded to, as a differentiation of the original set of actual or potential farmers. In general, most of the descendants do not relinquish their ties to the land, and most certainly not land ownership.

It must finally be added that in spite of the relevance of these trends, the direction in which they will guide St Lucia's evolution in the years to come is not clear. Other sets of rearrangements are taking place in the urban areas with the development of tourism and enclave manufactures. The convergence of these trends will be responsible for the ability of the country to respond to a third system of processes, namely international trade and politics.

Conclusion

Suffice it to say that the developments of a counter-plantation system has not yet gone through a full process of evolution. History has shown, however, that the restrictions facing the group of rural wage earners have prevented it from taking its place as the vanguard of social change in the society. Conversely, the ferment of social change, as in many of the Caribbean islands, is to be found among those who have attempted with varying success to extricate themselves from the relationships based on the plantation as a key economic institution.

It is suggested that the insertion in the society of the enslaved and of social groups which evolved from their practices presents specificities which are not immediately accounted for in current sociological theories. Thus there remains the necessity for further research to arrive at theories more relevant to this specific Caribbean experience.

In spite of the apparent set of new social relations which have evolved since the inception of the banana industry, one has to acknowledge the continued existence of new forms of "plantation" and "counter-plantation" systems. One can only speculate as to what further developments will yet take place — whether the "counter-plantation" system will make further progress in its establishment as the major sector of the rural economy of St Lucia. This can be achieved either by modernising or revamping the non-market sector; by the initiation of alternative economic and social models more appropriate to St Lucia; or the use of science and technology and relevant techniques of modern management which would offer a suitable balance between outward-looking and inward-looking activities.

4

PLANTATION DOMINANCE AND RURAL DEPENDENCE IN DOMINICA

P.I. Gomes

Background

While there is a sufficiently wide recognition and general understanding of the macro-structural factors in the underdevelopment of plantation economies, increasing attention needs to be paid to an elucidation of the social dynamics accompanying the plantation dominance and rural dependence manifested in concrete case-studies of definite historical periods.[1] Some of this work will necessarily rely on the already available historical analyses of rural conditions in Caribbean societies during slavery and indenture.[2] Also helpful in this regard will be social structural analyses, at the micro-level, of specific local situations. It is into this latter category that the present discussion is to be placed as a case-study from Dominica of a rural community and its neighbouring plantation on which the residents depended for their livelihood. This presentation is part of a wider examination of a rural sector study which was commissioned by the Caribbean Agro-Economic Society as an "integrated" rural development project.[3] As we pointed out in that Report, a wider consideration of national priorities and appropriate policies for the development of the agricultural sector as a whole are the essential context within which the development of a specific community is to be situated. Here we will address the historical context in which the social relations of the study-area developed, its demographic structure, the village economy and modes of subsistence, social

1. See G. Beckford, *Persistent Poverty* (Oxford University Press, 1972); a particularly perceptive treatment of these questions appeared in *Latin American Perspectives*, vol. 5, nos. 3 and 4, 1978, under the theme "Peasants, Capital Accumulation and Rural Underdevelopment", in which examinations of the agrarian social structures in Brazil, Mexico, Colombia, Guatemala and Chile are provided.
2. W.E. Riviere, *Active Resistance to Slavery in the Caribbean*. St Augustine, University of the West Indies, 1972; cf. also W.E. Riviere, "The Emergence of a Free Labour Economy in the British West Indies 1800–1950", Ph.D. thesis, University of Glasgow, 1968.
3. Caribbean Agro-Economic Society, *Rural Sector Case-study Report with Proposals for Development of Geneva Estate, Grand Bay, Dominica*, April 1976, p. 157.

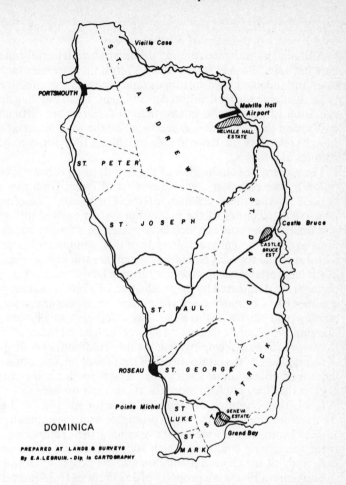

DOMINICA

PREPARED AT LANDS & SURVEYS
By E.A.LEBRUIN. - Dip. in CARTOGRAPHY

status and the class structure. The implications for change and development of the area are also identified, and some limited generalisations are made on the pre-requisites for the planned transformation of that and similar situations in the Caribbean.

The historical context of Dominica and Grand Bay

Within the Lesser Antilles of the Caribbean Archipelago, Dominica, a British colonial territory from the time of the Treaty of Paris in 1763, was granted political independence in 1977 and became a sovereign state within the (British) Commonwealth of Nations. Situated between the two French Overseas *Départements*, Martinique and

Guadeloupe, the island has an area of 750,582 sq. metres (289.8 sq. miles), and a population of 80,000 persons.

Although larger in area than all the other Eastern Caribbean countries including Barbados, the island's terrain is extremely mountainous and indented, and this topography reduces the effective land space available for agricultural development. Road building and the provision of other basic infrastructural facilities are difficult and costly, and this problem is exacerbated by the wide dispersal of the island's relatively small population inhabiting fifty or more villages, hamlets and towns.

The pattern of colonisation of the island, or its economic exploitation by the colonisers, was somewhat different from that experienced by the sugar colonies of the Caribbean. Therefore the ownership structures of the plantation system evolved differently, and many of the estates which have passed into foreign hands have done so only in recent years. In spite of this, a number of important features of the colonial plantation system are still in evidence. Most of the large estates occupy the best farming lands, and their cropping patterns are dominated by the production of a few important export commodities. In most cases the estates are owner-managed, and employ paid workers, who might have their own smallholdings on marginal lands, or be tenants on a parcel of land on the estate where they work. Seasonal employment is fairly common, as is the perennial complaint by the estate-owner of the lack of reliable labour. The pattern of utilisation of some of the estates has led some critics to suggest that they are held more for status than for use.

It was the perception of land held more for speculation than for the development of people which prompted a village population to a form of insurgency as a means of overcoming their dependency. This is the underlying condition which will be discussed in the present case-study of the Geneva plantation and the people of Grand Bay.

The Geneva Estate is a property of 552 hectares (1,380 acres) located in the parish of St Patrick on the south-western coast of Dominica (see map). The village is approximately 6 miles (9.6 km.) to the south of·Roseau, the country's capital, and is accessible by a steep, narrow, pitched road, winding its way circuitously, and in some ways very dangerously up to a height of about 2000 ft. The area generally referred to as Grand Bay is made up of several small hamlets, the main and most populous one being Berricoa (Berekua).[4]

4. The name results from a creolisation of the French *"Belle Croix"*, beautiful cross. Early attempts by French Jesuits to convert the indigenous population are said to have met with severe resistance. All wooden crosses which the priests erected were consistently destroyed. Eventually a large cross was hewn from solid

The Grand Bay area in general, and the Geneva Estate in particular, have had a tradition of turmoil and unrest, the underlying cause being the socio-economic conditions under which the community has struggled for survival. The estate provided the main source of sustenance and employment for the neighbouring village. As a privately-owned estate, Geneva's returns were subject to changing fortunes, related both to the market conditions facing the crops which were cultivated from time to time, and to the policies of management.

During its heyday the estate is believed to have absorbed a workforce of nearly 300. Apart from Geneva, there is very little cultivable land in the immediate environs, and alternative forms of employment are almost non-existent. (This is also the case with other plantation holdings.) In a real sense the villagers of Grand Bay have been made dependent on the fancies and fortune of the Geneva Estate and its management. In recent times, the prospects for employment have continuously declined as the socio-economic needs of the rural population began to increase. In such a situation it is not surprising that the simmering problem of uncertainty and unrest should have reached explosive dimensions.

In 1974, two years before our fieldwork began, the plantation was subjected to a spate of violent eruptions marked by arson in which five buildings, including the manager's office and owner's house, were destroyed. As a consequence all operations and employment on the estate were terminated. A chain of events demonstrated the fury of the populace, and the then government was forced to acquire the estate and place it under the control of the state-run Land Management Authority. To appreciate the context of these events, we will summarize recent incidents.

On 30 March 1974, the *New Chronicle*, a weekly Dominican newspaper, carried the headline story entitled "Grand Bay in Turmoil". There it was reported that the village of Grand Bay, which had been in the news during the Carnival celebrations the preceding week, had erupted into violence. There had been several incidents of destruction of property on the estate, which was owned by a Syrian who had lived in Dominica for several years. It was claimed that during this period cattle were stolen, other livestock were killed in the vicinity of the estate and their entrails left on the ground, and several coconut trees, the main crop of the estate, were cut down.

With increasing disturbances on the estate, it was found necessary

---

stone and this withstood attempts at destruction. The area thus took its name from this beautiful stone cross, which can be seen to this day in what became the village cemetery.

to send a contingent of police, who arrested a young villager, suspected of being the principal instigator of the incidents. However, following his arrest and subsequent escape, the situation at night in the village became increasingly turbulent. One of the workhouses used for cocoa storage was burnt down. Telephone wires were cut, thus preventing contact between Grand Bay and the police in the capital, Roseau. A shop was looted, trees were felled across the Geneva Road to prevent police contingents arriving from Roseau, and generally an acute state of unrest was emerging. Throughout the following week, the conflict heightened, and the situation in Grand Bay was one of near-chaos; during that week, the Geneva Estate House was completely destroyed by fire. On Wednesday, April 3, a state of emergency was proclaimed. Also destroyed were the estate diesel tanks and a coconut drying shed, and firemen who attempted to contain the arson were stoned. By this time, the public was forced to see the social conditions of Grand Bay in a new light: the 4,000 and more villagers were reliving features of Grand Bay's history.

The historical records of the village revealed a pattern of violent encounters between the masses and the landowners. As early as 1778, some eleven years before the French Revolution and thirteen years before the Haitian revolt, there was a violent slave uprising in the Geneva-Grand Bay area. Incessantly during the early nineteenth century up till *ca.* 1814, wars of Black Maroons, escaping the bonds of slavery and attempting to survive in the hills, had encompassed the village. In 1932, when the plantation was under the management of a Mr Lockhart, who had proved to be a paternalistic and benevolent employer, an incident over tenancy rights again escalated into widespread arson. In 1949 a Syrian merchant acquired ownership of the estate and adopted a policy of evicting tenants of long standing. This attitude of the new owners sowed seeds of resentment which blossomed forth in 1953 with strikes and outbursts of violence as retrenchment of labour and the systematic "running-down" of the plantation presented a direct threat to the future livelihood of residents in the surrounding villages. The intolerable situation persisted and it was widely believed that the estate was to become a source of land speculation with the view of attracting a housing development, not far from the capital. Such a use of the plantation and its land was the very opposite to a manner of surviving as smallholding farmers and an agrarian proletariat by which the people of Grand Bay had tried to meet their basic human needs over almost 200 years.

Among people well acquainted with resistance and rebellion against what they see as frustrating and unjust conditions of life, it was clear that long-contained feelings of discontent had exploded. Only a month earlier, in *The New Chronicle*, a villager from Grand Bay had written of the village:

Failure of agriculture there is due largely to the failure of large estates to work the land that they hold, or lease land available to those people who desire it. Another setback is inaccessibility of land and the type of soil that village people are confined to. An additional source of earning from straw plaiting brings but little income to many residents. Population increase and the number of young people who find themselves without work grow as an army.

In an attempt to restore order, and resume normal operations of the estate, the Land Management Authority encountered great hostility from the villagers. A militant section of the community claimed that the estate had been acquired for them, and that it should immediately be passed to them for management and control. Failure to meet their demands led to widespread larceny, and animals were let loose to roam the estate and destroy the plantation. Consequently, in its first year of operation, the Authority sustained a loss of *c.* $19,000 (EC).

By 1976 the estate had an undetermined number of squatters, and 120 tenants, 107 of whom operated ½-acre units. The regular crops grown by these are dasheen, tannias and plantains. The government was forced to search for a strategy that would prove viable and meet the community's approval. It is with a view to formulating such a strategy that the following discussion will be provided on the social relations arising from the structure of rural underdevelopment and the modes of subsistence production to which the broad majority have been subjected. Because of the limited available data, our remarks will be confined to the situation in that portion of the Geneva Grand Bay Area, considered as the village of Berricoa. We begin by looking at its demographic structure.

Population composition and distribution

Table I below shows the population of Grand Bay Village (Berricoa) by age and sex. Over 60% of the population is of school age, and 13% over fifty-five years. Thus, there is a large dependent population in the village, even when allowance is made for the fact that many in the post-primary age group are out of school and employable, and many 'senior adults' are engaged in active farming and far from retirement. When the age distribution is further examined, the problem of unemployment among youth is brought into sharper focus.

More important than the greater absolute number of females is the relatively higher proportion of females in the 35-54 age group, in which there are twice as many females as males. This difference is partly explained by the fairly large number of males who have traditionally migrated out of both the village and the country in search

Table 1. POPULATION DISTRIBUTION BY AGE AND SEX,
GRAND BAY VILLAGE (BERRICOA)

	Male	Female	Total	% of Village
Kindergarten (<5 years)	305	304	609	19
Primary school age (5–14)	541	513	1,054	33
Post-Primary (15–19)	133	171	304	10
Total school age population	*979*	*988*	*1,967*	*62*
Young adults (20–34)	157	250	407	13
Adults (35–54)	123	249	372	12
Senior adults (55 and over)	162	244	406	13
Total village	*1,421*	*1,731*	*3,152*	*100*

Sources: 1970 Population Census.

of employment. Over the last ten to fifteen years or so, the main
countries of outward migration were initially the United Kingdom,
the United States, Canada, the Virgin Islands and, on a smaller
scale, the neighbouring French Overseas *Départements* of Martinique and Guadeloupe. Recently, these areas of migration and jobs
have become almost closed, due to new immigration policies. During
our investigation in the village, it was a regular occurrence to meet
"returnee-migrants", particularly young men in their late 20s and
early 30s, who had become accustomed to what some refer to as
"good money" and a "fast way of life", and who on returning
home, had become immersed in a social environment that was stagnant and frustrating. The potential social impact of such returnee-
migrants assuming militant leadership roles was of considerable
significance in the subsequent development of a state of conflict.

With such migration outlets becoming increasingly restricted, it
was naturally expected that the village would show an ever higher
proportion of unemployed young men, acutely frustrated and
depressed, who could comprise a strong force in the demand for
social change. One would not need to spend long at Grand Bay
before encountering groups of such persons, doing little more than
idle their time away between gambling, dominoes, draughts or casu-
ally reclining at the doors of the many shops that dot the main street
(L'Allé) of the village.

Even a brief examination of the age differentials in the population
helps us to readily grasp a feature of long-term significance for an
authentic development of the human resources of the community. It
is almost an understatement to say that there is an acute division
along age differences. Some 62 per cent of the total village is less than

20 years of age, and 13 per cent more than 55 years. Perhaps even more revealing, is the fact that some 75 per cent of the village can be classified as *young adults and of school age.*[5]

The Grand Bay Primary and Junior Secondary School, an imposing structure built in 1972, from funds provided by the Canadian government, presently accommodates approximately 1,100 students. From the 1970 data, it was found that there were 1,054 persons in Berricoa alone, who were in the relevant age group — 5–14 years — for attending school. Not only does this indicate the likelihood of a present shortage of school places at this level, but should make us wonder what, in fact, is the present condition of post-primary school-leavers from the village. Our investigations revealed that 60–80 students may be classified as attending secondary schools in the capital, receiving technical and vocational training or serving as trade or craft apprentices. But this still left a sizeable portion of 500–600 between the ages of 15 to 30 as the main component of rural youth, without access to schools, training or jobs. It is not difficult to see why they constituted a growing mass of restless youth, perceiving nothing but a bleak and wasteful future ahead of them. To them, the plantation society had offered only the opportunity to be "social rejects".

The occupational structure and modes of subsistence

The history of Berricoa reveals the experiences of a rural population, whose livelihood depended mainly on selling labour to Geneva Estate, or becoming small cultivators of food crops, primarily for domestic use, and selling any further surplus in the market. If this was generally how the bulk of the population subsisted, it does not deny the fact of several medium-size farmers, working family lands, either freehold, or as tenants on a rent or share-cropping basis. To the extent that this tradition persists, viz. that of agricultural workers and small and medium-sized farmers, it should be explicitly recognised and taken into consideration for any development planning of the Geneva Estate. It is to be hoped that data from the Farmer Registration Programme will provide an empirical basis for the manpower resources and utilisation to be rationally divided.

At the time of our investigation, a sizeable portion of the male working-age population was unemployed. This was because Geneva had not been working at the same level as previously since the 1974 disturbances. Moreover, unemployment is a chronic problem of the

5. These data are based on the most recently available census figures of 1970 and probably conservative estimates in 1976.

entire economy, and one estimate indicated that in 1970 about 35%
of the labour force was without work.[6] Estimating the labour force
unemployed in Grand Bay on the basis of the 1970 population
figures, we get a number around 350, aged 20–64, which is similar to
35% on the national level. This rough estimate can serve as a guide to
the volume of jobs one would have to create in working Geneva
Estate fully again, if a significant impact is to be made on the major
economic problem of the area.

Economic subsistence for some residents is provided by small-
scale cultivation of bananas, ground provisions, cocoa, limes and
food crops. In general, such cultivation is hardly above subsistence
level. Farmers criticised the lack of proper marketing facilities and
low prices which make production unprofitable. Quite noticeable
and pronounced was the general complaint that the cost of production in bananas was prohibitive. Some farmers were able recently to
receive fairly reasonable returns from the cultivation of Chris-
tophene (*sichium edula*). In general, the condition of the small
farmer is hardly encouraging, and it can in no way serve as an incen-
tive for the younger generation, in whose minds farming is work
which their parents and ancestors had to endure, at the price of
extortion and exploitation.

In addition to subsistence farmers and agricultural labourers, a
small number of medium-size farmers can be identified in the
village, whose socio-economic standing is considerably better. On an
even higher economic level are the sizeable number of shopkeepers,
some 12–15 of whom are seen by the villagers as "doing pretty well".
It is fairly common to find that the shopkeepers do not depend
entirely on retail trade as the source of income. Very likely they will
also own or rent a piece of land, on which a tenancy or sharecropping pattern is operated. They might also own a few houses that
are rented, and/or cultivate a backyard garden on their premises.
Some 20–25 villagers are employed as schoolteachers, and another
12–15 earn their living as civil servants, sales clerks, skilled labourers
or craftsmen.

While a large number of females are employed in household activities, keeping a backyard garden, or assisting in small-scale cultivation, about a dozen young women are able to earn some money in
handicraft work. This mainly consists of preparing portions of straw
mats or basket weaving from the Vertiver or Screwpine grasses,
which are grown in the village. These activities seem to possess the
potential for a substantial handicraft trade. About 12–15 young

6. E. Sylvester, *The Promotion of Agricultural Producers and Marketing Co-
operatives as a Basis for Rural Community Development* (mimeo, n.d.).

women were found occupied, on a part-time basis, with needlecraft, mainly smocking parts of a dress, which were sold to a textile manufacturing concern overseas. The rate of pay for these jobs is minimal, but no doubt provides an additional source of income for a few households. The remittances sent by relatives who had migrated to the United States, Canada or the Virgin Islands were also considered an important source of economic support.

On the whole, therefore, the villagers rely on working the land, either as labourers or cultivators, as their main mode of subsistence. Conditions today reveal a striking contrast to what several persons recall as a fairly substantial agricultural production of vegetables, food crops and milk for the market in Roseau. To see their village return to such a situation was the main concern of the majority of residents, in whose view the great economic need is "jobs" and "land".

Classes and social status

To understand the relative position of members and groups in the village, if only in a preliminary way, was one of the important objectives of the investigation. Not only was this thought to be indispensible in identifying the leaders and influential individuals on whom the responsibilities for development would be placed, but knowledge of sources of power and authority will also be necessary for the attainment of development goals and to isolate forces which might be inimical to those goals.[7]

Power and authority can be considered as stemming from three distinct bases, economic, political and moral, even if these may not be factually separate in individual instances. It seems that the shopkeepers, as a quasi-class, occupy the highest rung in terms of local or national political power. For instance, as the village council chairman or a political party candidate for national elections, an individual would have access to two combined sources of status. As a group, shopkeepers are not seen as exercising high moral status.

Second in importance in the power-authority structure of the village are schoolteachers, hardly identifiable as a quasi-class, but comprising a group with moral standing and influence. Retired or older teachers were found to occupy a position of high socio-

7. In the interviews, a self-reporting method was used to collect responses to two questions, which served as main indicators of influence and authority. These were: (*a*) Whom do you consider to be the three most influential persons in Grand Bay? (*b*) Which three persons in Grand Bay do you think can command the greatest amount of confidence of the people?

economic status, not merely because of their salaries as senior teachers, but they would very likely have acquired their own homes, and would own or be working land, and have children overseas as sources to supplement family income. Quite pronounced were the emerging influence and power, particularly in terms of moral authority and appeal, now possessed by some younger school-teachers. Three of these teachers, in particular, were frequently mentioned by both old and young villagers as capable and trusted leaders.

At the bottom of the social structure one has to place the majority of subsistence small farmers, landless labourers, the unemployed and the young adults. The last of these ought to be considered as a distinct group, without being formally organised, but sharing similar aspirations and views on the social conditions. Those of low social status tend to have intense feelings of resentment towards the few, highly visible "better-offs". Here one finds a clear social division in the village, and both groups utilise sterotypes in dismissing the other. In the eyes of the rich, the poor are "lazy, unwilling to work, envious of the little we have acquired through hard work" and "inclined towards disruption", while to the poor, the rich are "corrupt", and "have sucked the little we have acquired through hard work" and "interested only in themselves", and "unwilling to see anyone else get ahead".

In terms of age and political affiliations, there also seem to be clearly divided positions in the village. Some of the older heads write off the young people as destructive, bent on disorder and violence, and supposedly under the influence of "communists". Political differences tend to be quite pronounced and cause acute rivalry. At the time of our investigation, several references were made indicating the general threat that the conventional parties perceived in the Movement for a New Dominica (MND). Efforts were therefore made to discredit any individuals — particularly among the young — who were suspected of being sympathetic or involved with the MND. The more important point is that, irrespective of formal membership, a significant number of young people are examining the social, political and economic conditions of their country, in a sufficiently serious way to warrant an understanding of the root causes of the problems. This, perhaps, has given rise to fears on the part of those whose interests are secure within the present *status quo*.

It should be recognised at once that no effective programme for integrated development will reach very far without significant participation by the younger people and their spokesmen. It is also necessary that co-ordination of such a programme should be sensitive to the potential conflicts across age differences and political affiliation.

Institutions, ideology, religion and social networks

On the administrative level, the two most important institutions are the Village Council and a recently formed Village Improvement Committee. Discussions with some executives of the former were revealing. Being all older persons, their opinions and attitudes tended to reinforce our earlier observations on their resistance to, and stereotypic dismissal of, the young people in the village. One can only wonder how effective the Council is and whose interests and purposes it serves.

The Village Improvement Committee, on the contrary, seems more dynamic; its chairman is a young schoolteacher, articulate and commanding much respect and confidence. For instance, their proposals on the future of Geneva, even if not clearly worked out at the time of our investigation, should certainly be given some attention, and their participation in strategies for development will definitely be necessary.

Some eight religious institutions are to be found in the village. These include churches of the following denominations: Roman Catholic, Methodist, Gospel Mission, Pentecostal, Yahweh Church, Seventh Day Church of God, Worldwide Church of God and Jehovah's Witnesses. Of these the Roman Catholics have the largest membership. There was no case of specific resistance to crop cultivation or animal husbandry resulting from religious beliefs.

The Catholic Church is formally entrenched in Grand Bay as in other communities in Dominica. However, its role appears to be passive in relation to cementing the conflicts in the society, and building a strong foundation for development. The Church could assume a more dynamic function, inspiring confidence and commitment as values beneficial for mobilizing a community, and playing an active part in bridging the gap between young and old.

The existence of a Parent Teachers' Association at the village school has not proved beneficial to the educational needs of the students and the professional needs of the teachers. No evidence could be found regarding its plans or programme of activities.

Of course, the school occupies a position of tremendous importance in the life of the village. Parents are clearly oriented towards their children doing as well as possible; but very few students will receive an opportunity for secondary education. Already, a growing number of young people are forced to leave school "half-baked", to use the words of a retired schoolteacher, and become frustrated and depressed by the lack of meaningful job opportunities.

Youth and their concern for change

It was previously indicated that a significant portion of the people in the village (75%) are less than thirty-five years of age. The aspirations of many young people are now well beyond what they are likely to achieve, and this increases their frustration and feeling of powerlessness. They have adopted an attitude and ideology whereby they search for the underlying political and social causes of the dependence to which they are subjected. They are therefore politically conscious and are exploring political solutions. Whether these will come through established movements and parties or through violent and spontaneous outbursts cannot be readily answered.[8]

In the immediate future, as well as for long-term development, organization and orientation of the creative energies and skills of the present adolescent group must be placed high among the priorities of a development strategy. As mentioned earlier, about 500–600 persons, within the 15–30 age-group, are without training or jobs. It is important that we understand the significance of this demographic phenomenon, both in national and village terms.

Dominica, like several other Caribbean societies, and indeed like many underdeveloped countries, has a population, a large proportion of which is under twenty-five years. In some instances, this section amounts to 60–70% of the total population. The conventional approaches to the population aspects of economic development which emphasise birth control measures and efforts at providing more and more "schooling" have not proved a great success. Not only are the costs prohibitive, but even increased school places and junior technical education do not solve the problems of inadequate job opportunities, nor do they provide means for an improved standard and quality of life for the rural poor. In general, the search by rural youth for an authentic way of life is hardly satisfied by so-called improvements in school curricula or longer periods in classrooms.

Notwithstanding the manifestations of reluctance to work, or the so-called general attitude of laziness, young adults undoubtedly demand an effective opportunity to assume a respected and meaningful role in shaping the kind of future, in the sort of society, that they consider desirable. Discussing problems of rural development, and the effects on groups of rural youth who had received little or no

8. The Prime Minister was removed from office in July 1979 following spontaneous protests and organized civil disobedience against charges of corruption and the proposed introduction of repressive legislation in the face of growing disenchantment.

primary education, a study in Kenya indicated, among other things, that "the 4-K experience has helped to discredit the familiar cliché that school leavers have a distaste for manual labour and that they only want white collar jobs. They understandably do not want to return to a life of unreformed agriculture, but there is strong evidence that when farming proves profitable, children are very eager to work at it."[9] On the assumption of their potential for adult responsibility and readiness to work in situations which are not dehumanising or exploitative, it might be possible to adopt a positive attitude towards the young people and devise with them experimental or pilot projects, providing a form of apprenticeship in which they can train and earn money at the same time. What kinds of pilot projects these will be must still await further discussion and the collection of all relevant data. However, current initiatives in the village can offer a basis for reflection.

Two possibilities seem to suggest themselves. One is already the subject of discussion, and seems to be supported by basic commitments on the part of a group of young people. The members of what is known as the Berekua Farmers' Co-operative strongly supported the view that a portion of the Geneva Estate should be allocated for their use as an agricultural producers' and marketing co-operative. An educational programme to bring about understanding of the principles of co-operatives has already begun, and there is contact between the group and staff at the Ministry of Agriculture. However, it will be necessary for specific and concentrated attention to be given, not merely to understanding co-operative principles and selecting the most economically profitable crops, but also to building group solidarity among members. It will also be necessary to provide them with a community awareness and with concrete opportunities for playing a strategic role in the village's overall development. These are all fundamental pre-requisites for agricultural co-operatives to be effective in rural development.

A second possibility could be in the direction of technical and industrial arts, along the lines of a woodwork and metalwork centre. Such an agency would provide training, and at the same time manufacture furniture for use both in the village concerned and throughout the country. The matters of available resources, costs of

9. P. Fordham and J.R. Sheffield, "Continuing Education for Youth and Adults" in James R. Sheffield (ed.), *Education, Employment and Rural Development*, Nairobi: East Africa Publishing House, 1967. "4-K Clubs" (meaning *Kuunga* [to unite], *Kufanya* [to work], *Kusaidia* [to help] and Kenya — supervised by Agricultural Extension Staff, provided training on modern farming methods and running projects (e.g. vegetable or poultry farming) to earn money.

production, desirable types of furniture, and marketing outlets will have to be considered in detail before any decisions can be made on such a project. [10] While these possibilities might primarily appeal to the young male population of the village, discussions should be re-opened on the feasibility of a Handicraft Centre, utilising Vertiver and Screwpine reeds, which could benefit a portion of the unemployed females. [11]

Conclusion

Our case-study has attempted to offer a comprehensive overview of the structural factors and salient social relations associated with the pervasive dominance of the plantation system in a specific locale of a particular Caribbean island. However it would be unscientific and misleading to build wider generalisations on plantation dominance and rural dependence from the analysis presented. However, it has been possible, for instance, to identify useful information on household life. The significance of the age and sex structure of the village inhabitants has also been well established. Both at the individual and family level, access to and control of the productive forces, primarily the land, were clearly identified by the inhabitants as crucial factors determining the livelihood of all the groups in the village. In this sense, the fundamental importance of the material conditions in general and such specific factors as the mode of land tenure was explicitly revealed in the awareness, perception and attitudes of the people of Grand Bay towards the plantation. Thus it was by no mere theoretical assertion that the relationship of the economic substructure and consciousness of the villagers was so vividly expressed, but rather in a long and consistent historical pattern of intervention and in their actual practical behaviour.

At a practical policy level, the outcome and prospects for change and development of Grand Bay were known to be subject to the interests of those exercising power over the Land Management Authority, who resided in the island's capital. In the course of our study it became clear that neither farmers, as a group or class, nor the youth were organized or linked with sources of power in the wider national political culture in a way that would have enabled

10. With further thought given to the utilisation of red cedar on the Geneva Estate, the linking of the woodworking and furniture manufacture to the use of such resources would require a small local sawmilling enterprise as an additional benefit.
11. See L.A. Simon and R.E. Riviere, *A Report on a Feasibility Survey for Proposed Handicraft Centre, Berricoa, Grand Bay, Roseau*, Social Development Division, 1969.

them effectively to pursue their demands along a path of development likely to satisfy mainly their own interests.[12] This course is an issue that may have consequences not merely for Grand Bay but for farmers and young people in other parts of the island as well as in other islands of the Caribbean.

Limited as they are, the kinds of conceptual categories employed in the analysis of Grand Bay are applicable to any holistic appraisal of social relations in the rural sector. As such studies are accomplished, it is to be hoped not merely that relevant information is obtained, but that opportunities are utilised for heightening the consciousness of the masses of the rural poor. Thus their capacity to organize themselves in pursuit of their interests will be extended. To abolish the structures of rural dependence at the local level is but one aspect of the wider process that will eliminate both the imbalance between urban and rural sectors and the exploitation of classes in the society as a whole. It is the goal of "integral" development.

12. This observation is supported by the fact that 6 years elapsed before the political directorate, with assistance from the Organisation of American States, agreed to a comprehensive programme of development. The author has since learnt that "popular participation" by the community will be incorporated in a settlement scheme being devised by the OAS.

5

ECONOMIC BEHAVIOUR OF PEASANTS IN TOBAGO

Carlisle Pemberton

Introduction

Agriculture in the Caribbean region has been characterised by a dualistic nature. On the one hand, there is the plantation sector devoted to the production of crops mainly for export (particularly sugar cane). On the other hand, there are a larger number of small farmers producing mainly food crops and livestock for domestic consumption and in a few important instances crops for export (e.g. sugar cane farmers in Trinidad and banana-growers in the Windward Islands).

The dualism is accentuated because, while in the plantation sector there has been the large-scale adoption of modern technological inputs in production and marketing, farmers in the small farm sector have remained largely traditional with the minimal utilisation of modern inputs. Important exceptions to this trend however exist. In particular, in cases of small-farmer production of some export crops (especially sugar cane and bananas) there has been a high level of adoption of modern technological inputs. There is therefore a dichotomy between the plantation sector and those small farmers engaged mainly in domestic food production (Demas, 1971). In this study this sub-sector of small farmers is defined as the peasant sub-sector.

The aspects of the dualistic nature of Caribbean agriculture that have received the greatest attention by Caribbean researchers have been associated with the impact of colonialistic exploitation on the patterns of land distribution, economic underdevelopment and dependence. Foremost among these works have been those of Beckford (1972), Best (1968) and Marshall in Chapter 1 of the present work. Much less effort has been devoted to investigation of the economic behaviour of the peasants, particularly as reflected in the low levels of adoption of improved technology on their farms and high levels of off-farm employment. This study aims to find an explanation for this 'lack of dynamism', and since it is the economic behaviour of the peasants that is being considered, there will be an attempt to investigate the determinants of that behaviour within the motivational structure of the individuals.

76

The agricultural sector of the island of Tobago was chosen to test the explanatory model developed in this study. The island's society is largely rural, and structurally its agricultural sector is in keeping with the general situation described earlier for the Caribbean as a whole. The Report of the Tobago Planning Team (1964, p.4) for example, provided this description of Tobago's agricultural sector:

The large estates of 100 acres and over are situated on the better and more productive soils. They are generally more efficient in management practices than the small farmer, but have not, except in a few cases, used their lands in a manner that will give the maximum returns in yields and provide the greatest employment. . . . The income from agriculture in Tobago has, naturally come largely from the production on large estates. . . . The peasants have not been able to contribute much to the economy . . . [and] their efforts are in large part a waste of resources — land and people. Years of low production and productivity have made them become 'subsistence' minded, thinking only in terms of producing enough to live on and not in terms of producing large surpluses for sale which could lead to an increase in their standards of living. In this connection, a contributory factor has been the absence of a proper form of marketing surplus. As a result, the young regard peasant agriculture and poverty as synonymous. . . .

A detailed investigation of the technological conditions on farms in both the peasant and plantation sub-sectors of Tobago's agriculture carried out in 1971 supported the general conclusions given in the above Report. This study, reported in Pemberton (1972), involved surveys of 37 peasant farmers and 16 plantation-owners (or managers).

As for the plantation sub-sector, of the 16 farms surveyed only five used fertiliser, nine had tractors (with a mean of three tractors per farm) and related mechanical attachments, and 14 had buildings devoted exclusively to farm operations. On seven farms there was specialised crop-drying machinery for coconuts and cocoa. Considering only crop enterprise, the mean capital stock per farm was $24,678 or $87.90 per acre cropped. The yields of the crops were low. This situation was blamed on the low plant production densities resulting from loss of trees by Hurricane Flora in 1963, and on low returns making the high cost of establishment of trees uneconomical.

As for peasant farms, the average yields of the crops were very low, particularly in thé cases of root crops and cocoa. The low yields resulted largely from inadequate use of improved inputs in production. Of the 34 farms with crop enterprises, only six used fertilisers, applying on average 141.8 lb. per crop acre. None of the farmers used herbicides and only three used insecticides. No farmer owned a tractor or machinery of any kind. Only four farmers rented the services of tractors to prepare their lands for planting. Thus, on most farms there was inadequate land preparation. There were only hand tools on the farms (cutlasses, forks etc.) and in one case a spray can. All crops were grown without irrigation on peasant farms, annual crop production being concentrated in the rainy season — May to December. There were no buildings on the farms used for crop production, as little input or produce was stored. Considering only crop enterprises, the mean capital stock per farm was $28 or $4.30 per acre cropped. The productivity analysis showed that for all resources (land, labour and capital) on the farms, the productivity of resource use on the large farms was higher than on the peasant farms. It also showed that large farmers should use more labour and put under cropping a greater amount of their idle lands (estimated at 37.5% of total farm acreage) to utilise their capital stock more fully and improve its productivity.

The study found that all the resources on the peasant farms were being used inefficiently. In particular, land productivity was very low, with 29.6% of the lands remaining idle. The study suggested that the peasants should increase their use of capital inputs in crop production so that greater acreages could be farmed, to improve the productivity of their labour.

The results of the 1971 study revealed a peasant sub-sector with little technological advancement, low crop yields and inefficiency of resource use. The next section presents a brief background to Tobago's agriculture to examine the historical context in which this situation developed, following which the analytical framework for this study will be elaborated.

Review of the modern history of agriculture in Tobago

The first phase of the modern history of agriculture on the island of Tobago began with the arrival of the European settlers in the seventeenth century. The first notable settlement started in 1642 with colonists from Courland (now Latvia). The Dutch arrived and settled in 1654, and at first lived on amicable terms with the Courlanders. The Dutch certainly undertook sugar-cane cultivation and sugar manufacture (Niddrie, 1961, p.16). However from 1658, hostilities in Europe found their expression on the island of Tobago by a series of changes of sovereignty.[1] Cultivation of the island in this

---

1. Woodcock (1867), Ch. II, presents a detailed and vivid description of this turbulent era of Tobago's history. Another interesting account is given by Williams (1962), Ch. VI.

first phase was apparently not extensive, since no single metro-politan power had a long enough span of control to develop the island's agriculture.

The second phase of Tobago's agriculture (1763–1838) could be termed the 'golden age of Tobago's agriculture':

By the ninth article of the definitive treaty of peace, signed at Paris on the 10th February, 1763, this much disputed claim of the Crown of England was fully guaranteed: The English were confirmed in their possession of Tobago, and the foundation was laid of the first permanent colony that through a train of disastrous circumstances had ever been permitted to flourish within its shores (Woodcock, 1867, p. 34).

The British immediately set about planning the settlement of Tobago. A Commission was appointed to subdivide the island into rectangular blocks of between 100 and 500 acres.[2] Settlers soon arrived, and by 1770 some 54,408 acres had been sold, mainly on the lowland coral plains and the alluvial flats of the Windward coast. In that same year (1770), the first shipment of sugar from Tobago left Studley Park. Cotton and indigo estates were also established.

By 1776 exports of sugar totalled 2,357 tons, with an estimated total value of £20,000 (Woodcock 1867, p.188). In that same year a plague of ants spread across the island causing great destruction to the cane fields — an event which encouraged the production of cotton. In 1780, Woodcock (p.188) reports, 3,000 hogshead of sugar (1,950 tons), 1,619,000 lb. of cotton and 27,000 lb. of indigo were shipped from the island.

From 1781 to 1793 the island was again in French hands. From all indications, agriculture continued its development under the French, although it would seem that cotton production declined from 1788 when a production of 1,475,600 lb. of dry lint was produced. The island was recaptured by the English in March 1793 and thereafter remained British.

Exports of agricultural commodities from Tobago for the period 1794–1809 are given in Table 1. Production of cotton fell rapidly from 1794. However the cotton produced in Tobago was of the highest quality known in the cotton trade — we quote below a description by Woodcock (pp.188-9) of the quality of Tobago's cotton, as well as his explanation of the decline in cotton production:

We are told in the 'Encyclopedia Britannica' edition of 1854 . . . that 'The cotton of the finest quality ever brought to the English market, or probably

---

2. A forest reserve was also created in the mountainous centre of the island as well as a strip of land 66 feet wide around most of the island was maintained by the Crown for defensive purposes (Niddrie, 1961, p. 16).

ever grown, was that . . . raised on the island of Tobago between the years 1789 and 1792, upon the estate of Mr Robley. That gentleman carried the cultivation of this article to some extent, but the price of cotton falling very low, and the cultivation of sugar becoming extremely profitable, in consequence of the destruction of sugar plantation in the French islands, he was induced to convert his cotton grounds into a sugar plantation.'

Sugar production expanded rapidly from 1794 (Table 1 and Fig. 1). With the high prices for sugar, Tobago's agriculture was very lucrative, so much so that Niddrie (p. 17) reports that a current phrase in London at that time was 'as rich as a Tobago planter'.

Table 1. EXPORTS OF PRODUCE FROM TOBAGO, 1794–1809

	Tons sugar	Puncheons molasses	Puncheons rum	Puncheons shrub	Weight cotton (lb.)
1794	5,406	91	4,998	–	454,500
1795	3,946	301	4,368	1	327,150
1796	4,840	42	5,693	1	401,100
1797	4,978	4	4,893	–	73,650
1798	6,365	–	7,415	1	25,950
1799	8,890	151	7,669	4	7,950
1800	6,679	1,383	6,429	5	9,000
1801	7,417	662	7,686	24	31,000
1802	8,645	585	7,864	80	24,150
1803	5,279	95	3,435	15	26,400
1804	7,179	381	6,390	14	19,200
1805	8,590	920	8,621	15	35,400
1806	8,177	655	8,192	29	29,250
1807	6,786	686	9,000	24	28,050
1808	7,004	206	7,934	22	20,400
1809	7,248	73	7,663	19	34,350

The golden age of Tobago's agriculture ended and its third phase started with the end of Apprenticeship and the unconditional freedom of slaves on 1 August 1838. Production of cotton had ceased by 1827 and the economy depended from the start of the nineteenth century on sugar production. Production of sugar started to decline slowly from 1813 (Fig. 1) owing largely to soil fertility loss. With the freedom of the slaves there was the immediate departure of a substantial proportion of the labour force, which resulted in a marked drop in sugar production. A further serious blow to the island's economy was the hurricane which struck the island on the night of 11 October 1847,[3] causing damage valued at £150,000 on the island, especially to sugar factories and dwelling houses. Hurricane loans were granted by the British Treasury to help rebuild the economy,

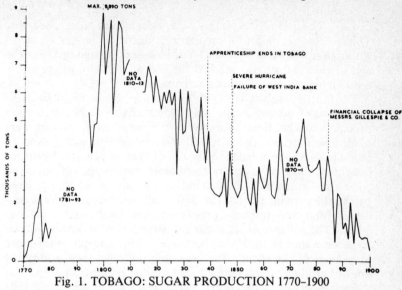

Fig. 1. TOBAGO: SUGAR PRODUCTION 1770–1900

Source: David L. Niddrie, *Land Use and Production in Tobago*, Geographical Publications, Bude, Cornwall, 1961.

but this measure only served to increase the indebtedness of the sugar planters. By 1847, also, sugar production itself had become much less profitable because of higher labour costs and increasing competition for the commodity from foreign cane sugar (grown with slave labour) and beet sugar. By 1854 many estates had gone bankrupt. An Encumbered Estates Act was passed by the Tobago House of Assembly in January 1858 to facilitate the sale of bankrupt estates, and ten years later 16 such estates had been sold. Many abandoned estates reverted to the Crown and this land was released at 10 shillings an acre in lots of 5–10 acres to Grenadian immigrants and local peasants for the cultivation of cocoa and nutmeg.[4]

With the collapse of the financial house of Gillespie and Co. in 1884 came the final death pangs of the Tobago sugar industry (Fig. 1); because most of the estates had relied on this firm for financial support and advances on annual crops, its collapse meant their

3. Woodcock (1867)ˊ, Ch. V, presents a vivid description of this event.
4. Production of cocoa in Tobago over this period has been given as 1876 — 1 bag; 1881 — 14 bags; 1884 — 75 bags; 1888 — 147 bags; 1890 — 31 bags. (1 bag = 165 lb.) There is no evidence of large-scale nutmeg production as a result of this measure. However Williams (1962, p. 60) reports on earlier cultivation of nutmeg as follows: "The nutmeg was discovered in abundance in 1768 and 40 plantations were immediately started."

demise. The island's economy was so shattered after 1884 that Tobago lost its political singularity, becoming subordinated to Trinidad in 1889 and a ward of Trinidad and Tobago in 1898. The end of the century also marked the end of the third phase of the modern history of agriculture in Tobago.

The fourth phase of Tobago's agriculture saw the rapid diversification away from sugar cane and a radical change in the distribution of landholdings. Because many of the sugar estate owners were bankrupt, they proceeded to sell their estates for paltry sums to individuals who proceeded to dispose of them to peasants by sale or leasehold. The Crown also released more land to peasants in lots of 5-10 acres in the more hilly Windward region of the island. Even before their emancipation, the slaves cultivated smallholdings producing food crops (especially root crops) and small numbers of livestock.[5] The collapse of the sugar industry allowed this peasant class to become entrenched by the purchase of land cheaply in the more hilly areas of the island. The peasants continued their traditional lines of production, and grew cocoa as their major cash crop.

Estates occupying the coral lowlands and some of the alluvial flats on the Windward coast changed from sugar cane to coconut production, accelerating a trend which had started in the mid-nineteenth century. By 1920 the area under sugar cane had been reduced to 563 acres, and sugar production had ended by the late 1930s, according to a Report of 1957. Those estates remaining on the Windward coast that did not get into coconut production had started cocoa production by 1925, the rapid extension of cocoa production taking place about 1915 (Report, 1957).

The patterns of land distribution and use in Tobago established by 1925 remained substantially unaltered to the end of the fourth phase of Tobago's agriculture in 1963. These patterns of land distribution and use are illustrated in Tables 2 and 3. As we see in Table 2, in 1963, 49 landholdings in Tobago were of over 100 acres. This represented 0.03% of the total number of landholdings, but these landholdings occupied 45.5% of the total acreage in private land holdings. Landholdings below 10 acres numbered 3,280 comprising 80.2% of the total number, but they occupied 27.2% of the total acreage. As for land use, the agricultural sector was still geared largely towards the cultivation of export and other tree crops in 1963 (Table 3). On the small holdings, however, the tree crops were sup-

---

5. Williams (1962, p. 60) gives the following land use distribution for Tobago in 1790: '4,878 acres were in sugar, 14,436 in cotton, 134 in coffee, 2 in cocoa, 4,842 in ground provisions and 5,356 in pastures. . . . There were 3,030 sheep and goats and 441 pigs. . . .'

plemented by the cultivation of the traditional food crops. Cocoa and coconuts were still the predominant tree crops, coconuts being more extensively grown on the large holdings, with cocoa being the more important crop on the smaller ones.

Table 2. LAND IN TOBAGO HELD IN HOLDINGS
OF ONE ACRE AND OVER, 1963-64

	No. of holdings		Total Acreage	
Holding size (acres)	no.	%	no.	%
1-4	2,100	51.30	4,900	10.7
5-9	1,180	28.90	7,550	16.5
10-49	737	18.00	11,035	24.1
50-99	21	0.01	1,498	3.3
100-199	16	0.01	2,158	4.7
200-499	20	0.01	5,658	12.4
500 & over	13	0.01	15,000	28.4

Sources: Central Statistical Office, Trinidad and Tobago, *Agricultural Census, 1967, Summary of Results*, Publication no. 6, Sept. 1969, pp. 1 and 2.

Table 3. ACREAGE AND VALUE OF SALES OF MAIN
CROPS IN TOBAGO, 1963-64

Crop	Acreage	Value of sales[a] ($'000 TT)
Cocoa	9,308	59
Citrus	127	1
Coconuts	9,186	25
Coffee	10	–
Bananas	435	9
Plantains	246	10
All other tree crops	112	1
Pigeon Peas	2,145	30
Ground Provisions	1,212	44
All other non-tree crops	1,074	24

[a] Extensive damage to holdings in Tobago in 1963 accounts for the low value of sales of all tree crops. The data refer to the crop year ending 30 Sept. 1964.

Sources: Central Statistical Office, Trinidad and Tobago. *Agricultural Census 1963, Summary of Results*, Publication no. 6, Sept. 1969, pp. 8, 12, and 20-2.

The current fifth phase of Tobago's agriculture began in September 1963 when Hurricane Flora devastated the island, particularly its tree crops and housing, with effects on agricultural production shown in Table 4. All indications are that agricultural production has never recovered to pre-hurricane levels; indeed, since 1963 there has been a large-scale abandonment of cultivation on both small and large holdings.

Hurricane Flora also caused an increase in public sector activity on the island. Since 1958, with the start of the First Five Year Development Programme (1958–62), public sector expenditure was having an effect on agriculture. For example, "The commencement of the First Five Year Development Programme (1958–1962) coincided with a period of declining prices for agricultural produce especially cocoa. The programme of Government activity in construction . . . did more than arrest the decline in incomes that may have been caused by falling prices. This was particularly important for the small farming sector in view of the importance of cocoa as a source of income on small farms. This new source of income also caused many small farmers to neglect their holdings and few of them have subsequently worked as full time farmers," (Pemberton, 1972, pp. 21–2).

During the current period, increased governmental activity, especially in road and community development, has attracted many individuals away from agriculture, thus greatly reducing the labour available to those farmers who have remained in production. The modest development that has taken place in the tourism sector has also served to attract labour from agriculture.

With regard specifically to agricultural development, activity in the public sector in this fifth phase has been concentrated in two areas — the acquisition and rehabilitation of abandoned large estates and the establishment of farms on State (formerly Crown) Lands for dairy, pig and vegetable production. Activity in both these two areas has met with little success. On many of the State Lands farms that were established, production has been abandoned, and the majority of the acquired estates remain almost completely unutilised.

The peasants have continued production to the present time although they have become an ageing class in the society with few young recruits. Production in this sub-sector continues to be largely of food crops and cocoa. Pig production has fluctuated over the current period, and the peasants continue to rear small numbers of other livestock.

Table 4. ESTIMATED VALUE OF PRINCIPAL ITEMS SHIPPED FROM TOBAGO TO TRINIDAD, 1958–66ᵃ (TT$1000)

Commodity	1958	1959	1960	1961	1962	1963	1964	1965	1966
Cocoa	523	565	496	377	675	367	29	94	79
Copra	620	1,135	856	994	863	909	267	447	452
Ground provisions	20	21	31	17	86	8	–	10	12
Bananas & Plantains	13	5	–	–	–	–	–	–	–
Fibre	73	79	52	33	29	22	14	8	14
Cattle	148	86	95	46	12	3	1	5	3
Sheep and Goats	71	54	47	73	56	48	66	47	51
Pigs	185	116	110	175	98	111	47	64	120
Poultry	57	13	19	2	19	–	–	–	–
Other Itemsᵇ	977	1,256	1,274	890	1,297	716	637	507	363

ᵃ Data for 1958–61 from *Report of the Tobago Planning Team* (Government Printery, Trinidad and Tobago, n.d.) 2, 41. Data for 1962–6 from Trinidad & Tobago Central Statistical Office, *Quarterly Economic Report*, Oct.–Dec. 1967 (C.S.O. Printing Unit, Trinidad, March 1968), p. 53. With effect from 1st quarter 1967, these series of estimates of value of goods shipped between Trinidad and Tobago have been suspended. (—) means less than $500.

ᵇ Include mainly cars and personal effects.

Analytical framework

Agrarian (traditionally rural) societies have been thought to be characterised by a set of distinctive values and attitudes, summarised by England, Gibbons and Johnson (1979). First, the farmer is seen (and sees himself) as an independent actor, the equal of all other men, in partnership with God, and self-sufficient. Secondly, agriculture is considered to be the basic industry on which all progress and prosperity are based; and finally, farming is considered a way of life which is undoubtedly natural and morally desirable with the emphasis on hard work and asceticism. On the other hand, urban (largely non-agricultural) life is thought to produce an emphasis on the evils of leisure and materialism. In recent times, the concept of a traditional value and attitude system characteristic of agrarian society has been challenged. England *et al.* have presented a comprehensive review of the relevant literature which has as its main conclusion that societies are converging to a single value and attitude system. At the stage where such a system exists, a "mass society" is said to be formed.

Two main causal factors of the mass society have been industrialisation and the organizational revolution. Industrialisation, it is agreed, requires high occupational mobility, a break-up of the extended family, continued rapid social change and urban dominance. Agriculture itself becomes simply another industry and no longer a way of life. It is also argued that these effects of industrialisation are, as it were, reinforced by the organizational revolution — the world-wide increase in the number, size and power of organizations. With this revolution, values have been shifted from being *personal standards* to *obedience to the collective*. There have also been shifts from the indispensability of individuals to their dispensability and from voluntarism to paternalism. These developments, it is argued, become extended to rural as well as urban areas and cause an erosion of distinctive rural values, until there becomes a homogenisation of values across all areas and all groups.

In their own research, England *et al.* show that in the United States, while some developments in the direction of a mass society have taken place, agrarianism (or rurality) is still an important determinant of values. In the Caribbean, the emphasis on economic development since the Second World War has been on capitalist industrial development (Demas, 1971, pp. 7–8). However, one may argue that the limited success of these developmental efforts should mean that the effects of industrialisation on values of rural society may have been minimal. It should be useful nevertheless to determine the value system in agrarian areas in the Caribbean.

Although values and attitudes are guides to individual behaviour, they are not considered as directly explaining human behaviour, especially not the levels of attainment of different individuals.[6] Some psychologists have chosen particular motives in an attempt to predict the level of attainment in human behaviour. For example, McCleland and Winter (1969) have dealt with the motive "Need for Achievement" (N Ach) by the use of the measurement procedure of a Thematic Apperception Test. Other psychologists have explained human behaviour in terms of a generalised measure of both the strength of human motives and the expectancy of success. Such a measure is the "Level of Aspiration", as used by Haller (1968), Rushing (1970) and Hotchkiss *et al.* (1979). Other theorists have suggested that the environment affects individual behaviour by its role in the cognitive process — the process of knowledge in the broadest sense including perception, meaning, judgement and so on.

In the process of cognition, the environment plays a key role as it allows cues and motives to be denied, distorted or exaggerated. Thus the environment plays an important role in influencing the level of attainment in human behaviour along with the strength of motivation of the individual as measured (for example) by the level of aspiration: "Level of attainment or action (Ac) is a non-linear accelerating function of the level of aspiration (A) and the level of facilitation (F) offered by the environment of the aspiration (including both intra- and extra-personal elements)" (Haller, 1968). Or in other words: "Ac = G (A, (A, F) F)", where "both the first and second derivatives with respect to A and F are positive." Haller's position is accepted as an operational formulation of human behaviour, and forms the basis of the following analysis of the economic behaviour of peasants in this study.

In rural societies, when individuals compare their own position with that of urban dwellers, this could cause a reconcentration of their goal structures in a more materialistic direction. Braithwaite (1968) has put forward an argument along these lines to explain the state of peasant farming in the Caribbean. Braithwaite contends that there has been a lack of dynamism in the peasant sub-sector in the

---

6. Some psychologists even suggest no role whatever for values in explaining human behaviour. Cofer and Appley (1964), for example state with respect to concepts such as values and attitudes that: "These terms all represent complex resultants of many factors and it is not at all clear that they are, in any sense, motivational." It is argued here that values are primary factors in human behaviour although not as direct causal agents, but as guiding standards to the whole process of individual behaviour.

Caribbean because of the disorientation of the peasants' motivational structures. The island societies are very small; communication is relatively easy, and there is widespread rudimentary education. These conditions, he argues, have led to goal orientations and levels of aspiration on the part of the rural population that are predominantly economic (raising the standard of living) and fairly close to those of the urban, metropolitan-oriented population. However, because of historical impediments, farming has not been seen by the rural community as having the capacity to fulfil these goals and aspirations. This has resulted in widespread rural-urban migration, and in the migration of these rural people to the metropole — the more developed nations in Europe and North America. Demas (1971, p. 11) puts forward similar views.

The availability of technological innovations with the potential for increased productivity in farming has not had the anticipated effect of stimulating peasant farming in the Caribbean. Adoption of improved inputs would need the investment of human and financial resources, and for such investment to be undertaken, the peasants must perceive that farming is attractive in terms of attaining the goals they are attempting to achieve. In the Caribbean, the environment in which peasant farming takes place (especially the small size of holdings and their location on marginal, hilly lands) would be generally hostile to satisfactory performance. Thus, as Braithwaite has argued, it could not be expected that peasant farming would be considered an attractive occupation. But if it is not attractive, one would expect rural societies to search for alternatives with the potential to meet individual goals (Simon, 1959). As noted above, Braithwaite deals with the alternative of migration from rural societies.

Another alternative would be for the individuals to seek off-farm employment within the rural society, and the fact that some individuals do this and thus do not sever their identity with the rural society would indicate that their agrarian values and attitudes are still having some influence on their behaviour. This influence of agrarian values and attitudes may even be strong enough to make some individuals reluctant to stop farming. Thus one could expect varying degrees of farming to be pursued by the peasants largely engaged in off-farm employment — the phenomenon of part-time farming. The degree of off-farm employment should be dependent on the strength of the motivational forces causing non-agrarian occupations to be pursued.

The attractiveness of an occupation to individuals engaged in it (especially in closed rural societies) reinforces cultural prejudgements of its degree of attractiveness to potential entrants. This is particularly because those potential entrants may not perceive the occupation precisely or realistically, but only do so in terms of these vaguely generalised prejudgements, which are usually undiscriminating in application, resistant to modification and tend to be self-perpetuating and self-enhancing because of their selecting and modifying effect on current experience. Thus it would be expected that the patterns of behaviour established by the traditional peasantry in Caribbean rural societies would by this process of cultural inheritance be adopted by potential entrants (mainly school-leavers). Under these circumstances, one could expect to observe migration among school-leavers from rural to urban areas and thence to metropolitan countries, as well as the adoption of part-time farming by those school-leavers who elect to take up peasant farming. Again it would be expected that the degree of off-farm employment would depend on the strength of the motivational forces causing the nonfarming occupations to be pursued. The degree of off-farm employment should thus be a relevant dependant variable to measure the influence of motivational factors on the economic behaviour of peasants. For example, the degree of off-farm employment should be inversely related to the level of attraction of farming as an occupation, positively related to the existence of materialistic goals, and inversely related to the influence of agrarian values and attitudes.

The analytical framework that has been developed is provided in the Model given in Figure 2. The following section discusses the methodology used in the study to test the appropriateness of this model as an explanation of the economic behaviour of peasants.

The survey

To obtain information for this study, a survey of the peasant subsector of agriculture in Tobago was carried out in 1977. The random sample of peasant farmers was obtained from listings of landholders in Tobago, having under 99 acres derived from the 1970 Population Census of Trinidad and Tobago.[7] A total of 118 landholders in actual agricultural production were interviewed. The information collected included the goals and aspirations of the peasant farmers, agrarian values, off-farm employment practices, and characteristics such as age, income and family size.

The procedures used to obtain information on goals and aspirations of the peasants was based on the Self-Anchoring Scale Method of Kilpatrick and Cantril (1960). They define a Self-Anchoring Scale as "one in which each respondent is asked to describe, in terms of his

---

7.   This sample frame was the same one used in the study of resource use on peasant farms in Tobago discussed in full detail in Pemberton (1972, pp. 28–33).

own perceptions, goals and values, the top and bottom, or anchoring points, of the dimension on which scale measurement is derived, and then to employ this self-defined continuum as a measuring device." In the adaptation of this method used in the study, the following question is asked first: "All of us want to achieve certain things in our lives. Now when you think of the best possible life for yourself, what are your wishes and hopes for the future if you are to be happy?" Statements here are assumed to be meaningful life-goals. Then this question is asked: "Turning to the other side of life, what are your worries and fears of the future?" Statements here give clues to the respondent's goals, since they may be the opposite to the goals that he would like to achieve.

The respondent is then presented with a pictorial scale in the form of a zero-to-ten ladder and is instructed to let the top of the ladder represent the best possible life and the bottom the worst possible life for himself. He is then asked to indicate where he thinks his life is on the scale at the present time, and is then asked where he thinks his life will be after five years. The present life-score provides an index of the individual's evaluation of the current status of his life. The life-score after five years (hereafter referred to as the future life-score) provides a generalized measure of the respondent's level of aspiration. Similar procedures have proved useful in analysing motivational patterns of rural people in studies by Rushing (1970) and Pemberton and Craddock (1979).

Kilpatrick *et al.* (1964) utilised a Self-Anchoring Scale to obtain occupational value orientations of individuals. A modification of their method was used in this study to determine the agrarian values held by peasant farmers in Tobago. The respondent is shown another picture of a ladder, but this time the top of the ladder represents the best possible occupation, and the bottom the worst possible occupation to the individual. The respondent is asked: "Where on the ladder do you feel your occupation of farming is at the present time?" The answer to this question termed the Farming-as-an-Occupation Rank provides an indication of the status of farming to the individual respondent, who is then asked the following question: "What are the things [features] of farming that caused you to give it this rating?" Answers here provide a picture of the agrarian values and attitudes held by the individual, or alternately answers may indicate an absence of agrarian values and attitudes and illustrate the changing patterns of rural value orientations.

For off-farm employment practices, the respondents were first asked to state the other occupations besides farming that they were engaged in, and were then asked to state the amount of time (as a percentage of the total time spent working) they were engaged in other jobs besides farming. Farmers engaged in off-farm employment were then asked: "Would you like to be able to farm full time?", and to state the reasons for the particular response given. Respondents stating they would like to be able to farm full time would be indicating a desire for an agrarian life-style; and they would be expected to give as reasons for their answer one of the traditional agrarian values or attitudes detailed earlier.

A measure of the relative poverty line[8] for the individuals in Sample 2 was obtained as a response to the question: "How much money *per month* do you feel that a family of father, mother and two children needs to live comfortably in Tobago?" The propensity of the peasants to invest in farming activities was measured as a response to the question: "Suppose you made an income of $1,000 from farming this year, how much of it would you spend on your farming operations next year?"

Data analysis

Linear regression analysis was carried out to test the validity of the analytical model given in Fig. 2 (p. 92). The dependent variable (Y), "off-farm employment", is defined as the % of total working time spent on occupations besides farming. The explanatory variables used in the analysis are given in Table 5 with the *a priori* expectation of the signs of their respective regression coefficients.

Table 5. A PRIORI EXPECTATIONS OF SIGNS OF
REGRESSION COEFFICIENTS

	Explanatory variable	Expected sign of coefficient
X_1	Land owned	–
X_2	Land farmed	–
X_3	Family size	+
X_4	Age	–
X_5	Present life score	+
X_6	Future life score	+
X_7	Farming-as-an-occupation rank	–
X_8	Poverty line estimate	+
X_9	Farm investment propensity	–

The following results were obtained from the Survey and the regression analysis.

8. A relative poverty line may be defined as the level of income as perceived by a family or individual which divides the families of á particular size, place and time into the poor a..d the non-poor.

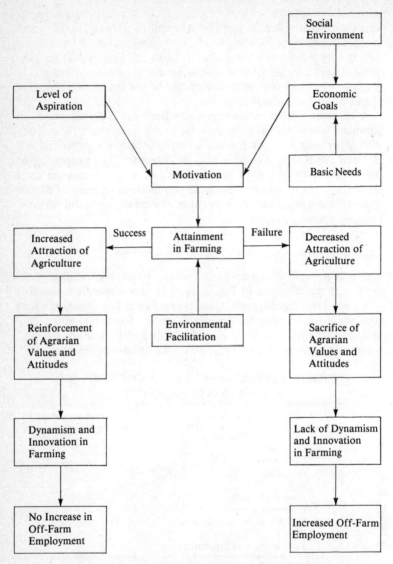

Fig. 2. EXPLANATORY MODEL OF OFF-FARM EMPLOYMENT
OF PEASANT FARMERS.

General characteristics of the peasant farmers

Table 6 gives for the sample of peasant farms, the % of farms and the acreage in actual production classified by the acreage owned.

Table 6. DISTRIBUTIONS OF THE PERCENTAGE OF FARMS AND TOTAL ACREAGE FARMED BY SIZE OF FARM

Size of farm (acres)	% of farms (n = 118)*	Total acreage farmed (n = 118)*
0–0.99	15.2	4.83
1–1.99	22.0	30.75
2–2.99	18.6	46.75
3–3.99	12.7	46.00
4–4.99	5.9	29.25
5–5.99	7.6	45.50
6–10	12.7	117.50
10	5.1	78.50

Mean Acreage Farmed, 3.38 acres.
Mean Farm Size, 7.49 acres.
Average total acreage unutilised on peasant farms, 55%.

* In this and subsequent tables, *n* represents the actual number of respondents or responses for the particular question. Where *n* is less than 118 respondents, the difference will represent cases of non-respondents; *n* may be greater than 118 in the case of questions where the respondents may state more than one response.

Table 7 gives the major enterprises on the peasant farms, in order of importance as stated by the farmers. The traditional pattern of production is still apparent, with cocoa and root crops being the most

Table 7. ENTERPRISES IN ORDER OF THE STATED IMPORTANCE ON PEASANT FARMS

Enterprise	% of Farmers* stating the enterprise as:		
	Most important (n = 111)	2nd most important (n = 103)	3rd most important (n = 80)
Cocoa	27.1	8.5	5.9
Root Crops	18.7	15.2	11.9
Sheep	16.1	7.6	5.9
Vegetables	10.2	15.2	12.7
Pigs	5.9	2.5	3.4
Dairy	3.4	5.9	2.6
Goats	2.6	7.6	3.9
Bananas	0.1	12.7	6.8
Other	9.3	11.9	14.4
Non-respondents	5.9	12.7	32.2

* % of all 118 farmers.

important enterprises, followed by small livestock and vegetable production.

The results in Table 8, giving the age distribution of the peasant farmers in Tobago, supports the contention that peasant farmers in Tobago are an ageing class with few young recruits. Table 9 indicates that 53% of the farmers had families of 5 or more members

Table 8. AGE DISTRIBUTION OF
PEASANT FARMERS IN TOBAGO

Age (years)	% of farmers (n = 118)
More than 80	5.9
70–79	15.3
60–69	32.2
50–59	25.4
40–49	13.6
30–39	5.9
Less than 30	1.7

Mean age of farmers, 59.4 years.

Table 9. DISTRIBUTION OF SIZE OF
FAMILIES ON PEASANT FARMS

Family size	% of farmers (n = 118)
1–2	25.4
3–4	22.0
5–6	17.8
7–8	16.1
>8	18.7

Goals and aspirations of peasant farmers

For the adapted Self-Anchoring Scaling Method, Table 10 presents the results for the question on wishes and hopes for the future while Table 11 presents those for the question on worries and fears. The results in Tables 10 and 11 show that the predominant goal of the peasant farmers is the acquisition of money. The other major goal of the farmers is the maintenance or recovery of good health. This goal perhaps reflects the fact, noted in Table 8, that the mean age of the farmers was 59 years, with 21% of them over 70.

Important results were obtained from the Self-Anchoring Scale.

For the present life score, 48% of the farmers (and 52% of those responding to the question) reported a score of 5 or lower on the 0–10 scale. Thus about half of the peasant farmers showed, at the least,

Table 10. GOAL ORIENTATIONS OF PEASANTS FARMERS:
WISHES AND HOPES FOR THE FUTURE

Response	% of farmers	% of responses
To have more money	50.9	30.0
To have good health	44.9	26.1
To have a happy and peaceful life	21.2	12.3
To have spiritual wellbeing	15.3	8.9
To possess more property and belongings	11.9	6.9
Not expecting more in the future	9.3	5.4
To bring about children's wellbeing	8.5	4.9
Other	10.2	5.9

Table 11. GOAL ORIENTATIONS OF PEASANT FARMERS: FEARS
AND WORRIES ABOUT THE FUTURE

Response	% of farmers	% of responses
Insufficient money to meet financial obligations	25.4	20.4
Poor health	11.4	8.0
Lack of suitable employment	6.1	4.9
Political uncertainty	5.3	4.2
Loss of possessions	5.3	4.2
Other worries and fears	14.9	12.0
No fears and worries	52.6	42.3

disaffection for their current status in life. The mean present life score was 5.11 and the mean future life score was 6.96. Thus peasant farmers can be classified as upward-oriented, aspiring to improve their lives by 36% over 5 years by achieving their goals in Table 10.

By way of comparison, in rural Manitoba, Canada, low, medium- and high-income farmers reported mean present life scores of 5.8, 6.4 and 6.7 and mean future life scores of 6.1, 6.6 and 7.3 respectively. Thus the high-income farmers showed the greatest upward orientation, aspiring to improve their lives by 9% over 5 years (Pemberton and Craddock 1979). Clearly the peasants in Tobago are demonstrating a greater desire for improvement in their lives.

Agrarian value orientation of peasant farmers

The results obtained from the adaptation of the Self-Anchoring Scale Method to discover agrarian value orientations of the peasant farmers are presented in Table 12, which shows that the major value of peasant farming was the provision of food. Other traditional agrarian values reported included: Farming is "a good way of life"; you are independent and "your own boss". Negative aspects of the occupation were also reported, especially the low income derived from peasant farming and the unfavourable environmental conditions such as poor infrastructure and lack of suitable inputs.

The mean Farming-as-an-Occupation rank of the peasant farmers was 6.25; in rural Manitoba, mean ranks of 7.4, 8.0 and 8.6 were obtained for low, medium- and high-income farmers respectively using the same (0–10) scale (Pemberton, 1976). As seen in Table 12, while 50% of the farmers still held exclusively positive and largely

Table 12. AGRARIAN VALUE ORIENTATIONS
OF PEASANT FARMERS

Responses	% of farmers (n = 113)	% of responses (n = 169)
Positive		
Provides food	28.0	19.5
Good way of life	23.0	15.4
Provides personal satisfaction and achievement	19.5	13.0
Is essential for human survival	11.0	7.7
You are your own boss	7.1	4.7
Income is derived	7.1	4.7
Other	2.7	1.8
Negative		
Too-little income is derived	15.0	10.1
Unfavourable conditions exist	12.4	8.3
Too old for occupation	8.0	5.3
Lack of suitable inputs (land, labour, etc.)	7.1	4.7
Other	7.1	4.7

Summary	% of all farmers (n = 118)
Farmers stating only positive responses	50.0
Farmers stating only negative responses	22.9
Farmers stating negative and positive responses	22.9
Non-Respondents	4.2

Mean Farming-as-an-Occupation rank, 6.25.

traditional agrarian values, 46% significantly did not. Thus a relatively low Farming-as-an-Occupation rank was obtained.

Off-farm employment of peasant farmers

Of the 118 farmers interviewed, 63 (53.4%) reported that they had off-farm jobs, while 54 (48.8%) reported no off-farm employment (there was one non-respondent). Table 13, giving the distribution of time spent in off-farm employment by the peasant farmers, shows that 83% of the farmers so engaged spent more than 75% of their working time in their off-farm jobs. The farmers with off-farm jobs may therefore be properly classified as part-time farmers.

Table 13. TIME SPENT BY PEASANT FARMERS IN
OFF-FARM EMPLOYMENT

% time spent in off-farm employment	% of farmers (n = 114)	No. of farmers (n = 114)
0	45.8	54
1–25	0	0
26–50	4.2	5
51–75	2.5	3
More than 75	45.6	52

Table 14, giving the occupational distribution of the part-time farmers, shows that employment in the public sector accounts for 71.4% of the off-farm employment. This consists mainly of unskilled jobs as labourers and watchmen.

Table 14. DISTRIBUTION OF OFF-FARM JOBS BY
PEASANT FARMERS IN TOBAGO

Job	% of farmers (n = 63)	No. of farmers (n = 63)
Labourer in public sector	36.5	23
Other jobs in public sector (watchman, driver, etc.)	34.9	22
Self-employed in service activity (shopkeeper, taxi driver etc.)	20.6	13
Self-employed tradesman (carpenter, butcher etc.)	4.8	3
Other employment	3.2	2

When the 63 farmers in off-farm employment were asked whether they would like to be able to farm full-time, 44 (or 70%) of them said "no" while 14 (or 22%) said "yes" (there were 5 non-respondents). The reasons stated by these farmers for their responses are given in Table 15. Here it is seen that half of the farmers who did not want to farm full-time gave the low income from farming as the reason for this position. These results support the contentions in the analytical model that the lack of a good income from farming is the major reason why peasant farmers seek off-farm employment.

Table 15. REASONS GIVEN BY PART-TIME FARMERS
FOR RESPONSE TO QUESTION: "WOULD YOU
LIKE TO BE ABLE TO FARM FULL-TIME?"

Reasons	% of farmers* (n = 44)	No. of farmers (n = 44)
For farmers responding "No"		
Not enough income from farming	50.0	22
Too old	13.6	6
No labour available	6.8	3
Poor resources (especially land)	6.8	3
Other	20.4	9
No response	2.4	1
	% of farmers† (n = 14)	No. of farmers (n = 14)
For farmers responding "Yes"		
Love of farming	50.0	7
Farming could be profitable	35.7	5
Other	14.3	2

* % of the 44 farmers responding "No".
† % of the 14 farmers responding "Yes".

The results given in Table 16 and those obtained for the relative poverty line estimates by the peasant farmers further support these contentions. From Table 16 we see that only 2% of the farmers obtained more than $5,000 p.a. from their farm operations. However, when asked to state their relative poverty line, 70% of the farmers gave their view that a family of 4 needed more than $6,000 p.a. to live comfortably in Tobago. In fact, the mean relative poverty line stated was $7,470 p.a., with only 9% of the farmers stating a relative poverty line below $4,800 per annum. Clearly, therefore, income from agriculture is insufficient to meet the material needs of the peasant farmers.

When it is also considered that only 22.7% of the farmers received more than $3,600 p.a. from off-farm employment, it is clear that peasant farmers in Tobago are poor and will be generally dissatisfied with their status of life, given their goal of making money to meet their family obligations. This contention is also supported by the results of the Present Life Score which were reported earlier.

Table 16. FARM AND OFF-FARM INCOME OF
PEASANT FARMERS, 1977

Income level ($)	Off-farm income % of farmers at level (n = 108)	Farm income % of farmers at level (n = 144)
250	51.9	52.9
251–500	2.8	18.3
501–750	1.9	7.7
751–1000	1.9	9.6
1001–2000	5.6	4.8
2001–3000	8.3	2.9
3001–5000	15.7	1.9
5000	12.0	1.9

From the regression analysis it was found that the five factors — age, present life score, the Farming-as-an-Occupation rank, the poverty line estimate and farm investment propensity — were significant in explaining the percentage of off-farm employment taken by the peasant farmers (Table 17). But the

Table 17. RESULTS OF THE REGRESSION ANALYSIS

No.	Explanatory (independent) variable Name	regression coefficient	Significant relationship to the dependent variable *
X_1	Land owned	−0.411	
X_2	Land farmed	0.800	
X_3	Family size	−0.814	
X_4	Age	−2.148	−
X_5	Present life score	6.270	+
X_6	Future life score	0.256	
X_7	Farming-as-an-Occupation rank	−7.159	−
X_8	Poverty line estimate	0.059	+
X_9	Farm investment propensity	−0.047	−

Dependent variable: % of off-farm employment
* At the 5% level of significance.
R^2 = 59.2%.

amount of land owned and the acreage farmed had no significant effect on off-farm employment. The significance of the age factor suggests that younger farmers are the more likely to be engaged in part-time farming. Moreover, on the basis of the poverty line estimate, i.e. the monthly income perceived as necessary for a comfortable life, the data show that farmers with high monetary dispositions (and thus with strong monetary goals) had high degrees of off-farm employment. The implications of these findings can now be further discussed.

Conclusions

The results indicate, first, that the majority of peasant farmers in Tobago are oriented to materialistic (mainly monetary) goals. These goals are at least consistent with the neo-classical economic goal of "profit maximisation", suggesting that traditional economic analysis could be used to explain some aspects of the peasant farmers' behaviour, particularly their supply response to prices. However, an explanation of other aspects of their economic behaviour, particularly their lack of dynamism in farming as well as their part-time farming activity, has required a more thorough examination of the totality of the individuals, particularly their motivational structure and their social psychology.

The majority of peasant farmers still hold on to some of the more traditional agrarian values such as self-sufficiency in food, independence and love for the agrarian life-style. However a significant minority of the peasant farmers do not. It is clear also that for the majority of the peasant farmers, the money obtained from farming is insufficient to provide the wherewithal for their current existence, and since goals provide stronger motivational forces than values, the younger peasants particularly are prepared to relegate farming to a part-time activity and become engaged largely in off-farm jobs.

The lack of dynamism and innovation in farming by the peasants is thus explicable in terms of the lack of attraction of the occupation, because it cannot provide enough money to meet their families' needs. This results from the fact that the manual methods of production employed do not generate economies of scale, resulting in sizeable amounts of unutilised land on even small-sized holdings.

It has been argued earlier that the lack of attractiveness of farming within the peasant sub-sector should be self-reinforcing by its impact on potential entrants particularly school-leavers. Braithwaite (1968) states that such a process of cultural inheritance in the Caribbean has led to agricultural communities that do not like and have a great bias against agriculture. The results of this study generally conform to his contentions. Thus the peasant sub-sector in Tobago consists largely of ageing individuals. The study has provided evidence to support the idea of peasant farming and poverty being synonymous, a view reportedly held by the youths in Tobago. Therefore migration of youths from the rural to urban areas, and their onward migration to metropolitan countries, is likely to remain a popular manifestation.

The above results provide considerable support for the explanatory model of peasant economic behaviour developed in this study, and all indications are that this model should be applicable to the wider Caribbean area and to other developing countries with similar historical, social and cultural conditions. To the extent that these behavioural patterns are present in the rural societies of developing economies, they will present formidable problems for authorities engaged in agricultural extension and rural development especially if no cognisance is taken of their existence.

REFERENCES

Beckford, G.L., *Persistent Poverty: Underdevelopment in Plantation Economies of the Third World*, Oxford University Press, 1972.

Braithwaite, L.E., "Social and Political Aspects of Rural Development in the West Indies", in G.L. Beckford (ed.), *Selected Papers from the Third West Indian Agricultural Economics Conference — April 1-6, 1968*, University of the West Indies, Mona, Jamaica, 1968.

Cofer, C.N., and M.H. Appley, *Motivation: Theory and Research*, Wiley, New York, 1969.

Demas, W.G., *The Political Economy of the English-Speaking Caribbean A Summary View*, Caribbean Ecumenical Consultation for Development, Bridgetown, Barbados, 1971.

England, J.L., W.E. Gibbons, and B.L. Johnson, "The Impact of a Rural Environment on Values", *Rural Sociology*, vol. 44, no. 1, 1979, pp. 119-36.

Evans, P., *Motivation*, Methuen, London, 1975.

Haller, A.O., "On the Concept of Aspiration", *Rural Sociology*, vol. 33, no. 4, Dec. 1968, pp. 484-7.

Hotchkiss, L., E. Curry, A.O. Haller, and K. Widaman, "The Occupational Aspiration Scale: An Evaluation and Alternate Form for Females", *Rural Sociology*, vol. 44, no. 1, 1979, pp. 95-118.

Kilpatrick, F.P. and Cantril, H., "Self-Anchoring Scaling: A Measure of Individuals Unique Reality Worlds", *J. of Individual Psychology*, vol. 16, 1960, pp. 521-45.

McClelland, D.C., and D.G. Winter, *Motivating Economic Achievement*, The Free Press, New York, 1969.

Niddrie, D.L., *Land Use and Population in Tobago*, Geographical Publications, Bude, Cornwall, 1961.

Pemberton, C.A., "Productivity of Resource Use in Agriculture in Tobago", unpubl. M.Sc. thesis, Un. of the West Indies, St Augustine, Trinidad, 1972.

——, "Goals and Aspirations and the Low Income Farm Problem", unpubl. Ph.D thesis, Un. of Manitoba, Winnipeg, 1976.

—— and W.J. Craddock, "Goals and Aspirations: Effects on Income Levels of Farmers in the Carman Region of Manitoba", *Canadian J. of Agricultural Economics*, vol. 27, no. 1, 1979, pp. 23-4.

Report of Team that visited Tobago in Mar./Apr. 1957, "Development and Welfare in the West Indies", Bulletin no. 34, Advocate Co. Ltd., Bridgetown, Barbados.

Report of the Tobago Planning Team, Govt. of Trinidad and Tobago, Central Statistical Office Printing Unit, 1964.

Rushing, W.A., "Class Differences in Goal Orientations and Aspirations: Rural Patterns", *Rural Sociology*, vol. 35, no. 2, 1970, pp. 337-95.

Williams, E., *History of the People of Trinidad and Tobago*, PNM Publishing Co. Port of Spain, Trinidad, 1962.

Woodcock, H.I., *A History of Tobago*, 1867, reprinted Frank Cass, London, 1971.

6

HIGGLERING: RURAL WOMEN AND THE INTERNAL MARKET SYSTEM IN JAMAICA

Victoria Durant-Gonzalez

Introduction

Higglering in Jamaica — or huckstering, its name in the Eastern Caribbean — is a highly visible manifestation of female participation in economic production throughout the English-speaking Caribbean. Female domination of the distribution of fresh farm products in the internal market system of Caribbean societies is somewhat paradoxical, for although it allows opportunities for women to combine economic and domestic roles, at the same time it competes with females participating in other areas of the labour force and in education.

Our purpose here is to demonstrate that higglering is a primary role of achievement for rural women. It provides opportunities for economic participation and self-fulfillment, and at the same time for conforming to the cultural expectation of childbearing and for meeting childcaring responsibilities. It will also show that higglering is an occupation that has effective methods of recruiting and training new members. We make the theoretical assertion that successful rural development is based on programs and development models which accommodate and draw upon existing economic and social contributions of all segments of a population. This assertion stems from the fact that female participation, as marketeers, in the traditional sector of the economy historically has made and continues to make essential inputs into the economies of Caribbean countries. It also recognises that much of the economic skill and knowledge which participants use in higglering is universal. This finding has important implications for planners of rural development. It suggests that higglers in the traditional sector have a potential, with their higglering skills, for easy integration into newly-created modern economic outlets.

This paper is documented and supported by data collected during eighteen months of anthropological fieldwork in a small farming community in the parish of St Mary, Jamaica, in 1974-5. During that experience, the author observed and participated with higglers in the local community (see Map), en route to market, and at the marketplace in Kingston (called "Town" by community members) Full participation was enjoyed in each aspect of the occupation: cultivating, collecting and gathering commodities for market, packaging them, carrying the load to the bus stop, riding the country bus with the higglers, and selling the commodities at the Princess Street Market.

Higglering profile

The social observer who comes to St Mary District even for only a short time becomes aware of the presence of the market woman. Wednesday is market-day for the majority of the women who are higglers. This is the day that the full-time higgler goes to the Princess Street Market in Kingston, where she will remain until Saturday evening. Market women are identified by their dress. Traditionally, higglers wear a pinafore or an apron with large deep pockets for keeping money and a plaid "tie-head", i.e. a scarf. The observer sees the activities that make up market day: the coming and going from bush to yard, the sorting and packing of fruits, vegetables, eggs — even an occasional chicken is included in the day's load. The observer is impressed by the way this is carried out, and in which individuals voluntarily assist with transporting the load from the yard to the bus stop.

An observer need not necessarily enter a yard to become aware of certain market-day activities. All one has to do is to enter the district from Junction Road where it crosses Grandy Hole and walk along the main road that passes through the middle of the district. On this journey the observer learns several things: which commodities are in season, which are being taken to market and in what quantities; the way they are prepared for transporting, and the containers in which they are transported. Should the observer be allowed to join the group of market women when they assemble at the bus stop, further insight into the higgler market business is gained from listening to the conversations that take place. These concern not only the market, but also the community in general and the nation itself.

Wednesday is a good day for observing the way that higglering permeates district life. The observer's attention is drawn to a group of small children approaching the bus stop. One child carries a butter pan filled with cherry tomatoes, another a small pan filled with ackee. A little later a young woman aged about twenty approaches with a large stalk of green bananas. She places this in the general area of the tomatoes and ackee; then she cuts a large banana leaf and places it over the stalk of bananas to protect the fruit from the heat

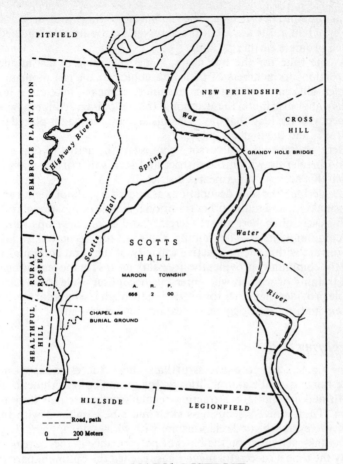

ST MARY DISTRICT

of the sun. The observer concludes that market-day involves not only the market woman, but many other people associated with her The appellations used makes it clear that some of these people are relatives.

The observer, continuing to linger at the bus stop, gleans more social information — for instance, the market woman is approached from time to time by other women, who ask her to bring items back from Town when she returns. As some of these requests are made, cash is handed over, but this is not always the case. Older women bring commodities such as a stalk of bananas, a sack filled with grapefruit or a basket of breadfruit which they give to a higgler to take to market for them. The full nature of these transactions is not apparent at the time, but the observer's curiosity is heightened, which prompts further probing.

As the time for the bus nears, some higglers give last-minute instructions to members of their household. At the last moment a higgler will remove a bag from her undergarments, take out a few coins, and distribute these among the school-age children who helped with the load that day. The bus arrives, the load is placed on the roof, and the higglers enter.

Here we have taken a cursory glimpse at the activities that surround higglering within the district and seen some of the ways in which this occuption permeates district life.

Higglering, like such occupations as midwifery, shopkeeping and dressmaking, and unlike other traditional female occupational roles such as schoolteacher, nurse, secretary and so on, develops within the community itself. The training, skills and tools required for higglering are within the productive capacity of the rural community, and the community provides the necessary means for the recruitment and training of women who enter this occupation while society as a whole provides the outlet for higglering through the internal market system and, to some degree, the export market system.

Higglering skills

Some higglers are more successful than others. Success is based on a wide range of skills and abilities — for example, in arithmetic, in profit-making and for attracting regular customers and keeping them. These universal business skills must be combined with the ability to establish good relationships with wholesale suppliers. Higglers rank each other on the basis of performance in these areas.

By the time a successful higgler has reached the optimum participatory stage of higglering, she has a secure relationship with her Town, and the suppliers of produce in the surrounding communities. She also, has an efficient system for collecting and gathering them. Typically, the load a higgler takes from the community to the internal market is augmented by buying wholesale produce from Coronation Market each night she is in Town. This market is within walking distance of Princess Street Market, and during the night higglers operate between the two markets — buying produce wholesale from Coronation Market to sell retail at Princess Street Market. The produce is usually transported by cart from wholesaler to the higgler's selling spot. At times higglers themselves will carry a wholesale load from Coronation Market to Princess Street.

The acquisition of wholesale produce in town is essential to the higgler's business and there is a vital skill attached to the manner in which she establishes her business relationship with a wholesaler. This process operates in the following way. A higgler buys from a number of wholesalers, and by thus spreading her purchases over several suppliers, she is assured of a constant source of available produce. I was told by higglers that if this practice of buying is not maintained and a higgler limits her wholesale buying to one wholesaler, she runs the risk of being boycotted by the other wholesalers when her supplier is out of farm commodities. Yet, I was told, each higgler nevertheless has a special wholesaler with whom a preferential relationship exists: this wholesaler provides credit when the higgler needs it and provides her with reasonable assurance of a supply of produce each week, while the higgler provides the wholesaler with a regular and consistent outlet for produce. This practice seems to be related to a general rule which governs the buying and selling of commodities at the marketplace — "You buy from me and I sell to you" — or the converse: "You didn't buy from me before, now I won't sell to you." This governing rule applies to wholesaler and retailer as well as to retailer and customer. This suggests that there is an emphasis on reciprocity at each level of the market system. Table 1 presents data on wholesale and retail prices and expected profit in October 1975.

Table 1. SELECTED DATA ON WHOLESALE AND RETAIL
COSTS*
(*Prices in Jamaican dollars*)

Quantity	Produce	Wholesale	Retail	Profit
100 lb.	Cassava	3.00	5.00	2.00
200 lb.	Cocoa	16.00	24.00	8.00
100 stalks	Sugar cane	9.00	15.00	6.00
100 lb.	Pumpkin	9.00	15.00	6.00
200 lb.	Plantain	10.00	16.00	6.00
Total		47.00	75.00	28.00

* These data represent an average week's transactions at the market for one higgler, and do not include the load she brought to market from her community. At the time of the study $1.00 (Ja.) = $0.90 (US).

The acquisition of what higglers call "my staunch customers" is another crucial element needed to succeed in this business. Steady customers are acquired over a period of time and the relationship between higgler and regular customers grows out of mutual need. Throughout the island there are almost always shortages of some kind. These range from items such as rice and flour on the shelves of modern supermarkets to red peas and onions at Princess Street Market, to soap, car parts, or telephone service. In the case of customer and higgler, the uncertainty of food is a basis of reciprocal ties. The higgler needs the security in her business of reliance upon a certain amount of fixed sales each week, and customers need the assurance of knowing that their higgler has saved a pint of red peas or a pound of onions during one of the perennial periods of scarcity within the country. Higglers go to great lengths to maintain the relationship with "staunch customers," as the following account reveals:

Miss Verne says, "If my staunch customers buy yams from me each week, I must have yams for these customers. Even if I am not selling yams, I will buy them from another higgler just so that my staunch customers get them."

Procuring these customers and the inter-dependence between them are illustrated in the following accounts.

Case no. 1

Higgler Miss Addy explained that she obtains her staunch customers through various techniques. She says that most of these customers she acquired over a long period of time. A customer would come to her each week making a sizeable purchase. This resulted in Miss Addy bringing something from her field for this particular customer. She says she doesn't do this each week, but only now and again. Miss Addy says that she obtained other staunch customers as a result of "our spirits just moving together well."

Case no. 2

Higgler Miss Verne says she has ten staunch customers. Six of these she has had for over five years. These staunch customers buy from Miss Verne each week, making purchases which total from 4 to 5 dollars. Each Christmas she receives gifts from her staunch customers. She showed me a white dress that a customer had made for her last Christmas. Miss Verne says this customer was somewhat reluctant to make her a gift of clothing, explaining that "You country people are so funny about accepting clothing." Thus the customer asked if she would accept such a gift before presenting it to her. The usual type of gift that customers make to higglers would be household items such as dishes, pots, pans or food items such as a Christmas cake.

Case no. 3

This veteran higgler is unable to go to market this week due to illness in the family, and she laments over the fact that her staunch customers will be disappointed. There was only one other occasion when this higgler missed going to market and this was due to her church obligations (she is a Mother in the church). She says, "There is a 'Coolie' gal (Indian) who has been buying from me for over five years. Each week she spends over 6 dollars. There is another staunch customer who last week bought 20 pounds of yellow yam from me (yellow yams sold for 35 cents per pound that week). This customer always spends between 7 and 8 dollars with me each week.'' I have observed these staunch customers, among others, buying from this higgler for more than eight months on a regular weekly basis, with only one week's absence, and this higgler's concern is not that she will lose these customers because of one week's absence, but that they will be inconvenienced. She says, ''Just the same, they will understand.'' She commented on the fact that the other higglers, especially the male higgler who sells directly across from her, will be happy over her absence. ''They can sell to all of my customers.''

Skill in the techniques of securing and maintaining wholesale suppliers and steady customers is acquired over time and on a trial and error basis. However, most of the techniques and skills are transmitted by observing and consulting with veteran higglers. Often within the community a beginner higgler will consult with a veteran higgler concerning some problem that has arisen with her wholesaler or with a customer. These are situations that place the veteran higgler in the role of advisor and teacher. An illustration of these advisory positions was demonstrated when junior higgler Miss Cutey came to veteran higgler Miss Bertie for advice:

This situation concerned a breach in a trust [credit] arrangement that Miss Cutey made with a Town wholesaler. The account of this agreement, as told to Miss Bertie by Miss Cutey, is that she bought yams, sweet potatoes, and plantain on trust from a wholesaler at Coronation Market. The agreement was that she was to pay the wholesaler at the close of market day. Well, Miss Cutey didn't make the amount of profit she anticipated when she made this agreement and therefore was unable to pay her trust and have enough money to buy the things she needed to purchase for her family, like sugar, rice, salt beef, etc. Miss Cutey said that she tried to explain her position to the wholesaler and promised that she would make good her trust the following market week. The wholesaler became vexed over this incident and began to curse ''a whole heap of bad words''.

The veteran higgler listened carefully to the details of this situation without commenting, and then asked in a stern tone: ''What kind of fool-fool market woman are you?'' She went on to point out that this was serious business and that a higgler should not create bad feelings with her wholesaler by not making good a trust. Miss Bertie said that this could result in Miss Cutey's getting a reputation at the market for not making good her word, so that she would be prevented from buying trust from other wholesalers. Also, everybody at the market would begin to talk about her, and such a reputation would make it impossible for her to participate in ''throwing a partner'' (a revolving credit system). ''The shopkeepers won't give you trust and you are a woman with little pickney [children], you cannot be careless so.'' After admonishing the junior higgler by showing her all the possible ramifications of this breach of trust, Miss Bertie said she that would lend her the money to pay the wholesaler, and this she advised Miss Cutey to do first thing on reaching the market the coming Wednesday.

It should be noted that Miss Cutey and Miss Bertie have no kinship ties. Miss Cutey is from outside the community while Miss Bertie was "born and grow" in St Mary's District. The man that Miss Cutey is "along with" is also from outside this community but he was reared there. Also, they have no strong church ties; Miss Cutey is not a member of Miss Bertie's church, but she does attend church on some occasions. The significant bond is that they are higglers, and it is through higglering that they are able to provide for their respective families.

The lack of compe'ition that this relationship suggests is due to the difference both in the ages of the two women themselves and in the length of time they have respectively worked at their occupation. Miss Bertie is 68 years old and has been higglering for fifty years; while Miss Cutey is forty and has been in the business full-time for only twelve years. Another factor which reduces competition between the women is that they are part of a support system, and the service that Miss Bertie is rendering to Miss Cutey is part of this mutual support between women and transcends economic competition. The fact that Miss Cutey has come to the older higgler seeking a solution to her problem reflects this bond between them. At the marketplace, however, and during the actual selling procedures, Miss Bertie and Miss Cutey engage in competitive selling and buying.

Other areas of higglering knowledge are more standardised or universal. These are the ability to count correctly and quickly, to make correct change, and to bargain effectively. Opportunities for these skills are part of the occupation, for most of the skills mentioned are acquired on the job. As is apparent from the cases described below, higglers generally receive little schooling and many of them are unable to read; nevertheless, their computation skills are highly developed. After observing the proficiency with which higglers compute sums of money and perform their bargaining techniques, it is difficult to believe that many of them are unable to read. Higglers manipulate the performance of computing skills between themselves and customers by exerting control over how this is carried out. When a customer attempts to confuse or outwit a higgler by out-computing her or calculating the sum of a purchase for her, the higgler simply stops the transaction. She does this by rearranging her produce, returning to the shelling of gungo peas, or simply by turning to her stall neighbour and engaging in talk about some aspect of the market. While she is engaging in such diversionary techniques she is at the same time computing the purchase. The customer usually gets the message and the transaction is reinitiated with the higgler in control.

One higgler told me that the manner in which cash is actually handled is important to her business. She conveyed that keeping track of cash and its usage is an important skill. Some bookkeeping techniques are involved, as is shown in the case cited below.

Miss Tah-Tah says that when she is selling she separates her money so that she will know when she has made back her "stand" [expenditures]. "After I made back my stand, then I start on my profit." She explained that she keeps track of her money by going to the toilet and counting it, always keeping the profit separate from the "stand" for this is the money [profit] she uses to buy things for her household and for little goodies for the "pickney them". Miss Tah-Tah says that money is counted in the toilet to avoid theft. This is a frequent occurrence at the market, not by other higglers, however, but by the "criminals" [this is a term used throughout the island for persons who break the law].

Higglering recruitment

In Caribbean small-scale farming communities such as St Mary District, there is an effective and efficient system for recruiting new members to the internal market business. I participated in and observed the way in which children under the age of 5 are socialised into the business of higglering.

This socialisation is informal and takes place simply as an outgrowth of daily life. Introduction and exposure to higglering is accomplished in subtle ways, some of which take place when "muma" (mother) goes to the nearby bush with her 2-year-old to gather fruits and vegetables that will eventually be distributed within the internal market system. Often muma is observed instructing a 3-or 4-year-old to fetch some of the needed items in preparing her load for market, such as string or cord to tie a burlap sack filled with breadfruit, or a piece of red cloth to use as an identification mark on her load. Another muma is observed sending a 5- or 7-year-old who happens to be in her yard at the time to a neighbour's yard to fetch the mortar and pestle she needs to produce country chocolate from cocoa seeds. A 5-year-old is observed alerting a higgler that a hen has just laid an egg under the house; then quickly goes off to fetch it. It will be added to the higgler's supply of eggs that she is taking to market.

All such incidents take place among the children who happen to be in the yard at the time. Some are children of the higgler and some are from other yards who have gathered to play. But each child is drawn informally into some aspect of this economic activity. At about the age of 7, participation takes on a dimension of formality, which is related to the availability of assistance, for higglering is a labour-intensive occupation. For instance, Miss Mable is a single parent with five school-age children. She recently returned to the community after an absence of 24 years; she had left as a teenager with her mother, who had separated from Miss Mable's father. As a result, her community support system is not extensive, and she is forced to rely almost exclusively on household members for aid generally and for assistance in the collecting and gathering of farm produce.

On a particular Wednesday, Miss Mable keeps three of her children home from school to help her collect and gather gungo peas and cabbage from a distant field that she cultivates. These she will sell to higglers who are going to market in Town. In contrast, Miss Patience is a member of a household that consists of herself, her husband, their three children (two of school age), and two adult sons from an earlier stage in her childbearing career. Her adult sons move in and out of wage labour employment and the household. Another contrasting factor is that Miss Patience has lived continuously in the community for fifteen years and her spouse was "born and grow" there. As a result, her support system is extensive and well established. When the adult members of her household are available, as well as members from other households, children are not called upon to remain home from school to help their higgler mother.

When children are kept home from school to help with the higglering business, their participation is no longer viewed as informal participation and they are then considered formal participants. At this level children perform a needed and useful service in the market business. For such services they receive small sums of money, presents brought back from Town, a new dress, a new shirt, a pair of shoes, candy, and the like. Some of these items would of course be provided under other circumstances, but a distinction is made between the situations when a higgler gives a present on certain occasions and when she is providing the necessities. In any event these rewards function as incentives for continued contribution of children to the higglering workforce. On the other hand, children are punished if they do not help in the tasks of marketing. This is done by withdrawing certain rewards and privileges.

During the initial processes of socialisation into higglering, there is no division of labour by sex. This division becomes pronounced when higglers start to take teenage daughters to the market. Typically, they take only daughters. I observed no instance where a mother took her teenage son to the market; however, teenage sons do visit the marketplace on their own initiative. It was a common occurrence during school holidays to see a group of young girls waiting at the bus stop on Wednesday with their higgler mothers, ready to go to market in Town. These girls are well dressed, well scrubbed, with neatly combed and braided hair; in short, they are ready for an excursion. And an excursion it is, for these girls are on "summer" holiday from school, and the marketplace is full of excitement and bustling with colourful characters. Everyone looked forward each week to seeing Rocky, who had become the Princess Street Market mascot. Rocky once performed on the concert stages of New York, Boston, Philadelphia and Chicago — if his tales of fame and fortune are to be believed. Nowadays, however, he is found wandering around the markets, dressed in layers of clothing: a pair of pants covered by a suede skirt buttoned down the front and topped with a printed shirt in bright colours. On top of this is a sweatshirt with the sleeves removed; and finally the entire outfit is covered by a sleeveless overcoat. All these garments are worn in the 80–90° temperature. Rocky carries a car aerial which he uses as an imitation microphone when rendering songs for all those who are willing and able to make a small contribution. The young people return to the district with detailed descriptions of Rocky's physical appearance and his performances.

For the higgler mothers of these young girls this is no mere exposure to city life and some of its colourful characters. The mothers are indirectly preparing their daughters for what is most likely to become their economic and social way of life. These trips to market with muma also provide supervision for some young girls who otherwise would be left in the yard with no immediate adult supervision, which fathers and other adult males who share the household and are away working cannot provide. These two purposes — learning and supervision — are seemingly incidental to the main business of selling. I have no evidence that at any time muma sits down and discusses the underlying nature of these trips to market with her daughter, yet these purposes are clear and well understood by household members as well as by other community members, for it has become a custom for mothers to socialise daughters into the business of higglering in this excursion-like manner which is filled with fun and excitement.

When I asked higglers why they take their daughters to market, the usual response was, "I need the help, she is a big pickney now and can be of some help to me at the market. School is on holiday and there is no one in the yard to look after her while I am at the market." On further probing, some mothers indicated that they are being far-sighted. This is illustrated by the statement, "She is a gal pickney and some day she may need to know the market." Informally and among themselves, mothers discuss the fact that this is a protective measure for maintaining supervision over young girls; but they were reluctant to discuss this explicitly with me.

The practice of taking puberty-age daughters to market also enables women to show off their young girls to their business friends in Town. When the young girls arrive at the market, a big fuss is made of them; women remark on how pretty and well dressed they are, and how much they have grown. These compliments serve as means of reinforcing and reaffirming to members of the market community that higglering provides opportunities for women to childrear and childcare.

The cases described below provide some ethnographic accounts of the way that higglers are recruited, and bear on other topics discussed in this paper: motivational factors for entry and the conditions that generate persistent participation in the occupation of higglering. These cases also illustrate an important element of success, the transmission of higglering skills and knowledge.

Case no. 1

Miss Lovie says she has worked as a higgler for "many, many years". In fact, she has just given up fulltime participation in this occupation within the last two years. She entered higglering through her grandmother, who is still remembered as a higgler of exceptional ability. Miss Lovie, now 65 years old, was phased into the higglering occupation at two levels: one, assisting in gathering, collecting, and preparation of the load; and two, by accompanying her granny to market. She recalls that she used to go with her granny to Coronation Market, Redemption Market, and Sugarfoot Market. As Miss Lovie grew into a woman and began to have children, she entered the occupation as a independent higgler.

Case no. 2

Miss Verne is 47 years old, the mother of seven children. She started higglering during her late adolescence, aged about nineteen, and it came about when her mother, a higgler, was unable to go to market due to illness. The mother sent her load with her daughter, who went with her cousin, an experienced higgler. Before this incident, Miss Verne's mother had been reluctant for her to go to market, but afterward the two began to go together on a regular basis. Her mother taught her the skills of buying and selling and the method of acquiring steady customers.

Case no. 3

Miss Ven is 39 years old, the oldest of seven children, and has been a higgler for as long as she can remember. She completed the first grade in school, dropping out to take care of household chores when her mother became ill. At this early age she took charge of the washing, cleaning, and cooking. She is unable to remember her exact age at the time she started higglering, but believes it was during early adolescence. She learned the skills of higglering from her mother and other higglers in her district.

Case no. 4

Mada Pinkey's parents died when she was about 12 years old and she was reared by her grandparents. Her yard was close to that of a very successful higgler, and this woman taught her the "knowledge" of higglering. "As a youth I followed her to the market, and little by little I learned how to buy and sell." That was more than forty years ago. Today Mada Pinkey is considered one of the successful higglers in the district. Other higglers, usually younger women, come to her for advice and suggestions about higglering.

These four cases show that women phase gradually into higglering in two ways: by following a higgler to market (already discussed) and by substituting for a higgler who is unable to go to market and who sends a younger female from her household in her place. She does not send the substitute to market alone but pairs her with a veteran higgler who assists the neophyte as she takes charge of the household's load. Sometimes young girls are launched into the business of higglering when a mother sets up a roadside stand to sell fruits and vegetables to motorists who pass through the district, and puts her ten- to fifteen-year-old daughter in charge. This provides an opportunity for young girls to learn some of the skills of trade in the home environment. The higgler in charge shares the money earned from these roadside stands with the girls. Young girls from different households can be seen calling out the qualities of their produce to motorists as they pass, and they attempt to arrange attractive stalls as they compete with one another to attract customers.

Motivations for higglering

Higglering is not the lowest-ranking job within the occupational hierarchy open to women in the Caribbean. Edith Clarke, writing on the topic of occupations and the status conferred by certain occupational roles, says: "The higgler ranks socially above the domestic servant or labourer; she is independent as compared with the wage-earner and wears an apron as the badge of her calling. It was noticeable that many of them lived on family land which in itself confers status in the community" (1957:152-3.) These observations, coupled with the fact that higglering is labour-intensive, making it an occupation that can accommodate a large workforce, are important motivations for entering the market business. Other social pressures that influence women to work as higglers are economic — the need for cash income, a lack of job opportunities for both men and women, the women's familial role, the opportunity and desire to broaden women's social base, and the flexibility of the role. The first three of these economic pressures — need for cash income, lack of job opportunities, and familial role — are intertwined. The cases cited below reflect these influences.

Case no. 1

Miss Aggie has three children, aged 8 to 22. Her spouse works sporadically doing whatever jobs are available in the district: working for the Public Works Department cleaning, repairing and building roads; and hiring himself out to cultivators in the district. This search for employment even takes him outside the country, and he does farm contract labour in the United States and Canada. His work history is marked by periodic unemployment. Miss Aggie says that because her husband is unable to find steady work she goes to market; she also says that she higgles because she likes it and it makes her independent. She explained that by going into Town each week she can buy the things she needs for her family. "And higglering is all I know."

Case no. 2

Miss Verne says she has continued higglering after marriage because oftentimes her "hubby" cannot find work. "So I go to the market." She went on to explain, "I have seven "pickney" to look after; by going to market I can get them a little something. One "pickney" is very bright and I am trying to do right by her and see that she gets the proper schooling."

Case no. 3

Miss Macka has worked as a full-time higgler since she was twenty-five. She is now 35 with seven children. She says that there are few jobs in the district for men, and because of this her husband is often out of work. So that the family will have something to live on, she goes to market each week.

Case no. 4

Miss Vanny explained that after she had so many "pickney" her mother told her that she had to work to help herself. Her husband, who she says is not like her because he can read well, has been unable to find steady work over the years (they have been married fifteen years). He works when he can, and has done farm contract labour in the United States. She says, "My hubby he doesn't work. During these times he cultivates, and I go to market."

These cases show how higglering originates from the configuration of economic pressures combined with the lack of job opportunity and the familial role of mother. These factors are so patterned among higglers that they can serve as a model for phasing into higglering and continuing to pursue it. This pattern can be stated as the need for cash income, the lack of permanent work for men, limited job options open to women with few saleable skills, and children to support. Even when men can find wage labour — be it at the local, the national, or the international level — work is temporary and sporadic. The unsteady nature of a work history of this type functions as an influence on women to enter and/or remain in higglering.

Men in this district are subject to frequent periods of unemployment. Higglering then is often the one source of cash coming into the household on a regular basis. Katzin writes about higglering as follows:

. . . The woman has a more regular source of income, even though her weekly earnings are less than those of the man when he is working. The household is thus assured of food necessities during the frequent periods of unemployment. . . . (1960:323)

These findings on motivational factors in higglering are further supported in the work of William Davenport:

With respect to the economic system of the island as a whole, most of the jobs for wages are for men, while the women are limited to the kinds of personal services upon which both sexes of all ages depend. The one major exception to this is the important role the women play in the marketing system, which takes them into a specialized sphere of economic exchange. . . . When the productive potential of men is limited or completely absent in a household, the women are able to take over their economic function. . . . Or the women can expand their marketing activities in order to provide a cash income for their household group (1961:437).

Besides economic pressures, there are other equally significant determinants in the recruitment of women into higglering. Among these are the fact that higglering offers women the chance to broaden their social base, and furthermore their sense of independence. Here independence has more to do with individual control over action and behaviour and the means to opportunities for achievement than with economic materialism. In the case of Miss Aggie cited above (p. 116), the higgler explicitly articulated independence as a factor which made her carry on in this occupation: "I like it and it makes me independent." This notion of a sense of independence was revealed through many conversations with higglers. My hostess and I had many discussions about higglering, and she repeatedly stated this as one explanation for continuing as a higgler. "Miss Vic, you are a woman, and I am a woman. You have a hubby and I have a hubby, but we must always remember that if your hubby gives you a

10 cents, you find a way of making a 10 cents of your own.'' What she was revealing in this statement was not solely an economic fact of having an independent source of income but something more, namely the position of a woman in relation to her mate, and the fact that she has something which she controls and over which she has authority. This contributes as much to women's higglering as the economic pressures from lack of jobs, need for cash, and the necessity of providing for children. This sense of independence, along with the other factors, causes a large number of women in the district to sleep on concrete three nights a week, to risk being attacked, and to endure unsanitary conditions.

To arrive at the manner in which higglering acts as an agent for broadening women's social base, we must first examine this social base and its boundaries within which the relationships that comprise higglering are carried out. The district and its physical boundaries can be seen as the social field of women, and the yard as the centre of that social field. Even though the boundaries of the district also bound the female's social field, many restrictions and limitations have been placed on her physical and social movements within those boundaries. For example, she is restrained from socialising at the shops, drinking rum in public, playing dominoes and smoking, all of which are defined as non-female activities.

After puberty, restraint is placed on young girls to discourage them from assembling at places other than the yard. All movement of women within the boundaries of their social field has a definite purpose: they go to the bush and to the garden to gather vegetables, fruits and root crops; to the river to wash clothes; to the shop to make a purchase; to the roadside water pipe to collect water for household use; or to a neighbour's yard for some specific reason. Even when a woman crosses the physical boundaries of the community her actions are again purposful: to church; on an errand for a family member; to the next district to assist at a wedding; to town to look after some household business. When an attempt is made to extend the social field, this effort is connected with the yard and/or the community. When women leave the district to seek employment, this is done through kinship and/or friendship ties in the community.

The market serves as one means whereby women can break away from some of these social restraints placed on their movement and behaviour at the community level. Katzin, writes of higglers:

Higglers and country people make the trip to market every week, not out of economic necessity, but because they enjoy it. As the story goes, if one meets a country higgler on her way to the market with a big load while she is still near her home, and offers to buy the whole load and pay more than she can expect to get for it at the market, she will refuse to sell. The reason for the refusal, according to those who tell the story, is that she wants to go to Kingston for some high life, to be able to do things that would not be approved by her rural neighbors (1960:316).

The male's social field, and his movement within this field, contrasts sharply with that of the female. His social field encompasses the entire island rather than just the community. He is free to move about the island at will; he can seek employment without a community link; he can follow his peers about the island seeking adventure. His movements are not restricted, and consequently he is often seen huddled with other male friends in social settings outside the yard, sitting on a rock, under a tree, or on the hillside; or at the rum shop drinking rum and/or playing dominoes. This last pastime starts at an early age, from ten years on. These are expected behaviour practices for males and are socially defined as unacceptable behaviour for women and/or puberty-age girls. There is a Jamaican patois expression that has a different significance according to the sex of the speaker: "me gone" (I am going). The male can leave the yard or the community with no more explanation than "me gone", with his destination undetermined, unknown and unconnected to his household or to the district. The female is restrained from moving about under these same conditions. She may say "me gone", but only after her destination and purpose have been cleared and sanctioned by household and/or district members.

The marketplace changes some of this. There, as in the yard, the woman's social position shifts from that of backstage to centre-front stage. In her role of higgler she performs a primary role, supplemental to none, and obtains preferential treatment from her household members and from her customers. The latter often rank socially above her, but her role as higgler turns this ranking system on its head for three days each week.

It is at the marketplace that she can break free from the rules which restrict her movements and behaviour in the district, as Katzin tells us, "to be able to do the things that would not be approved by her rural neighbors." It is a place where her identity takes on a more private and more individual element; where she has some control over how much of her private life and familial ties is revealed. In the social field of the marketplace, the chances are that her stall neighbour does not know all her family history and does not care to know it; here she is known as higgler, wearing her plaid "tie-head" and apron, described by Edith Clarke as the "badge of her calling". The domain of the marketplace provides her with opportunities for achievement and a place to build, by her own abilities, her reputation as a businesswoman; it is the place where her status is based on this role. Her trips to Town each week give her access to certain goods and services, and to greater knowledge, all of which contributes to elevating her within the community.

When veteran higgler, Miss Bertie, reminded her junior, Miss Cutey, that "you are a woman with little pickney, you cannot be careless so" she was explicitly reinforcing an important cultural value in the region: the high value placed on the mother role. The work by Madeline Kerr on social life in Jamaica emphasises a particular aspect of this: "An almost universal belief is that each woman is destined to have a certain number of children and she will not have good health unless she does. If she does not have this correct number she will be nervous, have headaches, or even go insane" (1963:25). Because of its flexibility, the role of market woman accommodates fulfilment of this cultural expectation by enabling women to continue to work while pregnant and while caring for young infants. Women accomplish this by rearranging the level at which they participate in higglering, and through the help of a higglering support system. This system operates "like so", to borrow a phrase from the St Mary District: women continue to go to market until the last stage of pregnancy, usually up till the seventh or eight month health permitting. They then stop going to the market until the breast-feeding period is coming to a close or has become regulated so that the women can return to market on a limited time basis. The higgler reorganizes her participatory activities by selling to other higglers and by sending a load with a friend. This is the nature of her support system. These two methods were employed by three higglers who gave birth while our research was in progress: each of them was a full-time higgler, each breast-fed her infant, and two started to return to the market when their infants were eight months old. However, they gradually staged re-entry by going to Town one evening and returning the next evening, thus women combine work outside the home with the traditional form of breast-feeding and achieve compatibility between two primary roles: occupational and familial. Other higglers talked of using this method during childbearing and childcaring.

It should be understood that women higgle not because of any one of these factors — need for a source of cash, lack of job opportunities for both sexes, to gain independence, to childbear and childcare, or to broaden the social base and widen the social field; but rather, all these factors are combined. This configuration of economic and social influences affects each higgler differently, and at different times in her life cycle and stages in the higglering occupation. For instance, a granny who is receiving remittances from children abroad, who is a veteran higgler with several "staunch customers", might not be under the same economic pressure as a beginning higgler who is at the prime of her childbearing career, whose mate is out of work and whose household thus has no other income.

Work conditions

Higglering is a physically taxing occupation. As we have seen, full-time higglers are at the market from Wednesday evening through Saturday evening. They sleep at the market in conditions that are extremely harsh and inadequate, when the service they perform as major food distributors for the nation is considered. Women are to be seen sleeping on cold cement floors, on top of boxes, or nodding off while sitting on stools. Some protection from guards is available, but it is minimal; as a result the higglers are constantly exposed to thieves and violence. The lack of security obliges higglers to be cautious in the way they handle cash. Usually, it is visible only in small sums; it is tied in handkerchiefs or plastic bags, or placed in a small bag and kept out of sight. The money visible at any given time is that being used in actual at-the-moment transactions. Large sums are kept in what is known as a "thread bag" (cloth draw-string bag), which is kept under the clothing and close to the body for safety. While there are many other reasons for handling money in this way, the danger of theft is the main one.

At the marketplace, sanitary facilities are as poor as the sleeping arrangements and protection service. The street on which the market is located is covered with discarded fruits and vegetables. Disposal containers (if they exist at all) are hard to find, and there is a constant buzzing of flies. The sewage system is inadequate, and thus there is always stagnant water in the streets, the stench of which alone conveys its bacterial content. These are only a few of the poor conditions that higglers face in their work. Others are the lack of any type of worker benefits or organization, and of adequate transport services. Such conditions make higglering an occupation that women do not opt for, but rather one to which they are relegated due to the lack of other economic opportunities.

Conclusion

Our discussion has shown that higglering is an occupation that provides women with access to a wide range of skills and knowledge, and with opportunities for some individual achievement and social recognition. It allows for childbearing and childcaring and for intergenerational co-operation. It is also an integrative force in the community and among household members. However, in spite of these positive features, higglering, in its present arrangement, does not foster social and economic growth either for its participants or for the nation as a whole.

A primary obstacle is the duality of the agriculture system of Caribbean economies. Typically, the agriculture sector is divided into a modern sector and a traditional sector. The former is devoted to export crop production under conditions of modern technology and management, while the latter produces for the domestic market in conditions of low levels of technology and management. Historically, there is a bias in favour of creating conditions for growth in export crop production. This modern-traditional dichotomy has in some instances given rise to the view that both the organizational arrangement and the participants in the traditional sector are backward. This view does not recognise that occupations in the traditional sector, such as higglering, facilitate the acquisition and use of universal skills and knowledge that can be transferred to the modern sector. A consequence of not distinguishing structural features in the traditional sector from individuals who make up that sector is a tendency to create programs for development that do not draw upon existing human resources.

In this paper, we have a common sense approach for reversing that tendency. It is suggested that change can be achieved by adopting the assumption that a community of people have and engage in effective means of carrying out daily life; this assumption presents a challenge to students and planners of rural development. The challenge is to create a mechanism for identifying effective social and economic elements in aspects of the social structure and the members of the population who possess such resources. Once these are identified they can form the basis for creating new programs and schemes for development that reflect both continuity and change. This common sense approach, if applied to the internal market system, has the potential of maintaining female participation in an essential sector of the economy and its consequent benefits. At the same time, this approach can lead to changing the occupation of higglering into one that fosters social and economic growth for the individual and the nation.

7

TOWARDS AGRICULTURAL SELF-RELIANCE IN GRENADA: AN ALTERNATIVE MODEL

*Robert Thompson**

The inability of dependent capitalist development in the Caribbean to meet the needs of the majority of the population has resulted in considerable interest in alternative development models. Further impetus to this interest was sparked by the 13 March 1979 overthrow of the Gairy regime in Grenada and the subsequent four and a half years of New Jewel Movement (NJM) attempted to undertake a socialist transformation of the island society. Despite its regrettable collapse, the "experiment" of the Grenada Revolution provided a unique opportunity to examine both the theory and practice of development and to discover both the potential and the limits of alternative models in the modern Caribbean and indeed the entire Third World.

This article begins with an examination of an alternative "model" and the implications of the works of such authors as C.Y. Thomas of Guyana and Samir Amin of Senegal, who advocate economic and social reorganization towards self-reliant (although not necessarily self-sufficient or autarkic) development, based on a dynamic of domestic production for basic needs or mass consumption, rather than the standard models of export-led growth or import substitution (Thomas, 1974; Amin, 1977). In particular I have looked at food consumption and production in Grenada within the framework of Thomas' "two iron laws of convergence", and will argue that any progress towards self-reliant development must focus upon the interdependent linkages which exist between the structures of (1) class; (2) food consumption and nutritional needs; and (3) agricultural resources for food production.

An analysis of the failure of dependent capitalist development in the Caribbean is beyond the scope of this article, but is crucial to an understanding of the importance of alternatives. Studies of Caribbean social formations by many authors such as Eric Williams, Arthur Lewis, William Demas, Lloyd Best, George Beckford,

Norman Girvan and Clive Thomas, to mention only a few, have amply documented the processes whereby the region is deprived of the fruits of its peoples' labours through the domination of production for export.

However, the study of flows of surplus and interaction between classes within a given social formation is frequently secondary to an analysis of the flows of surplus between different social formations. The very nature of social formations requires the study of both internal and external relations, and in particular the impact of external factors on internal structures. All social formations are based on a social division of labour which has evolved over centuries, beginning with simple hunting and gathering societies with little specialization, and evolving into complex modern social systems in which economic surplus is generated, circulated and disposed of through complex networks of institutions, political power, culture, ideology and class structures (Mansour, 1979: 199).

In the Caribbean, studies of the enormous drain of surplus from the region through the mechanisms of slavery and transnational corporations exist in abundance, while thorough reviews of the internal structures which inhibit development tend to be limited to simple descriptions of backwardness, which is often blamed on external or historical factors over which little control can be exercised.

The importance of internal factors has nowhere been more evident than in the reaction of the population of Grenada to the murder of Maurice Bishop and his colleagues and the subsequent US invasion of the island. The failure of Bernard Coard and his colleagues in that faction of the NJM to recognize sufficiently the importance of the internal class forces and class awareness which mitigated against acceptance of their centralist strategy is ample evidence of the failure of much traditional socialist and Marxist theory to recognize the importance of internal forces in deference to the rhetoric of anti-imperialism, however logical or appealing the latter may seem. This failure brings home the necessity of the search for alternative models of development for the region. The search for an alternative model begins with the failure of dependent, peripheral capitalism, dependence theory, orthodox Marxism and the Marxist theory of the Non-Capitalist Path to completely or even adequately explain, or resolve, the social and economic crises facing the Caribbean and Grenada today.

The failure of dependent, peripheral capitalism centres on the inability of the Grenadian bourgeoisie and petty-bourgeoisie to retain sufficient surplus from an internationally dominated export-oriented economy and thus accumulate enough capital to finance local capitalist growth. The weakness of dependence theory as a response to this lies in its neglect of the full complexity of class relations which puts limits on economic nationalism (one of the principal recommendations of dependence theory). This evasion of the full implications of class obscures the analysis of surplus flows and accumulation and the importance of classes in the ebb and flow of history. Dependence prescriptions have thus tended to be economistic and have failed to integrate social, political and ideological factors (Leys, 1977: 94).

The orthodox Marxist model relies on a stage of capitalist development to consolidate scattered private property, increase efficiency and develop the means of production through accumulation. But this did not happen naturally in Grenada. Therefore the orthodox Marxist approach falls into the same trap as neo-classical theory. It does not account for the unevenness of the spread of capitalism, and it provides no guide for progressive change in dependent peripheral economies. The theory of the Non-Capitalist Path has argued that a patriotic, nationalistic bourgeoisie can be persuaded to co-operate in the development of local forces of production. While this is happening, socialist awareness is being prepared for the next stage of full socialism, when these co-operative classes will be dispossessed. This theory has also assumed that the level and nature of assistance from the socialist world would be adequate to bypass the stage of capitalist accumulation. This assumption is tenuous at best, given the geopolitical realities of the Caribbean and the considerable differences between the needs of small agricultural economies such as Grenada's and the heavy industry and technological infrastructure of the Soviet and East European economies.

An alternative model

As an alternative to the organization of production primarily for export, Thomas and Amin have proposed an auto-centred, self-reliant development model which is well summarized by Mansour:

The results would be to reorient agriculture from producing raw materials for the world market to the production of foodstuffs and needed local industrial inputs on the one hand, and to raise productive efficiency on the other hand. Industry in its turn would be required to produce basic consumption goods, in particular those needed to raise agricultural efficiency. Certain proportions and balance have to be maintained between respective rates of growth of industry and agriculture and of the capital goods sectors. In highly developed capitalist countries, the market mechanism can be relied on to introduce such marginal structural changes as are called for, though of course not without its particular type of crisis and penalties. In Third World countries, where fundamental structural changes are indispensable, no such role can be expected from the market mechanism. Central planning is required, not only to initiate and carry out these changes in the balanced way, but to initiate and carry them out at all (Mansour, 1979: 232).

The comprehensive planning required by such a model is by no means simple. The control and/or co-ordination of capital, labour, raw materials and other inputs are subject to many influences which are specific to the historical context and conjuncture of each society. Thus there are no *a priori* formulas by which decisions can be made. Yet decisions must be made about optimal rates of accumulation or investment versus consumption, about the opportunity costs of different projects, about the allocation of scarce foreign exchange, about technologies appropriate to the particular mix of resources and industrial strategy chosen in the model and many other decisions.

In addition to such econometric decisions, political mechanisms must be developed which ensure a process of democratic parti-cipation in the determination of acceptable social costs of trans-formation. The willingness of the community to absorb these social costs and to increase accumulation for future growth is dependent on their participation in planning and all other aspects of govern-ment and social life (Thomas, 1974: 132). Although there may be substantial sources of extra surplus available once external drains are plugged or at least slowed, the remedying of low levels of con-sumption, nutrition, health and productivity resulting from decades or even centuries of neglect are certain to place a fetter on technically optimum rates of accumulation for further growth and structural transformation. Without an appropriate democratic political structure to mediate in disputes over the allocation of resources, political and social conflict will seriously undermine the process of transformation.

Planning under such a model cannot be based on existing demand or profit-oriented cost benefit criteria without merely reproducing existing price and income distribution patterns (Amin, 1977: 16). The simple projection of existing demand only serves to duplicate resource allocations which support existing unequal patterns of con-sumption, even if the forms of exchange and consumption change (Thomas, 1974: 20). Thomas argues that demand has been consider-ably distorted by unequal income distribution, imported tastes and a myriad of colonial, neo-colonial and other dependence relations which affect the choice of products consumed in both their quantity, quality and characteristics (Thomas, 1974: 59). The data on food consumption presented later in this article provide clear evidence of this divergence between demand and the nutritional needs of the majority of the population.

The model does not, however, advocate complete isolation from international markets in order to reduce or eliminate external diversion of surplus. Amin notes that an imposed autarky, if too drastic or total, could hamper self-reliance by involving excessive costs. He does not argue against any theory of comparative advantage, but points out that the unequal international division of labour invalidates the basic assumptions of such theories (Amin, 1977: 18). The need for foreign exchange and trade in a small society such as Grenada is obvious, but cannot be so easily conceded that the planning of its allocation is secondary or even ignored. Thomas notes that each project requiring foreign exchange must generate more foreign earnings during its lifetime than the capital and operational inputs necessary for its implementation. Import substitution must be evaluated on the basis of a reduction of imports greater than the foreign exchange investment required to replace them (Thomas, 1974: 244). There are certain to be problems of cash flow, especially at the beginning of any process of transition. However, the judicious allocation of export earnings and aid and the sequencing of investment can be incorporated into the planning process to deal with these problems (Thomas, 1974: 246). The critical role of foreign exchange makes it a potential obstacle, subject as it is to geopolitical influence, and may well be one of the major limiting factors in the application of the model.

A central factor in the creation of internal resource/consumption linkages is technology. The importation of technology and capital goods from either market or centrally planned industrialised economies determines the mix of inputs used in local industry. As noted above, technology developed for these markets reflects vastly different resource constraints, input availability and costs, and problems of development of productive forces which are of an entirely different order from the conditions found in the Third World (Thomas, 1974: 27). Appropriate technological models cannot be imported ready-made nor necessarily found in the history of the industrialized centres, as the theme of intermediate technology sometimes suggests (Amin, 1977: 17). Industrialization in the centre was based on a revolution in agriculture in seventeenth century Europe, whereas industrialization in the Third World must enable an agricultural revolution to take place in the twentieth century. Thus technological creativity and adaptability are the issues, and not just technology transfer (Amin, 1977: 17). The problems created by the transfer of inappropriate technology and the difficulties of avoiding such problems in Grenada's food industry are discussed below.

The development of Third World technological creativity and adaptability can be misinterpreted to require an indigenous science and technology research and development capacity far beyond the human and financial resources of most small nations. This is partly due to the sophistication of modern high technology and the mystification of it encouraged by transnational corporations in order to preserve patents and oligopolistic markets. However, the interdisciplinary structure of modern industrial production has resulted in the open publication of much basic scientific and technological research in North America and Europe, making technical information accessible to anyone with basic technical literacy and sufficient funds to subscribe to the thousands of specialist and popular journals.

Further, when colonial and neo-colonial assumptions about limited local capacity to master the environment in peripheral social formations have been subjected to a healthy scepticism, it has been discovered that the range of critically minimum levels of production are often much lower than optimum levels (Thomas, 1974: 305). The myths about economies of scale must rank near the top of any list of obstacles to development in small economies. Thomas argues that the test of feasibility with respect to self-reliance must consider whether the volume of output required for local consumption can be attained and whether the opportunity costs of such production are not excessive. Feasibility cannot be limited to a determination of whether the optimum level of output can be attained. Since the relative opportunity costs of self-reliant production are frequently overestimated as a result of neo-colonial assumptions, further research on technological alternatives is often not pursued. Thus opportunities are bypassed which could generate local production at only a slightly higher cost, but which would expand internal demand and generate other external economies in other related industries. The importance of central planning should be obvious here, since individual industrial or corporate plans may not recognize such external economies.

In an important paper on economic factors favouring small-scale, decentralized, labour-intensive manufacturing, Vail cites a number of studies which show how unit production costs in some sectors (e.g. small castings, machine tools, footwear, cement, diesel motors, and more) increase by only 2–9% in plants with half of the optimum capacity (Vail, 1975: 23; Silberston, 1972: 369). He goes on to argue that, since these studies were done on British industry which has evolved in response to factor prices quite different from those prevailing in the Third World, smaller-scale technologies might even be superior with relatively cheaper labour and more expensive capital. Other studies show that the "elasticity of substitution" between labour and capital in several manufacturing sectors is such that a range of technologies and (by inference) plant scales can be used efficiently (Pack, 1974: 394).

As an example of both the distortion of technology and the unrealized potential of the Caribbean sugar industry, Thomas' study *The Threat and the Promise: An Assessment of the Impact of Technological Development in the High Fructose Corn Syrup and Sucro-Chemical Industries* shows how it is theoretically possible greatly to increase the manufactured content of a traditional crop, even to the point where sugar could provide an alternative to petroleum as a chemical feedstock (Thomas, 1982). Farrell has argued that adequate intelligence on biotechnology might permit the Caribbean to take advantage of its traditional sugar production and, by increasing the manufactured content of its exports in carefully chosen market niches, could perhaps even reverse historically negative terms of trade (Farrell, 1982: 14). Both authors point out, however, that constraints on skilled human resources, inflexibility of the forces of production, lack of capital or access to capital, inadequate information systems concerning technology and external markets, and the absence of external economies of scale all make the achievement of such advances exceedingly difficult.

Technological difficulties are not only the product of transnational domination of world production and markets. For example, criticism can be raised of Grenada's acceptance of Cuban housing technology under the NJM since it is based on the use of imported concrete rather than local lumber as a basic material. Cuban cement is cheap and used throughout the Caribbean by governments of all political stripes because of its price; however, it is cheap because, as an energy-intensive industry, it relies on oil supplies from the Soviet Union at below world prices, a benefit which cannot be applied to Grenada's forest industry. The uncritical use of Soviet or any other foreign technology risks the selection of equipment and techniques which can divert factors of production away from local resources. This can have similar negative effects on the dependence and external orientation of the society in transformation to those caused by transnational monopolies, even though not related to "imperialistic exploitation".

The selection of this model, with its complex planning requirements and its vulnerability to political sensitivities on both internal and geopolitical fronts, risks being labelled as utopian. However, any less comprehensive approach to the problems of development in peripheral, dependent societies has been proven ineffective in the past several decades of experience in world development. We now go on to examine the structures of class, food consumption and agricultural resources which play a crucial role in the implementation of an alternative model.

The evolution of class forces in Grenada

The Grenada Revolution began in 1979 as a response to the repressive government of Eric Gairy, an ex-schoolteacher who rode to political power on his success as an organizer of farm workers in the early 1950s, and then used that power to further his own personal wealth and aspirations at the expense of the very workers he had led against the excesses of plantation agriculture. However, the poverty and political backwardness of Grenada under Gairy had roots in more than just the manipulation of one man. They are also the legacy of centuries of slavery and colonialism, and an economy and society organized around the production of food which Grenadians did not consume, in exchange for imported food and goods which they did not produce.

Grenada's economic history can be divided into three general periods: slavery (1600–1838), the "free" labour era (1838–1940) and the modern era (1940–79). These three periods have been marked by the development of increasingly complex relations of dependence in Grenada's links to the world capitalist economy. Foster-Carter has described this process well in reference to Jamaica, and his comments apply equally to the colonial history of the entire region:

The slaves' former subsistence production showed considerable resilience, eventuating into a peasant mode of production in a highly contradictory articulation . . . with a capitalism itself enmeshed in contradictions: structurally dependent on foreign monopoly capital, and first striving to 'break' the peasant mode in order to be assured of labour supplies, then incapable of developing enough to make use of that labour once it did begin to present itself (in torrents; ultimately diverted into emigration) (Foster-Carter, 1978: 234).

The external orientation of Grenada's economy features highly unequal terms of trade which amassed large fortunes for a few and left very little in the way of resources and capital to be invested in improved consumption and services for the people who produced this wealth. The plantation system of colonial agriculture, utilizing slave labour, was so profitable that it was cheaper to import food for the slaves than to devote even a few acres to local food production.

The exodus of peasants to the cities and factories of Europe as the Industrial Revolution advanced created such a demand for cheap food energy that sugar was called "green gold".

The development of Grenada's economy has been dominated by its interaction with the changing capitalist world economy over a period of three centuries, during which substantial surpluses have been transferred out of Grenada. Indeed, Wallerstein, Amin and Williams regard the Caribbean as an important element in the initial accumulation of capital in Europe and the world (Wallerstein, 1980; Amin, 1982; Williams, 1944). The initial development of Grenada to provide raw materials and capital for European, particularly British, industrialization has influenced (and still affects) current development and places serious obstacles in the path of a self-reliant development strategy today.

As internal European markets developed and the vast fertile lands of Brazil and Cuba provided cheaper sugar, Britain's Caribbean colonies lost their competitive edge in sugar production. The demand for cheaper raw materials created modernizing forces which required that slaves be replaced with more efficient machinery. But centuries of slavery had left deeply ingrained social structures, and the plantocracy resisted their displacement in the economy by the growing industrial capitalists. Through their control of politics, the landed aristocracy in Britain aided the plantocracy in the colonies in this resistance. Using the colonial state, they succeeded in restricting access to land, credit, technology and markets for the slaves who had been freed by the economic logic of the Industrial Revolution.

In Grenada, where the rugged terrain had made sugar even less profitable, it was replaced by cocoa and nutmeg in the late nineteenth century. These were export crops more suited to smaller estates and requiring less capital from the owners who had become indebted due to the competition with larger capital-intensive operations in the larger territories and colonies. This allowed smallholders to gain a small foothold and partly to reduce their dependence on the plantocracy. However, the emancipated slaves were only given sufficient land to grow a portion of their subsistence requirements. This had the effect of lowering wages and reducing the planters' food import bills, yet kept labour tied to part-time estate work. The legacy of this system is an economy in which a substantial proportion of the dependent "peasantry" are forced to sell some of their labour to the estates, while also having to rely on subsistence farming, jobs in tourism or service sectors, remittances from relatives abroad, barter, migrant labour, cash crops, petty commerce, mutual aid societies and a host of other mechanisms, in a complex network of multiple dependences and defence mechanisms.

The subservience of Grenada's economy to export markets resulted in a lack of linkages between local production and consumption. In that now classic phrase, Grenada produces what it does not consume, and consumes what it does not produce. This dependence leads to a drain on the economy through unequal terms of trade, whereby the prices of manufactured imports historically rise faster than the prices of commodity exports. Unless export production can grow faster than the increased prices of imports, and/or become more efficient, there is a drain on the economy. Grenada's small size makes increased production difficult and the historical drain of surplus from the economy has left insufficient capital for investment in increased efficiency.

The long-term drain on the economy had an important impact on Grenada's social structure. The collapse of sugar on the smaller islands such as Grenada reduced the ability of the plantocracy to accumulate capital and thus the wealth necessary to dominate the society. The dependent peasantry and the urban middle classes were similarly limited in their access to an independent economic base. The balance of class forces in Grenadian society was therefore fragile, and tended to favour whichever group was able to control the state, the only mechanism sufficiently powerful to allow control by one class or another.

The lack of an independent economic base for any one class which would permit it to accumulate sufficient surplus to dominate the society is a major feature of peripheral and dependent capitalist societies today.[1] One result is the creation of delicate class alliances and balances which frequently change as competing sectors of the politically dominant petty-bourgeoisie vie for control of the society, primarily through control of the state, often through the armed forces or police.

Flows of surplus are based, not only on economic relations such as the ownership of capital, but also on a broad social and political consensus (which includes cultural factors) that forms the basis for an acceptance of and sometimes resignation towards the role each class plays in generating and sharing the overall surplus. Changing alliances, both within the petty-bourgeoisie and with external actors, provoke many of the *coups* and counter-*coups* so prevalent in the Third World today.

1. C.Y. Thomas, in *The Rise of the Authoritarian State in Peripheral Societies* (Monthly Review Press, New York, 1984), provides the basis for an analysis which stresses the role and nature of the state as a mechanism for the *creation* of classes as well as (or in lieu of) the traditional Marxist view of the state as the object and tool of class *control*.

In addition to the economic, technological and infrastructural legacies of colonialism, which are discussed below in an analysis of food consumption and agricultural resources in Grenada, the fragmentation of class structures, forces and balances plays an important role in obstructing development today. This fragmentation continues today, and forms the basis for a political framework which limits consensus and generates more confusion than agreement on national development strategies.

Since control of the state depends on both political and economic factors, the granting of universal adult suffrage in Grenada in 1950 under pressure from anti-colonial forces led to a political shift in balance from the plantocracy to the urban middle classes between 1951 and 1979. In 1950 Eric Gairy formed a trade union to redress the grievances of agricultural workers who were losing their semi-feudal tenancy "rights" as capitalist relations of production and wage labour were forced on the plantocracy by the colonial authorities in the name of modernising production. Following a successful general strike for wage increases of over 50%. Gairy vaulted to political power and was able to develop a political and economic base for himself using the power of the state. Monopoly import privileges, tax breaks, government contracts, patronage, land expropriation and other legal and illegal incentives allowed him to control the expanding urban sectors of construction, tourism and small manufacturing.

Gairy also broke the economic base of the plantocracy once and for all through the expropriation or outright seizure of estates. Agricultural production fell by half (by volume) from 1970 to 1974 as a result of his land "reform" programme, which not only removed land from production to be distributed as patronage in tiny uneconomic plots, but also reduced investment and maintenance expenditures and thus productivity on those lands not actually seized but threatened by the atmosphere of intimidation (World Bank, 1982: 15; Cumberbatch, 1977: 12). Between 1961 and 1981, 43% of cultivated land, or 10,382 hectares, was taken out of production. Of the 13,697 hectares farmed in 1981, approximately one-third were not cultivated.

Gairy's resort to repression to reinforce his hold on the state eventually alienated the other substantial sector of Grenada's middle class organized around the Grenada National Party of Herbert Blaize (GNP). Not only did his actions reduce their own profits, but his repression also threatened the whole basis of Grenada's capitalist economy by provoking widespread unrest. The GNP allied itself in the 1976 elections with the New Jewel Movement (NJM), a grouping of left-leaning populist intellectuals with considerable support among Grenada's youth (some 50% of the population) and sectors of the working class and peasantry. Winning 6 of the 15 seats in parliament despite massive rigging by Gairy, this People's Alliance became the Official Opposition in Parliament, with Maurice Bishop as its leader.

However, Grenada's Westminister-style parliament, like many Caribbean parliaments, was dominated by excessively concentrated executive power. Meeting infrequently and never allowed more than cursory debate of legislation and budgets, it had little capacity to criticise or even monitor Gairy's depredations. This political vacuum, Gairy's repression and the fragmentation of political and economic forces facilitated the takeover of the state by the NJM on 13 March, 1979. Once in control, the NJM's domination of the state overshadowed the weak, divided economic and political bases of Gairy, the GNP and the plantocracy. As we have seen, however, realignments in internal forces, even within the NJM, are capable of producing spectacular changes in the balance of class forces in a small society like Grenada, with political implications which go well beyond minor adjustments.

It is evident that the development of classes in Grenada has been fragmented and uneven, with the result that cultural, ideological and structural obstacles endure which resist the reorganization of the Grenadian social formation. The importance of this class analysis lies in its identification of the particular relations of production which underlie the generation of economic surplus in Grenada. Without an understanding of the basis for these flows of surplus, it would be difficult to redirect them along the lines advocated by the alternative model of development outlined above.

The particular blend of economic and social factors which influence food consumption and agricultural production is the subject of the remainder of this article. The complex inter-relationships between class, food consumption and agricultural resources discussed below have a profound impact on development strategies under an alternative model or, for that matter, under the traditional model prevalent in the Caribbean today.

Food consumption and nutritional needs in Grenada

A study of food consumption in Grenada at the national level and in the poor village of La Poterie shows a marked difference between the demand for food and actual nutritional needs. Here I will argue that expenditures on imported foods and a demand structure which is heavily influenced by higher income consumption and tastes tends to divert resources from the supply of basic foods which meet the nutritional needs of as many people as possible at the least possible cost. This is the essence of Thomas' second "iron law of convergence", the necessity of matching local demand with the objective needs of the majority of the population. If demand is distorted to include goods which cannot be easily produced locally, then the convergence of demand with local production will be that much more difficult.

The data outlined below in Tables 1 and 3 shows that Grenada imports some 76% of its food energy and protein consumption, with the result that food is a commodity very much subject to the influences of international markets. As with all commodities, it is allocated largely on the basis of purchasing power, and, in the context of widespread poverty and unemployment, services the needs of the relatively better-off classes and groups (Thomas, 1982: 3). The current structure of food consumption is heavily influenced by two factors: (1) unequal income distribution and (2) Western consumer technology (e.g. packaging, processing and marketing). These factors operate in such a way as to create or maintain demand for end-products which can be linked to local resources and production only with great difficulty, thus obstructing self-reliant food production.

A detailed analysis of national food consumption in Grenada, when compared with a nutrition survey carried out in La Poterie, a poor rural village in St Andrews Parish, shows that consumption of meat and imported foods is much lower among rural low-income groups than it is for the national averages (see Table 3 below). From this discrepancy it would appear that a small, mainly urban, high-income group has a disproportionate impact on national food consumption as a result of its higher purchasing power (see Table 2 below for an outline of income distribution in Grenada). The La Poterie Nutrition Survey of 1972 was chosen for comparison with national statistics for two reasons: (1) as a rural area, La Poterie is more representative of the income and consumption patterns of the rural majority in Grenada; (2) it is the *only* detailed study of income and food consumption available for a lower-income group.

Western consumer technology is introduced by transnational corporations which dominate the international market, distort conditions in favour of their own markets and profits, and engage in large-scale demand-creation through advertising and other consumer technologies such as packaging and "convenience" food-processing unrelated to nutritional requirements.[2] These factors

2. For a good review of the impact of these factors on the food industry, see UNCTAD, "The Food Processing Sector in Developing Countries; Some Recent Trends in the Transfer and Development of Technology", TD/B/C.6/66, Geneva, 14 Oct. 1980.

influence Grenadian demand for food, not only through the dominance of imported foods in local diets, but also via the media, the tourist industry and contacts with Grenadians living abroad in the United States, Britain and Canada.

The influence of Western technology, designed as it is for affluent markets, makes it difficult for Grenada's food industry to find food-processing equipment and technologies appropriate to its particular mix of resources and inputs and thus to compete with imported food and Grenada's tendency to consume processed food imports instead of local produce is further reinforced by recent trends in the international food industry. These trends include increasing corporate concentration and a movement in the food processing industry to compete for disposable income through demand creation rather than cost reductions. These factors have influenced the technologies available to the Grenadian industry (and hence its competitiveness) as well as the particular structure of demand for food in Grenada.

Forced to compete for disposible income against manufactured goods because of relatively lower income elasticities of demand for food, the food industry has attempted to become more efficient in influencing tastes as well as in lowering production costs. The impact of advertising and the development of capital-intensive technologies designed for affluent Western markets have combined to trigger a process of corporate concentration which the food industry had hitherto resisted because of its sensitivity to local tastes, transport requirements and storage limitations. The quality, packaging and advertising standards against which local produce must compete are such as to discourage the development of a local food processing industry.

William Demas has made the following comment on the role of the media in promoting inappropriate consumer demand in the Caribbean:

Any honest and clear-minded view of the role of the mass media as they operate at present in the region will show them as instruments for selling metropolitan consumer goods produced either in the advanced countries or in the Caribbean under license, for homogenising the population of the region for induction into a second rate kind of mass commercial culture, and for effectively blocking the emergence of a genuine Caribbean identity (Demas, 1973: 21).

The international food industry has also penetrated the Grenadian market directly through advertising in the local and regional media, and indirectly through the influence of tourism on local tastes and expectations. The data presented by Dellimore and Whitehead on the agro-industry of the Eastern Caribbean shows that the media influences tastes towards foods with a high import content and a degree of processing which is nutritionally inefficient. Dellimore and Whitehead cite several concrete examples of inappropriate technological choice resulting from foreign-influenced technology and product choice. One is the demand for white, wheat-flour bread, which results in the importation of standard technologies and equipment for the baking of hard wheat flour only. These technologies make it difficult to begin a progressive substitution of composite flours (containing root crop or legume flours) as a means of saving foreign exchange and of stimulating local agricultural production. Another is the selection of multipurpose driers which rely on electricity and/or expensive fossil fuels. While they may be competitive for expensive processed or convenience foods, these driers are too costly to operate in the drying of inexpensive local fruit and vegetable products. Thus overcapacity in a small market cannot easily be offset by making the driers economically as well as technically multipurpose (Dellimore, 1979: 62, 63).

An interview with a senior employee of a transnational corporation illustrates the difficulties which can be expected when the transformation is attempted of that part of the industry that is foreign dominated.

He admitted to having access to the product formulations of all products manufactured by the TNC, both local and overseas, and was largely responsible for reformulating them to suit the local market. He also knew how to obtain equipment at half the cost paid by the subsidiary of the TNC. Yet, in spite of his privileged position in comparison to other would-be entrepreneurs, he indicated he did not feel able to take advantage of it by going into production in competition with his present employer. Though he could produce as good a product and had no strong feeling of loyalty to his employer, he felt that without an established brand name behind him, it would cost a fortune in advertising to enter the market successfully (Dellimore and Whitehead, 1979: 145).

The tourist industry is another factor which influences Grenada's food consumption patterns in addition to income distribution, technology transfer and the media. While food consumed by tourists is only a tiny portion of national consumption, tourism has a potential demonstration effect far beyond its quantitative impact. Of total "meal-days" measured for Grenada in 1980, only 0.76% came from stayover and cruise visitors (World Bank, 1982: Table 7.1). In 1978 this figure was 1.0%. Even allowing for much higher *per capita* calorie and protein consumption, say 9,600 calories per day versus

4,550,[3] tourist food energy consumption was only 1.6% of total "calorie-days" in 1980. The relative insignificance of tourist food consumption in terms of volume means that it is unlikely to be a substantial stimulus to local agricultural production. Increased local incomes and food consumption will have a much greater marginal impact on local agriculture than will tourism.

However, tourist demand can affect Grenada's food consumption and production in other ways which may be very significant. Tourist expenditures of an average US$50 per person per day influence local conditions in a number of areas: demand for highly processed foods with "international standard" quality; transfer of inappropriate technology to meet these "international standards"; importation of mass consumer technology to the extent that mass tourism forms at least a part of the Grenadian "market"; creation of a demonstration effect on wage and income expectations and therefore on local labour costs and supply.

The structure of food consumption in Grenada

Table 1 below provides a detailed outline of national food energy consumption in Grenada for 1980. Detailed import and production volumes were translated into food values and costs, and sub-totalled with the assistance of a computer. Consumption was analysed under 15 categories of food type and categorized by local and imported food, food energy, protein, and food costs. Consumption here is defined as being "disappearance" of food in the absence of adequate statistics to determine changes in inventories. Similar analyses were undertaken of protein consumption and foods costs and the overall results are tabulated in Table 3 below. Comparisons between the structures of total national consumption and expenditures and consumption in La Poterie are provided to demonstrate the differences in consumption at different income levels.

In comparing consumption in La Poterie and nationally, it is also necessary to take into consideration the relative amounts of animal-origin foods, since 7 plant calories are required to produce one calorie of food energy of animal origin (UNCTAD, 1980: 4). This

3. These allowances for *per capita* food energy consumption come from an adjustment of real calorie intake to highlight the greater meat content of high-income "tourist" diets. It has been calculated that 7 calories of plant food energy are required to produce one calorie of food energy of animal origin (UNCTAD, 1980: 4).

means that actual food energy consumption in Grenada and La Poterie, both direct and indirect, is 4,530 kcal./person/day and 2,547 kcal./person/day respectively; a ratio of 1:0.56 as against the direct energy consumption ratio of 1:0.73. It is interesting to note that total demand for food energy in the industrialized market economies in 1979 was 9,600 kcal./person/day indirect and 3,373 kcal. direct (UNCTAD, 1980: 4), or more than twice that of Grenada's national average and 3.8 times that of La Poterie.

It is clear from these figures that low-income diets, which tend to use food energy more directly, without the "waste" associated with

Table 1. FOOD ENERGY CONSUMPTION IN GRENADA, 1980
(*millions of kilocalories*)

	Local production	Imports	Exports	Local consumption	% of national total	La Poterie
Fish	1,750,000	1,305,035	17,490	3,037,545	3.46	3.2
Meat	2,741,435	4,081,100	149,140	6,673,395	7.60	3.6
Dairy & eggs	268,950	5,608,290	—	5,877,240	6.69	2.9
Flour/Wheat	—	27,944,607	1,733,721	26,210,886	29.18	30.2
Rice	—	3,219,810	—	3,219,810	3.67	—
Other cereals	1,620,234	7,148,336	—	8,768,570	9.98	—
Vegetables	1,791,611	929,608	—	2,721,219	3.10	9.0
Fruit	5,364,211	183,071	320,531	5,226,751	5.95	4.3
Root crops/ Starches	3,078,412	486,788	—	3,565,200	4.06	24.3
Sugar & Syrups	1,841,874	10,124,045	—	11,965,919	13.63	9.1
Edible oils	2,169,822	1,690,547	—	3,860,369	4.40	5.5
Margarine/ Shortening	—	3,204,618	—	3,204,618	3.65	—
Alcoholic beverages	1,786,003	812,273	—	2,598,276	2.96	—
Soft drinks	356,879	178,100	—	534,979	0.61	—
Miscellaneous	—	355,354	—	355,354	0.40	7.8
Totals	22,769,431	67,271,582	2,220,882	87,820,131	100.00	100.0

National percentages: 25.93% + 76.60% – 2.53% = 100.00%
Average food energy consumption in Grenada, 1980: 2,194 kcal./person/day (population 109,664; 365 days).
Average food energy consumption in La Poterie, 1972: 1,610 kcal./person/day.

Sources: Statistical Office, Ministry of Agriculture, St. George's; Imports by SITC, Central Statistical Office, St. George's; World Bank, *Economic Memorandum on Grenada* — Report No. 3825- GRD, 4 Aug. 1982, Washington, DC.; Caribbean Food & Nutrition Institute, Food Composition Tables, Kingston, Jamaica, 1974; CFNI, *La Poterie Nutrition Survey*, May 1972, p. 11.2.

140 *Robert Thompson*

Table 2. ESTIMATED INCOME DISTRIBUTION IN GRENADA, 1970

Annual income range	No. of wage earners	% of wage earners	Total est. income (EC$)	% of est. income
No income or not stated	21,695	49.1	0	0
0–1,500	17,036	38.5	12,914,000	44.1
1,500–5,000	4,891	11.1	11,769,750	40.2
5,000 plus	487	1.3	4,589,000	15.7
Total	44,209	100.0	29,275,750	100.0

Source: 1970 Census, University of the West Indies, St Augustine Trinidad.

Table 3. COMPARISON OF DAILY PER CAPITA CONSUMPTION OF IMPORTED, PROCESSED AND ANIMAL-ORIGIN FOODS

	Energy (kcal.)		Protein (gms.)		Cost (EC$)	
National						
(1) Imported	1,681	76.60%	54.6	76.60%	1.10	54.70%
(2) Processed	1,535	69.98%	47.9	67.13%	1.28	63.51%
(3) Animal-origin	389	17.75%	35.2	49.41%	0.69	34.0%
Total	2,194	100%	71.3	100%	2.02	100%
La Poterie						
(1) Imported	742	46.10%	22.1	50.50%	0.47	34.30%
(2) Processed	949	58.94%	23.0	52.55%	0.69	49.98%
(3) Animal-origin	160	9.96%	13.4	30.60%	0.47	34.10%
Total	1,610	100%	43.8	100%	1.38	100%

CFNI recommended; energy: 2,342 kcal. protein: 58.0 gm.
Cash income — Grenada (National) EC$320/yr. (1970)
            — La Poterie EC$160/yr. (1972)

Sources: Statistical Office, Min. Agriculture, St. George's; *Imports by SITC*, Central Statistical Office, St George's; World Bank, *Economic Memorandum on Grenada*, Report 3825–GRD, 4 Aug. 1982, Washington, DC; Caribbean Food & Nutrition Institute, *La Poterie Nutrition Survey*, May 1972, p. 11.2; 1978 Abstract of Statistics, Central Statistical Office, St. George's; Income Distribution Tables, 1970 Census, University of the West Indies, Jamaica, 1971.

Note: care must be taken in the comparison of food expenditures and income data since different years are involved. Discrepancies in inflation factors and retail price index weights from actual consumption patterns could distort the adjustments I have made in order to compare the data from the 1972 La Poterie Survey with the 1980 data.

meat production and excess processing, require fewer kilocalories and thus fewer resources than those needed to satisfy higher-income, higher-calorie diets. This diversion of resources to high-income consumption-patterns blocks or prolongs efforts to feed the entire population of Grenada adequately.

Food consumption in Grenada has been shown to be influenced by two major factors: (1) unequal income distribution (both international and domestic) and (2) demand creation and growing concentration in the international food industry. These factors operate in such a way as to create or maintain demand for end-products which can be produced using local resources and technology only with great difficulty and excessive cost. Without a restructuring of these demand patterns, the process of agricultural self-reliance will be slowed or even blocked. I do not argue here that Grenada should accept "second-rate" food in order to become self-reliant. The objective of this analysis however is to point out clearly the opportunity costs of maintaining inequitable income and consumption structures.

Agricultural resources in Grenada

In planning agricultural self-reliance along the lines indicated by the alternative model, the use of local resources for local consumption must be a major objective. This is Thomas' first "iron law of transformation", the convergence of resource-use with demand. In this section it will be shown that Grenada's pattern of land use, focused as it is on export production and based on a highly unequal distribution of land, creates particular problems for the convergence of local production and local consumption of food. These problems include the distortion of domestic agricultural productivity by international markets, as a result of the heavy focus on export production. They also involve the waste of a substantial quantity of land which is left idle because of circumstances introduced by internal class relations and by international market conditions.

Current land-use in Grenada is characterised by three main features: a highly unequal distribution of ownership, a devotion to export crops rather than local food crops and a high proportion of idle land. As can be seen in Table 5 below, land ownership is very unequal, with only 0.3% of all holdings, representing estates of 100 acres or more, containing 31% of the cultivated land in 1981. The dominance of export crops is demonstrated in Table 4, which shows that 80% of the 14,804 ha. estimated in cultivation at the end of 1981 was devoted to the three major export crops: banana, cocoa and nutmeg. With respect to idle land, the total cultivated acreage fell from 24,079 ha. in 1961 to 13,697 ha. in 1981; a drop of 43% over 20 years (Weir, 1979: 13; *Ag. Census*, 1981: 3). In addition to this land taken out of production, it has been estimated that approximately 30% of cultivated farmland (some 3,980 ha.) was lying idle in 1981. This estimate comes from a revision of Brierley's 1981 findings (5,704 idle ha.) with more current data on Grenada Farms Corporation land used for the larger holdings (Brierley, 1981: 28; GFCa, 1981: 26).

Grenada has a total land area of 34,000 ha. (including Carriacou), of which some 10,000 ha. is either primary forest, or under resi-

Table 4. FOOD/CROP DATA FOR GRENADA, 1980/81

	Area (ha.) 1981	Local production (kg.)	Exports (kg.) 1980	Imports (kg.) 1980	Domestic con- sumption (kg.)	Local prod. & dom. consum. %
Fish	—	1,590,909	16,140	507,853	2,082,622	76.4
Meat	848*	1,029,192	63,075	2,286,618	3,252,735	31.6
Dairy	—	0	—	1,632,210	1,632,210	0
Flour/Wheat	0	0	476,297	8,091,431	7,615,134	0
Rice	0	0	—	887,000	887,000	0
Other cereals	70	448,818	473,518	1,902,353	1,877,652	23.9
Pigeon peas	110	449,250	—	56,707	505,957	88.8
Other vegetables	59	850,329	22,394	518,851	1,346,786	63.1
Root crops	167	1,165,360	—	593,644	1,759,004	66.2
Breadfruit	190	1,749,318	—	—	1,749,318	100.0
Sugar	440	500,000	—	2,707,396	2,707,396	15.6
Citrus	588	3,533,203	38,013	187,467	3,682,657	95.9
Other fruits	688*	4,008,650	389,426	95,949	3,715,173	107.9
Banana	1,400	16,363,636	12,458,505	—	3,905,131	100.0
Cocoa	6,400	2,136,364	1,865,555	—	279,809†	100.0
Nutmeg	4,000	2,493,770	1,518,426	—	975,344†	100.0
Coconut	1,380	1,818,182*	—	5,000	1,823,182	99.7

Sources: Ministry of Agriculture/IICA, Nov.–Dec. 1981 crop survey, mimeo.; 1980 Production Estimates, Statistical Office, Ministry of Agriculture, St. George's; Imports by SITC, Central Statistical Office, St. George's.
* Estimated.
† Warehoused awaiting sale.

dential, industrial or infrastructural use (Ifill, 1977: 5). The 10,388 ha. of unused land mentioned above, plus 3,980 ha. of idle farmland, or 14,368 ha. in total, represents 60% of the 24,000 ha. of cultivable farmland in Grenada. The reasons for this considerable waste of resources lie in a complex mixture of historic, political and economic conditions.

Agricultural resources, primarily land and labour, while theoretically available in sufficient quantity to replace all food imports with local production (see Tables 6 and 7 below), are subject to a number of conditions which limit their quick or easy mobilization. Among these conditions are a highly fragmented structure of land ownership, tenure and productivity; international commodity markets which transfer inappropriate production technology to Grenadian agriculture; a historical neglect of agricultural investment which has reduced the productivity of land; and a legacy of social relations of production which has depressed labour productivity to very low levels. Let us look at each of these in turn.

As we can see in Table 5 (below) Grenada must cope with a highly fragmented organization of land tenure which has reduced the efficiency of food production. Small holdings (under 10 acres) contained 5,898 ha. or 43% of the cultivated land in 1981 and private estates and state farms held 45% and 12% respectively (Table 5 and GFCa, 1981: 26). Notwithstanding this highly skewed land distribution, farms under 10 acres produced approximately 50% of export crops (nutmeg, cocoa and bananas) and 85% of food crops in 1978, an indicator of the inefficiency and collapse of the estate sector, despite its political and economic dominance over the centuries.

The result of this fragmentation of ownership is a division of production which requires policies to tackle deficiencies in all three sectors, small holder, estate and state farms in an ongoing and interdependent manner. While investment in small scattered private holdings is often seen as less effective than in estates over which greater central control of inputs can be exercised, we must not lose sight of the fact that we are dealing with a social process as well as agricultural productivity. A dialectical approach is required which balances increases in small farm productivity (and therefore returns and buying power for the majority of the population), while at the same time maintaining and improving the productivity and foreign exchange earnings of the estates. Not an easy task, but necessary nevertheless.

Since 80% of Grenada's farmland is devoted to export crops, the dynamics of international commodity markets influence food production technology in much the same way as noted above for

Table 5. HISTORICAL DISTRIBUTION OF LAND HOLDINGS IN GRENADA

	1881	1891	1900	1911	1919	1929	1940	1945	1961	1975	1981
Under 10 acres	3,000	2,508	8,176	8,349	13,248	15,419	18,456	19,592	13,444	12,030	7,808
10–100 acres						426	457	383	560	469	365
		516									
Over 100 acres					143	138	125	130	92	65	24

Sources: Grenada Handbook, 1946, *passim;* Statistical Office, Ministry of Agriculture, St. George's.

Grenada's food-processing industry. In particular, the monopsony control of banana marketing by the transnational corporation, Geest, has introduced modern agricultural technology such as fertilizers, biocides and plastic sleeves. The expanded use of these inputs extends the cash economy to small growers and thus enlarges the market under which unequal relations of exchange drain surplus from the Grenadian economy. Geest benefits from this unequal exchange through its complete control of transport and wholesale distribution of West Indian bananas within Britain and its transport and supply of the modern inputs which it deems necessary if it is to maintain competitiveness and purchases of bananas.

It must be noted that, since this modern technology originates mainly from modern capitalist agriculture, it follows the logic of capitalist markets and favours increased productivity of fixed capital, particularly land. Since the distribution of land is unequal, this technology thus benefits one group of producers, the estates, more than others. Despite their privileged position however, the estates have been chronically undercapitalized, since their surplus was "consumed" elsewhere rather than reinvested locally. Following the collapse of sugar, Grenadian estates drifted to local ownership and lacked the access to markets and working capital which speeded up the transition to capitalist agriculture in Barbados, Jamaica, Trinidad and Guyana. Incentives for capitalist investment were also limited by the lack of significant industrial processing necessary for Grenada's export crops. The rugged terrain also posed limits to mechanization. In addition, what little accumulation did take place was set back by the destruction caused by Hurricane Janet in 1955 and the land "reform" policies of "Hurricane Gairy" in the early 1970s. As a result, investment in estate lands to modernize production lagged considerably and now requires considerable investment to catch up with the level of productivity necessary to compete in international markets and to reduce the opportunity costs of local vs imported food production. The state farms, a legacy of expropriations by Gairy, face similar conditions to those of the private sector and are confronted as well by difficulties of access to management skills since they must compete with other expanding state sectors. They do have some advantages however in improved access to training and social programmes for their workers which could speed the growth of labour productivity.

It is claimed by some authors that peasant or small holders are more efficient than estates in their efforts to justify increased investment for this sector (Greenwood, 1973). Beckford argues that the apparent efficiency of small farmers is the result of their highly intensive use of labour, which reduces the amount of idle land on small farms as compared to the estates (Beckford, 1972*b*: 33). This intense exploitation of family labour masks low levels of labour productivity through greater yields per acre owned (as opposed to per acre actually cultivated). Small holders have also been chronically starved of the credit, additional land and access to improved technology which could increase their labour productivity. These factors which influence small farm productivity are important, since the allocation of resources for increased food production under the model proposed here cannot simply maintain current conditions of efficiency which are based on an unequal sharing of resources such as land, credit and technology.

What is required is a dynamic view of efficiency, whereby the allocation of resources will be based on changing patterns of control over the means of production, and thus on changing rates of efficiency in the major sectors: small holders, co-operatives, estates and state farms. At the same time, this control must be consolidated so as to increase co-operation and an additional division of labour established in order to further increase efficiency. If increased division of labour and therefore increased productivity is achieved through the consolidation of holdings carried out or regulated by the state, it could easily conflict with the interests of the owners of scattered private farms unless the benefits of increased efficiency are passed on to them. This of course is one of the fundamental dichotomies which land reform must face.

To gain support for a greater degree of consolidation and therefore efficiency, educational programmes are needed which show how, in a complex dependent capitalist economy, cultural and ideological barriers, particularly those which surround private property, help to obscure the benefits of co-operative action and ownership. These barriers also help to maintain unequal income distribution through the confusion of small property rights with the "rights" of large property which dominate the economy. This is not to negate a role for small farm holdings however, since objectively, most food production and a large percentage of exports come from holdings under 10 acres in Grenada.

Since no single group has sufficient resources to meet all the demand for domestic food without drastically reducing export earnings and bankrupting the island's economy, increased food production must realistically come from both large and small farmers. A clear understanding of the situation of small farms, estates and state agriculture in Grenada is therefore necessary before policies can be discussed which balance increased production and productivity in all three groups against income redistribution policies which would favour small farmers over the other two.

The potential for import substitution

When calculations were made of the hypothetical extra acreage required to replace food imports, the difference in resource requirements between the current unequal structure of national consumption, and consumption by the poor rural majority (as represented by La Poterie) becomes clear. In these calculations it was assumed that adequate food energy would be provided to the entire population at the level of CFNI recommendations, but that the structure of national consumption would be that of La Poterie, rather than the actual structure which is "distorted" by the high-income sectors of the population. Based on this hypothetical situation, 6,874 to 7,560 ha. of extra cultivation would be required to replace 56% of food energy imports. At least 12,328 ha. or 79% to 63% more land would be required to replace the same percentage of imports if the current unequal national demand for food energy were to be met from local production. This does not include any allowances for more sophisticated agro-industrial investment which would be required to replace processed foods.

It is clear from these figures then that Thomas' second "iron law", that of the convergence of demand and need, is particularly relevant to the amount of resources required for agricultural self-reliance in Grenada today.

Table 6. EXTRA LABOUR FORCE & ACREAGE REQUIRED
FOR AGRICULTURAL SELF-RELIANCE

Demand assumptions	Ha. assumed needed for self-reliance	Labour force required
La Poterie Demand (based on most energy coming from Pigeon Peas)	6,874	5,130
La Poterie Demand (based on substitution of 15% of wheat consumption)	7,560	5,642
La Poterie Demand (based on replacement of all wheat)	11,344	8,466
National Demand (15% of wheat replaced)	12,328	9,200
National Demand (all wheat replaced)	17,330	12,933

Notes:

1. See Table 7 for an outline of the assumptions made in arriving at these figures.
2. The requirement of 5,130 to 9,200 extra agricultural workers can be compared with an agricultural labour force of 10,200 (Coard, 1983: 46), a total labour force of 37,930 and unemployment of 10,460 in October 1980 (UWI, 1980: 41).
3. The requirement of an extra 6,874 to 17,330 hectares of land can be compared to the 10,382 hectares of land lost to production in the period 1961–82.
4. Labour requirements were calculated on the basis of an agricultural labour force of 10,200 in 1980 (UWI, 1981: 13) and cultivation of 13,690 ha. (see Table 4), giving a labour intensity of 1.34 ha./worker.

Table 7. HYPOTHETICAL IMPORT SUBSTITUTION BASED ON CURRENT NATIONAL DEMAND STRUCTURE

	Kcal. demand 1980	Kcal. imports 1980	% Replaced	Kcal. new prod. requ'd	Assumed tonnes/ha.	Yields (kcal./ha.)	Extra ha. required
Meat	6,673,395	4,081,100	100	4,081,100		(1,095)[1]	3,727
Dairy 1.	5,608,290	5,608,290[2]	50	2,804,145		(1,330)	2,108
2.	5,608,290	5,608,290	100	5,608,290		(1,330)	4,217
Flour 1.	26,210,886	26,210,886	15[3]	3,931,633	7	(7,700)[4]	511
2.	26,210,886	26,210,886	100	26,210,886	7	(7,700)	3,404
Rice	3,219,810	3,219,810	100	3,219,810	1.1	(3,960)[5]	813
Other cereals	8,768,569	7,148,336	100	7,148,336	2.43	(8,772)[6]	815
Root crop/starch	3,565,200	486,788	100	486,788	7	(7,700)	63
Sugar	11,965,919	10,124,045	100	10,124,045	2.7	(10,071)[7]	1,005
Vegetables	2,721,219	929,608	100	929,608	7	(5,417)[8]	172
Ed. oils/shortening	7,064,987	4,895,165	100	4,895,165	7.7	(1,572)[9]	3,114

Totals 1. −56% of food 37,620,630   12m328 ha. energy imports
　　　　2. −93% of food 62,704,028   17,330 ha. energy imports

Notes:
1. Meat and Dairy yields per ha. were calculated from kg./carcass, ha./animal, kg. feed/carcass and litre/lactation data found in Blades and Motta, "A Preliminary Design for a Regional Livestock Complex", mimeo, CARICOM Secretariat, 1975.
2. No data was available for local dairy production and it is assumed here that all dairy supplies are imported. In actual fact, there is likely to be a small trade and home production of dairy products for which data was not available.
3. In the first case, it is assumed that wheat flour is replaced by 15% root crop or legume flours. While theoretically possible to go beyond composite flours and replace all wheat flour, the costs and nutritional disruptions incurred are likely to make such a policy politically disastrous, as the Government of Guyana is currently discovering.
4. Yields are for root crop flours, taken from Williams, The Agronomy of Major Tropical Crops, Oxford University Press, 1975, and local data.
5. Rice yields are for hill rice in Belize. Although test plantings have apparently been conducted in Grenada, and some 6,500 ha. of suitably wet good soils exist, officials are pessimistic about local rice cultivation due to the low yields of hill rice in comparison with imported Guyanese paddy rice. The estimate of suitable acreage available for rice cultivation was made by comparing soil and climate conditions on overlay maps made from data in the 1959 UWI Soil and Land Use Survey (Vernon, Payne & Spector, 1959).
6. The assumed yield here is for local maize production.
7. Sugar yields come from Grenada Sugar Factory production estimates.
8. Vegetable yields are averaged from local production data.
9. Oil/shortening data comes from local coconut/copra/oil production.

Conclusions

The circle of interdependent linkage between class, income, land ownership and food consumption should be evident from the material presented above. These relationships, and therefore the development strategies which attempt to modify them, are extremely complex, and often vex Caribbean politicians who would prefer to present simplistic solutions and rely on rhetoric rather than reason to attract their voters. This complexity is also a bane to those theoreticians and practitioners who tout the scientific correctness of their recommendations, without the flexibility to adapt and modify when faced with frequent changes in the political and economic conjuncture.

We have seen how food consumption structures are concretely connected to income levels, and how agricultural land is similarly linked to income. While not as concrete or easily measured as food consumption or agricultural resources, class relationships are obviously closely associated with income levels as well. In addition to the more objective influence of income, diets relate to class through the influence of cultural and social customs. The example of salt cod as a legacy of slavery is but one example, with many other examples to be found in folklore of the role of root crops, fish, rum, etc. as distinct manifestations of food and class. Similarly, the different roles of land, agricultural practices, tools, animal husbandry, landless farming and many other features of Caribbean peasant and estate agriculture highlight distinct class approaches to food production.

The co-existence of various forms of land tenure (e.g. "peasant" small farms, middle "peasants", landless labourers, mini-estates, plantations, state farms and co-operatives) requires that a diversity of solutions be found, since the resources required for self-reliant agriculture are beyond the capability of any one group or class (Thomas, 1974: 289). The quantity of output is not the only variable either, since, as we have seen, the quantity of land and labour needed for self-reliance is indivisibly linked to the composition of output. Quantum and composition of agricultural production are therefore inseparable for the purposes of planning as advocated by the model discussed here. The complexity of planning within this framework goes well beyond the econometric and agronomic variables normally considered in government planning offices. It must also include political and social factors as well.

As noted earlier, the process of decision-making which determines relative levels of consumption versus accumulation of scarce resources must be as democratic as possible if the majority of the population are to accept the sacrifices inherent in the transformation of the society against great odds. Thomas is one of the few authors in this area to stress the importance of democracy to socialist transformation. At the risk of being simplistic, one could argue that it was around this whole area of political organization that the process led by the NJM in Grenada foundered.

In addition, the reaction of external factors is a critical area of concern. The need for foreign exchange to purchase those capital goods required to transform local production creates vulnerability to those forces which control access to most of the international liquidity available for development projects today. The availability of aid for the international airport in Grenada provided a limited breathing-space and fuelled much of the economic growth which took place during the Revolution. The near-completion of its construction and the consequent reduction in cash flow which offset the historical drain of surplus through commodity exports, were of considerable concern to Grenada's planners and politicians. Maurice Bishop, in his trip to Eastern Europe and the Soviet Union just before his murder in October 1983, had secured an agreement to study the feasibility of a second deep-water harbour in Grenville on the island's east coast. It may be that the NJM hoped to buy further time for the transformation of the economy through the influx of funds for another large construction project.

In the end however, it was not the restriction of foreign exchange receipts, but military conflict, both internal and geopolitical, which restricted the advance of the Grenada Revolution. Military intervention, by both a faction of the NJM and the United States has led to a dominance of external military power in Grenada (and the entire Caribbean) on a scale never seen or required during its colonial occupation. The resources diverted to military concerns now reduce the investment available to tackle the urgent problems of underdevelopment in agriculture. Politicians now tend to be guided by priorities which have little to do with the study of the complex food problems discussed here, since their external "benefactors" reject the need for self-reliance. It may be some time before the potential of this alternative model can again be tested against the reality of the Caribbean's development problems.

BIBLIOGRAPHY

BOOKS

Bettelheim, C. & Sweezy, P. (1971), *On the Transition to Socialism*, New York: Monthly Review Press.

Coard, Bernard (1982), *Report on the National Economy for 1981 and the Prospects for 1982*, St. George's: Government Printing Office.

—— (1983), *Report on the National Economy for 1982 and the Budget-Plan for 1983 and Beyond*, St. George's: Government Printery.

Craig, Susan ed. (1982) *Contemporary Caribbean: A Sociological Reader*, Port of Spain: published by the editor.

Cumberbatch, Edward (1977), *Agro-Industrial Science and Technology Needs in Grenada*, Washington: O.A.S. Studies in Scientific and Technical Development No. 33.

Dellimore, J. & Whitehead, J. (1979), *Secondary Agro-Based Industries: ECCM and Barbados*, Barbados: Caribbean Technology Policy Studies Project I.

Demas, William (1973), *The Political Economy of the English Speaking Caribbean: A Summary View*, Barbados: Caribbean Ecumenical Consultation for Development, Study Paper No. 4.

EPICA (1982), *Grenada: The Peaceful Revolution*, Washington: Ecumenical Program for Inter-American Communication and Action.

Farrell, Trevor (1982), *Small Size, Technology and Development Strategy*, Trinidad: Caribbean Technology Policy Studies Project II, UWI.

Gittens-Knight, E. (1946), *The Grenada Handbook and Directory, 1946*, Barbados: Advocate Co. Ltd.

Gonsalves, Ralph (1981), *The Non-Capitalist Path of Development: Africa and the Caribbean*, London: One Caribbean Publishers.

Greenwood, D.S. (1973), *The Political Economy of Peasant Family Farming: Some Anthropological Perspectives on Rationality and Adaptation*, Ithaca: Cornell University Rural Development Occasional Paper No. 2.

Marshall, W.K. (1967), "Metayage in the Sugar Industry of the British Windward Islands, 1838–1865", Barbados: Dept of History, University of the West Indies (mimeo).

Post, Ken (1978) *Arise Ye Starvelings: The Jamaican Labour Rebellion of 1938 and its Aftermath*, The Hague: M. Nijhoff.

Thomas, C.Y. (1974) *Dependence and Transformation: The Economic of the Transition to Socialism*, New York: Monthly Review Press.

—— (1982), *The Threat and the Promise: An Assessment of the Impact of Technological Developments in the High Fructose Corn Syrup and Sucro-Chemical Industries*, Trinidad: Caribbean Technology Policy Studies Project II, ISER/UWI & IDS/UG.

Vail, D.J. (1975), "The Case for Rural Industry: Economic Factors Favoring Small-Scale, Decentralized, Labour Intensive Manufacturing", Ithaca: Cornell University Institute on Science, Technology and Development (mimeo).

Vernon, Payne and Spector (1959), Soil and Land-Use Surveys, No. 9: *Grenada*, Trinidad: Imperial College of Tropical Agriculture.

Wallerstein, Immanuel (1980), *The Modern World System II: Mercantilism and the Consolidation of the European World Economy, 1600–1750*, New York: Academic Press.

Williams, Eric (1944), *Capitalism and Slavery*, New York: Capricorn.

Williams, C.N. (1975) *The Agronomy of the Major Tropical Crops*, Oxford University Press.

Articles

Amin, Samir (1977), "Self-Reliance and the New International Economic Order", *Monthly Review*, 29, 3, pp. 1–21.

Beckford, George (1972*b*), "Land Reform for the Betterment of Caribbean Peoples", *Proceedings of the 7th West Indian Agricultural Economics Conference*.

Best, Lloyd & Levitt, K. (1968), "A Model of a Pure Plantation Economy", *Social and Economic Studies*, 17, 3, pp. 283–326.

Dellimore, J.H. (1979), "Select Technological Issues in Agro-Industry (I)", *Social and Economic Studies*, 28, 1, pp. 54–96.

Foster-Carter, Aidan (1978), "The Modes of Production Controversy", *New Left Review*, 107 (Jan.–Feb.), pp. 47–77.

Girvan, Norman (1973), "The Development of Dependency Economics in the Caribbean and Latin America: Review and Comparison", *Social and Economic Studies*, 22, 1, pp. 1–33.

Hart, Richard (1982), "Trade Unionism in the English Speaking Caribbean: The Formative Years and the Caribbean Labour Congress", in Craig (ed.) *Contemporary Caribbean: A Sociological Reader*, Vol. 2.

James, C.L.R. (1980), "The West Indian Middle Classes" in *Spheres of Existence: Selected Writings*. New York: Lawrence Hill & Co.; London: Allison and Busby.

LeFranc, E. (1980), "Small Farming in Grenada" in *Small Farming in the Less Developed Countries of the Commonwealth Caribbean*. Barbados: Caribbean Development Bank, pp. 1–56.

Lewis, Arthur (1949), "Industrial Development in the Caribbean", *Caribbean Economic Review*, 1, 1 & 2.

—— (1954) "Economic Development with Unlimited Supplies of Labour", Manchester School of Economics and Social Studies.

Lewis, Gordon (1981), "The Caribbean in the 1980's: What We Should Study", *Caribbean Review*, X, 4.

Leys, Colin (1977), "Underdevelopment and Dependency: Critical Notes", *Journal of Contemporary Asia*, VII, 1, pp. 92–107.

Mansour, Fawzy (1979), "Third World Revolt and Self-Reliant Auto-Centred Strategy of Development" in *Towards a New Strategy for Development*. Rothko Chapel: Pergamon: pp. 198–239.

Pack, H. (1974), "The Employment/Output Tradeoff in LDCs: A Micro-economic Approach", *Oxford Economic Papers*, 26, 3.

Shanin, Teodor (1983), "Late Marx and the Russian 'Periphery of Capitalism' ", *Monthly Review*, 35, 2, pp. 10–24.

Silberston, A. (1972), "Economies of Scale in Theory and Practice", *Economic Journal*, 28.

Thomas, C.Y. (1982), "From Colony to State Capitalism: Alternative Paths of Development in the Caribbean", *Transition*, 5, pp. 1–20.

Whitehead, Judy (1979), "Select Technological Issues in Agro-Industry (II)", *Social and Economic Studies*, 28, 1, pp. 139–98.

Documents

CARICOM (1975), "A Preliminary Design for a Regional Livestock Complex" by H. Blades, & S. Motta., Georgetown: Caribbean Community Secretariat.

CARDI (1980), "A Profile of Small Farming in Antigua. Montserrat and Grenada". Trinidad: University of the West Indies — Caribbean Agricultural Research and Development Institute.

CFNI (1972), *La Poterie Nutrition Survey*, Trinidad: Caribbean Food and Nutrition Institute.

—— (1974), Food Composition Tables for Use in the English-Speaking Caribbean. Kingston: Caribbean Food and Nutrition Institute.

—— (1976), *The Nutritional Status of Young Children in Grenada*. Trinidad: CFNI-T-36-76.

—— (1979), *Food Production and Availability in Grenada* by Colin Weir. Trinidad: CFNI-T-72-79.

—— (1980), *Background Data on Rural Development Policies and Programmes in Grenada*. Trinidad: CFNI-T-55-80.

DTRC (1980), *Grenada Visitor Expenditure and Motivation Survey, Summer and Winter 1979* by J. Belfon. Barbados: Caribbean Tourism Research Centre.

ECLA (1977), *Agricultural Sector Plan for Grenada*, 1977–81 by Max Ifil. Trinidad: Economic Commission for Latin America. ECLA/CARIB 77/3, vol. 1.

—— (1978), *Land/Man Relationship in the Caribbean: With Special Reference to Grenada*, by Max Ifil. Trinidad: Economic Commission for Latin America, ECLA/CARIB 78/1.

—— (1979), Report on a Farm Survey Conducted in Grenada, by Max Ifil. Trinidad: ECLA/CARIB 79/12.

Grenada (1978) Abstract of Statistics — 1978. St. George's: Central Statistical Office.

—— (1979) Abstract of Statistics (First Quarter) — 1979. St. George's: Central Statistical Office.

—— (1980) Imports by S.I.T.C. — 1980. St. George's: Central Statistical Office.

—— (1981a) Agriculture Sector Report — June 1981. St. George's: Ministry of Agriculture.

—— (1981b) Agricultural Production Estimates — Quantity and Value, 1977–1980. St. George's: Ministry of Agriculture Statistical Unit.

—— (1981c) A Preliminary Investigation of Idle Land in Grenada, with Special Reference to the Grand Roy Valley, prepared by John Brierley. St. George's: Ministry of Agriculture (mimeo).

—— (1981d) Agricultural Census — 1981. St. George's: Ministry of Agriculture.

—— (1980) Wages in Grenada — September 1980. St. George's: Ministry of Labour.

—— (1980) Proceedings of the First Grenada Conference on Science and Technology. St. George's: Ministry of Planning.

GFC (1980) Project Profile for the Development of the Grenada Farms Corporation. St. George's: Grenada Farms Corporation.

GFCa (1980) Addendum One, Project Profile for the Development of the Grenada Farms Corporation. St. George's: Grenada Farms Corporation.

IICA (1982) Acreages of Crops Cultivated in Grenada. St. George's: Interamerican Institute for Co-operation in Agriculture (excerpted from an unpublished survey dated November–December 1981).

International Monetary Fund (1981) Grenada — Recent Economic Developments. Washington: IMF CGCED-81-23, March 12, 1981.

—— (1981) Grenada — Staff Report for the 1980 Article IV Consultation. Washington: IMF SM/81/55, March 12, 1981 with corrections to May 7, 1981.

UNCTAD (1980) The Food Processing Sector in Developing Countries: Some Recent Trends in the Transfer and Development of Technology. Vienna: U.N. Commission for Trade and Development, TD/B/C.6/66, October 14, 1980.

UWI (1980) Grenada: Unemployment, Employment and Household Survey, 1980. Trinidad: Department of Economics, University of the West Indies.

World Bank (1979), Current Economic Position and Prospects of Grenada. Washington: World Bank Report No. 2434-GRD, April 19, 1979.

—— (1982), Economic Memorandum on Grenada. Washington: World Bank Report No. 3825-GRD, 4 Aug. 1982.

8

TOWARDS THE SOCIALIST TRANSFORMATION OF CUBAN AGRICULTURE 1959–1982[1]

Brian H. Pollitt

Introduction

The tempo of the transition from private to social ownership of land and other means of agricultural production in post-revolutionary Cuba was extraordinarily rapid. The First Agrarian Reform Law, promulgated in May 1959 and substantially implemented by the summer of 1960, generally lowered the ceiling on the size of private farms to approximately 400 hectares(ha.). In October 1963 the Second Agrarian Reform Law expropriated, with some exceptional cases, the total area of all farms exceeding 67.1 ha. In the late 1960s, the area under private cultivation was further eroded by the sale or renting of such land to and by the state, accompanied by the negotiated integration of other private agricultural producers into the production plans of the local "People's Farms". From 1977 new emphasis was placed on the collective pooling of individual private landholdings and means of production in "production cooperatives", and these comprised some 30% of the one-fifth of Cuba's farm-area remaining in the private sector in 1982.

Pre-revolutionary organization of land and labour

The speed and scale of the transition to socialist forms of post-revolutionary agrarian organization reflected, in large measure, an earlier process of agricultural development in which specialised commercial farming, primarily for the export of cash crops (principally sugar-cane and tobacco), was predominant. The expansion of sugar production from 1 to 5 million tons between 1901 and 1925, primarily financed by US capital and primarily destined for US markets, was decisive in the development of large-scale farming units employing predominantly wage labour during the opening decades

1 This essay is reproduced from the *IDS Bulletin*, vol.13, 4, 1982, where it appeared under the title "The Transition to Socialist Agriculture in Cuba: Some Salient Features." The kind permission of the publishers is hereby acknowledged.

Table 1

Economically active population (14 years and over) in agriculture, forestry and fishing in Cuba in 1953

category	active population, male and female (000s)			percentage of all agricultural labour reported
	total	men	women[1]	
Farmers and livestock breeders	221.9	220.5	1.5	27.5
farmers	217.9	216.5	1.4	
livestock breeders	4.0	4.0	...	
Agricultural workers, gardeners etc	568.8	558.7	10.1	70.4
administrators and foremen	9.2	8.8	0.4	1.1
agricultural wage-workers	489.0	480.5	8.5	60.6
non-wage family labour[2]	66.7	65.5	1.2	8.3
gardeners etc	3.9	3.8	...	0.5
Fishermen, hunters and trappers	6.0	5.9	0.1	0.7
fishermen	5.7	5.7	...	
hunters and trappers	0.3	0.3	...	
Forestry workers	10.8	10.6	0.2	1.3
Total	807.5	795.7	11.8	100.0

[1]The number of women is grossly understated because the Census enquired as to the 'primary' occupation of those enumerated. Women performing occasional seasonal work (including as wage-labour) and sharing in small peasant farm-labour (most conspicuously in tobacco farms) are normally classified as 'housewives'.

[2]Non-wage 'family labour' refers in general to the sons of peasant farmers employed on the lands owned or rented by their fathers and not paid a money-wage.

... = less than 0.5

Source: *Censos de Población, Viviendas y Electoral*, 1953 from Table 54, p 204; (Population, Housing, and Electoral Census, 1953).

Table 2   **Occupational structure in 1957 of those interviewed in 1966**

ZONES

OCCUPATION IN 1957		San Luis	Güines	S.A. de las Veras	Manguito	Cabai-guán	Escam-bray	S. Spíritus	Florida	Florencia	Alto Songo	Bayamo	total	% of all agri-cultural workers
Farmers and graziers	owners	5	9	6	5	13	11	11	1	41	11	13	125	12.5
	cash-renters	1	15	7	—	15	3	3	—	8	1	1	55	5.5
	sub-renters	—	—	3	—	—	—	—	—	—	—	—	5	0.5
	share-croppers	22	9	5	—	28	18	—	—	27	3	2	114	11.4
	squatters	—	—	1	—	1	—	—	—	—	—	1	3	0.3
	others	—	1	1	—	—	—	—	—	—	—	—	2	0.2
	sub-total	28	34	23	5	57	33	14	1	77	15	17	304	30.4
Semi-proletarians	farmer/A.W. and R.W.	12	3	1	9	2	3	8	7	12	27	13	97	9.7
	farmer/R.W.	21	1	—	—	1	—	—	—	4	—	1	28	2.8
	sub-total	33	4	1	9	3	3	8	7	16	27	14	125	12.5
Non-wage agricultural workers	permanent non-wage A.W.	1	6	2	4	6	13	1	2	9	1	3	48	4.8
	seasonal N.W.A.W. and S.A.W. or S.R.W.	4	1	—	3	1	6	2	5	—	3	4	29	2.9
	sub-total	5	7	2	7	7	19	3	7	9	4	7	77	7.7

													Total	%
Agricultural wage-workers permanent A.W.-skilled	1	6	1	3	—	—	9	1	—	—	7	28	2.8
permanent A.W.-unskilled	4	12	13	10	13	8	19	15	2	1	22	119	11.9
seasonal A.W.-skilled	1	—	—	—	—	—	4	—	—	—	3	8	0.8
seasonal A.W.-unskilled	15	31	10	46	19	35	36	42	9	22	23	288	28.8
S.A.W. and S.R.W.	18	1	3	5	6	5	6	5	—	1	—	50	5.0
S.A.W. and S.U.W.	1	—	—	—	—	—	—	—	—	—	—	1	0.1
S.A.W. and S.R.W. and S.U.W.	—	1	1	—	—	—	—	—	—	—	—	2	0.2
sub-total	40	51	28	64	38	48	74	63	11	24	55	496	49.4
In agricultural work Total	106	96	54	85	105	103	99	78	113	70	93	1002	100.0

Legend:
A.W.   = Agricultural Worker
S.A.W.   = Seasonal Agricultural Worker
N.W.A.W. = Non-wage Agricultural Worker
R.W.   = Rural Worker
S.R.W.   = Seasonal Rural Worker
U.W.   = Urban Worker
S.U.W.   = Seasonal Urban Worker

Figure I   **Proportion of total farm-area per farm-size group
with proportion under crops and composition of
output value, 1945**

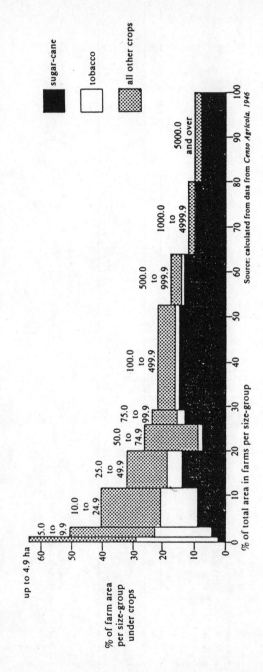

Table 3

Number of farms in Cuba, 1945, classified by principal source of income

principal source of income	number of farms in 000s	% of all farms	% share in total farm income	% of income from principal crop or activity*
Sugar cane	29.1	18.2	41.6	86.6
Livestock	28.8	18.0	20.9	82.2
Tobacco	22.8	14.2	10.2	75.9
Cereals and beans	26.8	16.8	9.4	63.8
Root crops	15.7	9.8	6.7	60.7
Coffee	9.3	5.8	2.7	75.6
Tree fruit	4.8	3.0	2.0	70.6
Garden truck	1.2	0.9	0.9	62.1
Other crops	11.4	7.1	5.0	73.9
Forest products	0.9	0.6	0.6	79.3
	9.1‡	5.6‡		
Totals	159.9	100.0	100.0	

* That is, the percentage of the total income of farms of each type which comes from their principal crop or activity. For example, farms whose principal crop was sugar obtained 86.6 per cent of their income from sugar; farms whose principal activity was cattle raising obtained 82.2 per cent of their income from cattle — and so on.

‡ No income reported.

Source: *Censo Agrícola, 1946.*

Table 4

Socialisation of means of production and services in the Cuban economy, 1961-77[1]

(percentages)

sector	1961	1963	1968	1977[2]
Agriculture	37	70	70	79[2]
Industry	85	95	100	100
Construction	80	98	100	100
Transportation	92	95	98	98
Retail trade	52	75	100	100
Wholesale and foreign trade	100	100	100	100
Banking	100	100	100	100
Education	100	100	100	100

[1]Figures in the table refer to property not to production. In 1976, the output of the private sector represented about 4 per cent of national output (excluding trade) with the following shares by economic sector: 25 per cent in agriculture, less than 7 per cent in transportation, and less than 1 per cent in communication. (The per cent in the latter statistics refers not to national output but to the private share of output in each economic sector.)

[2]Private farmers owned about 33 per cent of the cattle and produced 80 per cent of tobacco, 50 per cent of coffee, 50 per cent of vegetables and fruits, and 16 per cent of sugar.

Source: C. Mesa-Lago, *The Economy of Socialist Cuba,* University of New Mexico Press, 1981:15.

of the twentieth century. A "pure" form of plantation system, in which both agricultural and milling operations of the sugar industry were integrated in ownership and in which mill and field workers formed part of the wage-labour force of the same enterprise, was never predominant in modern Cuba; however, on the eve of the Revolution of 1959, the bulk of the agricultural wage labour force derived its primary source of money income from employment in large-scale cane farms.

Cuba's highly differentiated agrarian class structure, with a majority of wage-earning agricultural proletarians, distinguished her pre-revolutionary agrarian system from most, if not all, other agrarian societies which subsequently experienced transitions to socialist agriculture. As is shown in Table 1, of an (underestimated) total of some 800,000 persons defined in 1953 as 'economically active' in agriculture, forestry and fishing, less than 30% were classified as "farmers and livestock breeders" and of the remainder, some 60%, were classified as "agricultural wage-workers".

Most Census procedures yield statistically simplified rural occupational structures which exaggerate the delineation in clear-cut "class-boxes" of more complex agrarian classes or strata. Table 2 shows the pre-revolutionary agricultural occupations of a sample of 1,061 married male household heads, aged between 25 and 55, as reported for eleven rural zones in Cuba in a survey directed by this writer in 1966.[2] It indicates the spatial variations to be encountered in the balance of agrarian classes or strata; shows the diversity of pre-revolutionary tenure arrangements to be found among "farmers and graziers"; indicates the existence of a significant "semi-proletariat" that combined both wage and non-wage labour in agriculture; and suggested the diversity of non-agricultural wage work activities undertaken by those formally classified as "agricultural wage workers".

Figure 1 shows the concentration of Cuban farm lands in relatively large-scale units, according to data extracted from the comprehensive Agricultural Census conducted in the island in 1946. It shows that as farms increased in size (passing from predominantly "non-wage" or "peasant" to predominantly "wage" or "capitalist" forms of agricultural organization), the general intensity of cultivation of the farm area decreased and the aggregate level of

2   See B.H. Pollitt, "Agrarian Reform and the 'Agricultural Proletariat' in Cuba, 1958–66: Some Notes", University of Glasgow, Institute of Latin American Studies, Occasional Papers, no. 27, 1979; also B.H. Pollitt, "Agrarian Reform and the 'Agricultural Proletariat' in Cuba, 1958–66: Further Notes and Some Second Thoughts", University of Glasgow, Institute of Latin American Studies, Occasional Papers no. 30, 1980.

productive specialization increased. At the extremes of farm-scale, it could be seen that 63% of the area in farms, less than 5 ha. in size, was under crops. By contrast, less than 15% of the total area in farms of 1,000 ha. or more was sown to crops. It could be seen that less than half of the value of crops sown on farms less than 75 ha. in size corresponded to sugar cane, with tobacco and other crops generating a greater proportion of crop-values. On the other hand, sugar cane comprised 75% of the value of all crops sown on farms over 100 ha. in size.

Pasture-land (and hence livestock production) was not represented in the diagram (Figure 1); its importance, with that of certain other crops, is more clearly shown in Table 3. Nonetheless, the diagram permitted certain productive characteristics of the lands expropriated under the post-revolutionary agrarian reform laws to be predicted.

Agrarian reform, economic strategy and labour shortage, 1959-63

The First Agrarian Reform Law formally abolished rents in cash and kind for some 100,000 smaller farmers who had cultivated their lands under diverse tenure arrangements, and with varying degrees of security of tenure. It also abolished the controls over land-use commonly conditioning pre-revolutionary tenure agreements. These had been extensive for lands rented by cane-farmers and for those share-cropped by small-scale tobacco producers. It can be seen from Figure 1 that despite significant changes in the period 1945–58, the prime beneficiaries of this aspect of the agrarian reform were farmers who had produced an overwhelming proportion of the island's tobacco output and a disproportionate share of the value of all crops other than sugar-cane.

The Second Agrarian Reform Law of 1963, as is shown in Table 4, reduced the private sector of the national farm-area to approximately 30% of the total. Nonetheless, farms of less than 67 ha, which numbered some 170,000 or even more, continued to produce a more diversified range of crops (including the bulk of the nation's coffee) than did the larger farms expropriated over the period 1959–63. Moreover, the generally more intensive cultivation depicted in Fig. 1 in terms of the comparative sown area was maintained and, as was to be expected, partly reflected the generally greater inputs of non-wage family-labour per hectare in smaller farms *vis-à-vis* those of predominantly wage-labour in larger enterprises.

The largest farms expropriated under the First Agrarian Reform

Law were principally dedicated to cane production and to the extensive grazing of cattle, and possessed substantial reserves of under- or unutilised land, even when non-cultivable areas were discounted. While uncertainties as to when and how the law would be applied provoked demands for "land or work" from the agricultural proletariat historically employed as "permanent" or "seasonal" labour, there was no irresistable pressure from such workers for their sub-division for individual or loosely-organized private cooperative farming. Their organized pre-revolutionary struggles had generally been for better wages and more stable employment. Such farms were thus generally retained in large-scale enterprises and the "People's farms" — i.e. state farms in other contexts — formally organized to pursue production targets set by national and regional agricultural planning agencies, constituted the typical organizational form in the state sector of agriculture by 1962.

Between 1959 and 1963, Cuban economic strategy emphasised industrial growth and the diversification of agricultural production. Under-employed land was to be combined with under-employed wage-labour, primarily in the expanding state sector, to increase total agricultural output and employment and to produce a broad range of foods and industrial raw materials to substitute for imports and to contribute to industrial development. The myriad dislocative effects of the US political and economic blockade of Cuba vastly exacerbated the difficulties inherent in an already over-ambitious programme of industrialisation. Diverse measures of income redistribution in the towns sharply increased urban demand for food (particularly meat and poultry), while redistribution of income in the countryside, particularly in the smaller-scale farms that had traditionally supplied a high proportion of nationally produced urban food supplies, resulted in rising on-farm consumption at the expense of marketed surpluses.

The seasonal concentration of unemployment in the wet summer months — the "dead season" — distorted statistics of average annual rates of unemployment in agriculture and concealed the (not untypical) fact that the proportion of the agricultural proletariat which was unemployed in the months of the sugar harvest — which coincided with the sowing and/or harvesting periods of most of Cuba's other major crops — was relatively small. Expanding activity in the growing state sector of agriculture rapidly ran up against labour shortages as one branch of activity increasingly competed with another. Newly-created employment in the old "dead season", partly created by investment in agricultural diversification and in rural building construction, contributed to a reduction in the spatial mobility of labour in an agricultural system which, above all in the sugar harvest but also in that of coffee and tobacco, had traditionally required vast armies of seasonal migrant labour from both towns and countryside. State farms conferred the rights of full employment and other benefits on old "seasonal" as well as "permanent" workers, and this reinforced other factors tending to "freeze" agricultural wage-labour.

A sample of 1,061 male household-heads, interviewed in rural Cuba in 1966, were questioned as to the occupations of their brothers in that year and in the year 1957. Table 5 records the responses for 3,535 cases. A vertical reading of the columns shows the occupational groupings in 1957. It could be seen, for example, that of a total of 31 reported members of the army or police in 1957, only one remained such in 1966. A horizontal reading of the columns indicates the occupational structure in 1957 of totals reporting individual occupational groupings in 1966. From this, it can be seen that the total in the army or police in 1966 increased from 31 to 123, and that 59 of these had been agricultural workers in 1957. In the present context, the most important feature of the general swirl of inter-occupational movement reported in Table 5 was a comparative increase in the number of "small farmers" and "semi-proletarians" but a fall of some 20% in the number of "agricultural workers" reported in this sample.

Data obtained from respondents in the same rural survey showed that if the generally "landless" character of much of the "agricultural proletariat" in pre-revolutionary Cuba had been exaggerated by many writers, then the tendency of such workers to accumulate, by diverse means and for diverse motives, land plots within and without the state sector, increased notably after the revolution. Of 495 respondents reporting themselves to have been "agricultural wage-workers" in 1957, 188 — or 38% — reported ownership or access to a land-plot in that year. By 1966, land-plots were reported by 48.8% of the 367 state farm workers responding and 67.7% of 158 agricultural wage-workers without formal affiliation to state farms. Access to such plots increased household consumption of traditional food staples — now subject, together with virtually all other consumer goods, to a rigorous rationing system — but tended also to reduce the proportion of their workers' productive energies expended on state-owned lands. The combination of all such factors was a potent one and was made more so by a long-standing popular antipathy to manual cane-cutting when alternative employment opportunities were available. As is shown in Table 6, of a sample of 602 state farm and other agricultural workers and "semi-proletarians" interviewed in 1966, 212 reported that they had cut cane in 1957. Only half that number — 106 cases — reported that they had

Table 5   The occupational structure of a sample of male workers,   Cuba 1957 and 1966

1957-1966	farmers	semi-proletariat	agri-cultural workers	rural workers (non-agri)	urban workers	army or police	retired or sick	not working	school or university	other	not known	total
Small farmers	727	22	153	20	8	1	—	10	2	8	1	952
Semi-proletariat	19	90	24	5	—	—	—	3	—	—	—	141
Agricultural workers	40	11	1037	34	10	2	—	80	25	7	4	1250
Rural (non-agri) wkers	19	3	96	84	4	4	—	7	2	5	3	227
Urban workers	41	4	137	27	333	19	1	9	7	6	3	587
Army or police	5	1	64	6	10	1	—	26	2	7	1	123
Retired or sick	11	—	42	11	12	4	27	3	—	4	1	115
School or university	1	—	3	—	1	—	—	63	8	—	—	76
Other	18	2	24	2	4	—	—	3	—	8	3	64
Total	881	133	1580	189	382	31	28	204	46	45	16	3535

Source: 1966 Rural Surveys, from 'Employment plans, performance and future prospects in Cuba', by B. H. Pollitt, Department of Applied Economics, University of Cambridge, *Reprint Series* no 349, 1971.

Table 6   Occupation structure of sample of workers engaged in cutting cane and other agricultural work,   Cuba 1957 and 1966

occupation	1957			1966		
	cane cutters	others	total	cane cutters	others	total
State farmers	145	228	373	62	311	373
Agricultural workers	46	112	158	35	123	158
Semi-proletariat	21	50	71	9	62	71
Total	212	390	602	106	496	602
per cent	35.2	64.8	100.0	17.6	82.4	100.0

Source: B. Pollitt, 'Employment plans, performance and future prospects in Cuba', in *Third World Employment*, R. Jolly et al (eds), Penguin, London, 1973, p 256.

Table 7   Cuba: production, exports and export prices for sugar

	thousand of tons		US cents per pound	
	production	exports	price paid by Soviet Union	world market price[1]
1959	6,039	4,951	—	2.97
1960	5,943	5,634	—	3.14
1961	6,876	6,413	4.09	2.75
1962	4,882	5,132	4.09	2.83
1963	3,883	3,520	6.11	8.34
1964	4,475	4,176	6.11	5.77
1965	6,156	5,316	6.11	2.08
1966	4,537	4,435	6.11	1.81
1967	6,236	5,683	6.11	1.92
1968	5,165	4,612	6.11	1.90
1969	4,459	4,799	6.11	3.20
1970	8,538	6,906	6.11	3.68
1971	5,925	5,511	6.11	4.50
1972	4,325	4,140	6.11	7.27
1973	5,253	4,797	12.02	9.45
1974	5,925	5,491	19.64	29.66
1975	6,314	5,744	30.40	20.37
1976	6,156	5,764	30.95	11.51
1977	6,485	6,238	35.73	8.14
1978	7,350[2]	7,231[2]	40.78[2]	7.80[2]

[1] International Sugar Agreement prices

[2] preliminary

Sources: ECLA, on the basis of data from Cuba's annual statistical reports; Banco Nacional de Cuba, *Desarrollo y perspectivas de la economía cubana;* International Sugar Organization, *Statistical Bulletin,* and United Nations statistics. Reproduced from *Comercio Exterior* of the Banco Nacional de México, January 1981.

Note: The US dollar was devalued in 1972 from parity with the Cuban peso to approximately US$1.00 = $0.70 pesos but the change is not taken into account in relative Soviet and world market price statistics.

done so in the 12 months prior to their interview. It could be seen that the fall was disproportionately great for state farm workers.

The agro-industrial export strategy and agrarian reform, 1963–80

This "flight from cane" — or at least from its manual cutting — contributed powerfully to the fall in Cuban sugar production in 1961–3 shown in Table 7. This in turn was to accelerate the expropriation of farms over 67 ha. in size under the Second Agrarian Reform Law of October 1963. By that year it had become more than evident that the early post-revolutionary industrialisation programme was proving excessively costly in terms of imported capital goods and raw materials, and returns on exceedingly high rates of industrial investment were disappointingly low. The relative collapse of sugar production, accompanied by a sharp fall in the quantity and quality of tobacco exports, meant that rising foreign indebtedness to finance industrialisation was accompanied by a steep fall in the economy's capacity to maintain, let alone increase, foreign exchange earnings. In 1963, accordingly, a radically different development strategy was adopted. Its underlying economic logic (which prevails to this day) was that if the US blockade had destroyed Cuba's links with her major pre-revolutionary trading partner, the economies of the socialist bloc (and above all that of the USSR) comprised new, expanding markets for Cuban agricultural exports, of which sugar was overwhelmingly the most important, with favourable terms of trade for needed imports. As can be seen in Table 7, price stability characterised the Soviet-Cuban trading relationship in sugar from 1963 to 1972, in sharp contrast to the volatility of world market prices. Subsequently, Cuban sugar exports to the USSR were to be index-linked to the prices of Soviet exports to Cuba, including oil. From 1963, Cuba's rate of industrial investment was to be reduced while her export capacity was to be restored and further expanded. Renewed emphasis on industrial growth, and especially of industry related to the further processing of raw materials of agricultural origin, was to await the necessary build-up of an adequate infrastructure (including trained personnel) and would then be financed by a dramatically increased foreign exchange-earning sector. The latter meant above all sugar, with livestock, citrus fruits, tobacco, mining etc. in secondary roles.

This new strategy emphasised the apparent contradiction between an increasingly radicalised, and by 1961 explicitly socialist, revolutionary process and the continued private ownership of some 30% of farmland in operational units of up to 400 ha. in size. An 'agrarian bourgeoisie', enmeshed with the equivalent of the Russian *kulaks* or 'rich peasants', was rightly judged to be an active or latent enemy of the political trajectory of the revolution, and there was strong evidence of declining investment and production in this sector after 1961. Political factors apart, uncertainty as to the future of their holdings and constraints on what could be purchased with money income derived from private entrepreneurial activity in agriculture made an 'investment strike' in larger farms foreseeable by 1963. As could be deduced from Figure 1, the lands they occupied possessed productive characteristics of crucial importance for the new strategy of national development to be fuelled by agricultural and agro-industrial exports. Comprising some 10,000 farms, they embraced more than one-quarter of the area then sown to cane and a disproportionate share of the national cattle-stock and of quality pasture-lands. They were expropriated on 3 October 1963, modest compensation being paid over a ten-year period, and the farms so affected were integrated into existing or newly-founded state farms.

Labour shortage, mechanisation and large-scale state farms

While the Second Agrarian Reform increased to some 70% the farm area responsive to direct mechanisms of planning and resource allocation, it did not of course resolve the problems of labour shortage previously outlined. The solution to that was perceived to stem in the short-term from the mobilisation of voluntary labour, primarily for the sugar harvest, recruited from the army, students and the urban labour force. In the medium term, it would be resolved by the mechanised harvesting of the sugar-cane.

In the 1960s, however, technical problems of mechanising cane-cutting proved equally intractable both for Cuban and Soviet engineers. Neither possessed any accumulated practical expertise in the mechanised manipulation of such a heavy prime agricultural material over relatively protracted time periods in difficult operating conditions. Significant progress was made in the mechanisation of soil preparation for sowing and in the mechanised loading and de-trashing of manually cut cane in the first decade of the revolution. However, despite the deployment of significant numbers of combine harvesters best classified as 'experimental', a peak figure of only 3% of the total cane harvested in any year up to 1970 corresponded to mechanised cutting. In the context of endeavours to expand sugar production to 10 million tons by 1970 — i.e. to double the average level of production of the 1950s in the new market conditions prevailing, but with a professional cane-cutting labour force half or less than half the size of that active in immediate pre-revolutionary years — the primary consequence was an intolerable sharpening of the labour shortage crisis. In 1970 8.5 million tons of sugar were produced, but the quantity of labour employed and the record production achieved were such as to disrupt almost all other plans for economic growth in agriculture and industry.

The prime virtue of large-scale agricultural enterprises, from the time of the Bolshevik revolution and before, was envisaged by Marxists to lie in their receptivity to the application of modern agricultural techniques and high levels of mechanisation that would vastly increase the productivity of both land and labour. Such theoretical advantages were not generally realised in Cuba's large-scale state farms in the 1960s. In the 1970s, however, more sober planning procedures, accompanied by relative breakthroughs in the mechanisation of cane-harvesting, began to yield their potential fruits. As can be seen in Table 8, the national stock of cane combine-harvesters increased sharply, and the diverse types of machines — many of which had to be paid for in convertible currency (and hence from the proceeds of trade in unstable and generally less favourable commodity markets) — were progressively displaced by the KTP-1 combine. This was of Cuban-Soviet design and was initially imported from the USSR, but by 1977 it was produced or assembled in a Cuban industrial complex. By 1979, some 42% of the sugar harvest was mechanically cut and, as shown in Table 9, there was a sharp fall in the number of cane-cutters (above all, of relatively low-productivity volunteers) employed in the cutting of progressively larger harvests. Table 10 (page 170) shows a perceptible albeit erratic trend for per-hectare cane yields to increase for both state and private sectors.

By the end of the decade, better tillage practices (associated not least with traditionally greater per-hectare inputs of labour) of the private sector appeared to be increasingly offset by rising yields in the state sector. These generally corresponded to a greater and progressively more effective use of irrigation, fertilisers and herbicides; to a reduction in the damage to plantations caused by both indiscriminate pre-harvest burning of cane and by the deployment of heavy machinery and equipment, in the hands of initially inexperienced operators, in field conditions that were imperfectly prepared or were too wet during harvest operations. Such yields seemed susceptible to more or less sustained future improvements and the possibility of further expanding sugar production via increased per-hectare yields rather than by extending the area sown to cane was immensely important for non-sugar agricultural expansion. Large-scale state farms in Cuba, after two decades of costly experiment in both organization and technique, appeared to be at the stage of assuming

Table 8 **Combine harvester models**

	Massey-Ferguson 201	Libertadora 1400	KTP-1	total
1976	439	162	683	1,284
1979	407	157	1,734	2,298

Source: 'Memorias', Ministerio de la Agricultura, Havana 1980.

N.B. Massey-Ferguson and Libertadora have cane-top cutters which the
KTP-1 does not. Both the KTP-1 and the Libertadora cut green cane which
the Massey-Ferguson 201 does not.

Table 9

**Cane-cutters employed in peak-periods of the
sugar harvest, 1970-79 and percentage of cane
harvested manually, state and private sectors**

year	no of cane-cutters (000s)	% of harvest cut manually	total cane harvest (000s mn tons)
1970	350.0	99	81,514.9
1971	274.0	97	52,189.7
1972	210.5	93	44,303.0
1973	229.0	89	48,230.1
1974	200.3	82	50,373.3
1975	175.6	75	52,380.4
1976	153.3	68	53,783.9
1977	139.1	64	60,352.8
1978	153.9	62	69,652.9
1979	126.4	58	73.1 million

Source: Number of cane-cutters from 'Memorias', Ministerio de la
Agricultura, Havana, 1980, and percentage of manual harvest.
Total cane harvest from *Anuario Estadístico de Cuba, 1978*,
Ch V, Table 7, p 68 for 1970-78; 1979 from *Guía Estadística*,
1979, p 8.

Table 10

Cane-area harvested, total cane production, yields per hectare, state and private sector, and percentage of harvest cut by combines, 1961/62-1978/79

	cane area harvested (000s hectares)	cane production (mn of tons)	yield per hectare			harvested by combines %
			total (tons)	*state (tons)*	*private (tons)*	
1961/62	1,117.0	37.1	33.2	35.7	31.7	—
1962/63	1,074.9	32.0	29.8	31.0	28.9	—
1963/64	1,033.9	37.8	36.5	37.4	35.0	—
1964/65	1,054.5	51.5	48.9	48.9	48.8	2
1965/66	937.7	37.4	39.9	39.1	42.0	3
1966/67	1,081.1	51.6	47.7	47.9	47.3	2
1967/68	987.9	43.6	44.1	42.4	49.2	3
1968/69	944.4	42.9	45.4	43.6	50.9	2
1969/70	1,464.3	84.4	57.6	56.0	63.5	1
1970/71	1,255.7	54.0	43.0	42.1	46.7	3
1971/72	1,211.9	45.9	37.9	37.4	39.9	7
1972/73	1,072.9	48.2	44.9	44.4	47.5	11
1973/74	1,105.6	50.4	45.6	45.0	48.6	18
1974/75	1,181.4	52.4	44.3	43.6	48.0	25
1975/76	1,226.1	53.8	43.9	42.7	50.3	32
1976/77	1,137.5	60.4	53.1	51.1	62.8	36
1977/78	1,236.8	69.7	56.3	55.3	61.2	38
1978/79	1,304.1	73.1	56.0	...	...	42

... unavailable.

Sources: Cane area, production and yields. 1961/62 to 1977/78. *Anuario Estadístico de Cuba. 1978*, Ch V. Table 7, p 68. For 1978/79, *Guía Estadística*, 1979, p 8. Percentage of mechanized harvest. *Memorias*, Ministerio de Agricultura, 1980 for 1971/72 to 1978/79. For 1964/65 to 1970/71, 'Algunos aspectos sobre el desarrollo de la agricultura cañera en Cuba', O. Granda Balbona. Paper given at the Annual Conference of the Jamaican Association of Sugar Technologists. Kingston, Jamaica, MINAZ Doc no 1897. ATAC. November 1975.

the 'industrialised' attributes imputed to such enterprises by Marxist writers on socialist agriculture relatively early in the twentieth century.

'Socialist transitions' in the private sector of agriculture

If the weight of the state sector, both in agriculture and economic development strategy as a whole, is evidently decisive, the role of the surviving private sector and the various organizational forms promoted within it lack neither importance nor interest: 1 million tons or more of sugar originates in this sector. It was and remains the major producer of tobacco and coffee, and various root-crops, vegetables and dairy and other livestock products supplied by private producers continue to be important in urban and rural food consumption.

In the 1960s, private agricultural producers were organized into the National Association of Small Farmers (ANAP). This included more tightly organized 'Cooperatives of credits and services', notably among tobacco farmers, but the majority of producers belonged to looser associations in which effective state influence upon productive decisions, exercised via the supply of credits, inputs and purchases, was less marked. A semi-spontaneous peasant movement for the collective pooling of individual private holdings in Societies of Agricultural and Livestock Production (*Sociedades Agropecuarias*) was given erratic official aid and support. Most of these faded out in the second half of the 1960s primarily because the direct attachment of private lands to state enterprises (by sale, rent or other arrangements) was given greater government priority.

By the mid-1970s, however, great importance was attached to the promotion of Agricultural and Livestock Production Cooperatives (CPA) and it was given special impetus at ANAP's Fifth National Congress in 1977. These were a more carefully organized variation of the earlier movement to pool private holdings among the farmers forming their membership. In very explicitly coercing a peasantry into 'higher forms' of production, great emphasis was placed on the voluntary nature of the process of their formation; also on the careful, independent valuation of the contribution, in terms of land and other means of production, of their individual members so that each could be differentially reimbursed from common funds in a relatively brief period of time. The rudiments of financial accounting were required to be mastered with the formation of a cooperative. Exceptionally low rates of interest on state credits were offered to them and they were given preferential treatment in the allocation of agricultural machinery and equipment.

By March 1982, almost 30% of all farm land remaining in private hands was organized in CPAs with a continuing momentum for their further development. Their average size was small by comparison with some international ventures in peasant 'collectivism', and numbered some 25 individual households. Their success in terms of increased gross production and income was widely publicised, and was explained principally in terms of a more advanced division of labour in association with technically more advanced means of production and technique on lands now rationally devoted to their best crop-use. Stress was placed upon the improved access to electric-power supplies, pumped water and other social amenities attending the concentration of previously dispersed peasant households in small hamlets. Special emphasis was given to the improved situation of women in such cooperatives attending the breakdown of their social isolation, and to their heightened contribution to production and income facilitated by collective labour-organization and related child-care provision. All this reflected an important shift in the developmental 'model' for the private sector. In the 1960s, small-scale private farmers had generally been encouraged to see in the large-scale state farms the 'model' of the future, incorporating the most modern productive techniques available and realising the economies of scale viewed as essential for rapid increases in output and income. In the 1960s, however, the state sector was not conspicuously successful as a 'model' of productive efficiency. On the contrary, it was viewed by many farmers in the private sector as an example of wasted, scarce resources which they themselves would have used more productively. In the later 1970s, however, the 'model' for the private sector became its own CPAs. Modest in physical scale and agricultural techniques and the object of keen interest of neighbouring farmers and of organized visits from more distant areas, they showed every sign of appearing more relevant as institutions and more promising in terms of productive and social advance.

9

POLITICAL PATRONAGE AND COMMUNITY RESISTANCE: VILLAGE COUNCILS IN TRINIDAD AND TOBAGO[1]

Susan Craig

Introduction

In this essay, the state apparatus for promoting community development in Trinidad and Tobago is described and appraised in historical perspective. The core of the study is based on 183 unstructured depth-interviews conducted between 1970 and 1973 in some 40 settlements of varying ethnic composition throughout Trinidad and Tobago. Among those interviewed were Community Development Officers (CDOs) and aides (retired and active); members of youth groups, Friendly Societies, sports clubs, women's groups, religious organizations and political parties; County Councillors, Aldermen and Members of Parliament. Meetings of Village and County Councils were attended. To ensure confidentiality, I have not always given the names of persons interviewed.

The main research strategy — interviews and participant observation — has certain limitations, some of which deserve mention. First, with a study of this focus, it did not permit an exhaustive sociological analysis of the communities visited. Secondly, although notes and quotations were taken during interviews and meetings, much of the recording was done after the fact and the possibility of bias on the part of the researcher in reconstructing and interpreting events becomes acute. Thirdly, the permissibility of generalising from oral evidence and limited observations can be questioned. However, my belief is that the conclusions given are substantially correct. They are corroborated by all the written documentation that is available, by the striking testimony of persons from parts of the country not visited for this research who commented on this thesis, and by the

---

1. *Author's note.* This paper is extracted from *Community Development in Trinidad and Tobago, 1943–1973: From Welfare to Patronage*, Working Paper no. 4, ISER, Un. of the West Indies, Mona, 1974. The original essay described and evaluated the history and functioning of the Village and County Councils in Trinidad and Tobago from their inception in the 1940s to 1973. Because of the constraints of space, only the Village Councils are considered here, and many detailed examples and references in the original are omitted.

Prime Minister's critique of the government and ruling party, the People's National Movement (PNM), in his address to the PNM Convention of 1973. Until more systematic research can refute these findings, they provide an indication of the impotence and malaise into which the local institutions had fallen by 1973.

Social welfare in the 1940s

The social context. The appalling social and economic conditions that led to the uprisings of the working class and small peasants throughout the Caribbean in the 1930s have been well documented, particularly by imperial investigators (Moyne Report, 1945; Forster Report, 1937). So unresponsive was the colonial system to the needs of the population on whose labour it was consolidated that the majority were obliged to rely on their own resources to express their grievances and to procure some form of social welfare.

In Trinidad and Tobago, the calypso became "the most effective political weapon" (Brown, 1947) and a target for the censors. Apart from the fledgling trade union movement and the various informal types of mutual aid practised by the poor, a few of the ethnic-based organizations sought to provide for the needy. But the most energetic local formations which offered social security, in the form of sickness, maternity and death benefits, were the Friendly Societies, of which there were 317 with 83,000 members in 1947 (Wells and Wells, 1953, p. 28).[2]

Social security provided by the state was virtually non-existent before the island-wide rebellion of 1937, and welfare work remained the preserve of the churches and the wives and daughters of the commercial and professional élite. The leading organization in the field was the pioneering Coterie of Social Workers, founded by Miss Audrey Jeffers in 1921 (Maynard, 1971).

The Social Welfare Department. Colonial Development and Welfare, the Moyne Commission's answer to West Indian problems,

2. Since 1888, legislation had been passed to regulate the activities of Friendly Societies. Act no. 18 of 1950, by providing that longstanding members of these societies pay only half subscriptions (and in some cases no subscriptions at all) but receive full benefits, has led to their increased financial embarrassment. This, together with the growing importance of (mostly foreign) insurance companies and the new official National Insurance Scheme, has meant that the membership and strength of Friendly Societies are on the decline. Recent revisions of the 1950 Act have had no appreciable impact on the fortunes of the Friendly Societies. (Interviews with Mr F.G. Maynard, former President of the Association of Friendly Societies, 16 Nov. 1972 and 31 May 1983.) The Friendly Society movement was never very strong in Tobago.

was in essence a palliative. The recommendations on "development" suggested local food production by a more stable peasantry and diversification on the estates which would remain intact. Independence of Britain was deemed "irreconcilable" with the new programme; the Crown Colony system was to continue, albeit with the extension of the franchise and greater popular representation on local authorities (Moyne, 1945, pp. 287, 291). Development turned out to be what Gordon Lewis called "a multitude of minor schemes" (Lewis, 1968, p. 92).

Major importance was attached to "welfare". Although Trinidad and Tobago refused the assistance of the Colonial Development and Welfare Organization at its inception, a Social Welfare Department was established in 1939 to improve on existing social services. Its initial emphasis was on giving assistance to the chronically sick and aged and to needy children, reflecting the "relief" concept typical of the time (Lloyd and Robertson, 1971, p. 5).

Not until after 1943, when Miss Dora Ibberson assumed the position of Social Welfare Officer, was any policy for correcting social ills clearly spelled out in a document produced by an advisory Social Welfare Committee nominated by the Governor in 1944. Here the needs of the countryside were identified as the following: recreation and cultural facilities; "moral welfare and rescue work"; medico-social work; "women's work" — child care, nutrition etc.; cottage industries, poor relief, care of the aged, probation, "children's work" and attention to the social side of housing and land settlement (Council Paper no. 33 of 1945, p. 1). The practical recommendations called for a corps of officers, of whom the five senior ones would be British and responsible for training local recruits. The rest would include rural welfare officers — the first Community Development Officers (CDOs) — and staff to work with other departments. A voluntary, non-profit organization, Trinidad and Tobago Ltd., patterned after Jamaica Welfare Ltd. (which was led by Norman Manley), would take care of "rural work", cooperatives and cottage industries.

The early years of the Social Welfare Department were spent in cautious experimentation (Armstrong, c. 1955). Between 1943 and 1948, when the Department was closed down, its essential accomplishments were as follows. First, a corps of local men and women — among them Carlton Ottley, Eileen Armstrong, George Sinanan, Victor McIntyre, Olga Shurland and Jeremiah Saunders — almost entirely drawn from the teaching service — were sent to Mona to be trained. Through these officers, the Department was able to establish itself at county level. Particular devotion was paid to what is called "women's work".[3] Finally, a number of advisory Village Councils (VCs), then called Welfare or Community Councils, were established in various districts, as committees of representatives from all voluntary groups. The Councils organized the building of community centres on a "dollar-for-dollar" basis (half the cost being borne by the state); and classes in handicraft, nutrition and like subjects were conducted under their auspices. All of this activity by-passed the existing local government bodies. These programmes were essentially remedial, ignoring the fundamental arrangements of the political economy.

Much of this activity was well received by the rural villagers who supported the VCs in the hope that they would bring needed amenities. But in an era when the progressive forces in the Caribbean were demanding self-government, the imposition of a bevy of foreign senior officers was galling to several of the local politicians. Tito Achong, one-time Mayor of Port of Spain, remarked with typical acidity: "The official social welfare missionaries brought in [*sic*] the West Indies move among the people as whales among minnows." And he aptly observed that the assumption underlying 'welfare' was that "social happiness can flourish on a foundation of wage slavery with its corollaries — bad housing and disease, illiteracy and crime. [. . .] One of the immediate needs of Port of Spain is additional housing for the people as a whole. But the Comptroller of Welfare could hardly give any help . . . for housing, education and social medicine have been assigned to other hands" (Achong, 1944, pp. 203–4). Albert Gomes, Patrick Solomon, Ranjit Kumar and Chanka Maharaj were among those who criticised the emphasis on welfare as the panacea of the time.[4]

---

3. Activities with women's groups in the 1940s were often under the influence of the Governor's wife of the day, and of the European women who lived in the villages. "Lady Dorothy" at Plymouth, Tobago, and Mrs de Pompignon at Mayaro, Trinidad, were examples of the latter. Such women could use their influence among other proprietors to get gifts for "their" village. The building of the village hall at Mayaro owes much to Mrs de Pompignon and the Women's Institute. In 1948, the then Governor's wife, Lady Shaw, is said to have used her influence to ensure that a skeleton staff which would promote "women's work" would be retained after the Social Welfare Department closed down (interview with Miss Olga Shurland, retired Community Development Officer, 7 May 1972). See also Molly Huggins (1967) for her intervention into "women's work" in Jamaica. One of her concerns was for the infrequency of legal marriage among the Jamaican poor. She imported 2,000 gold wedding rings and assisted a coterie of middle-class women, led by Mrs Mary Morris Knibb, to organise a series of mass weddings throughout the country (*ibid.*, p. 117). See also Louise Bennett's comments in 'Mass Wedding' (1966, p. 30).

4. Patrick Solomon and Ranjit Kumar, quoted in *Trinidad Guardian*, 6 Mar. 1948,

Opposition from the politicians was matched by that of the churches and the Coterie of Social Workers. The latter resented the introduction of expatriates to do essentially what they had been doing all along, and feared official control over their activities. Certainly, Miss Jeffers of the Coterie confessed in 1948 that she "shared no sorrow" at the departure of the British welfare officers (*Trinidad Guardian*, 6 March 1948, p. 2). In addition, the Social Welfare Department suffered from serious disabilities: it was unable to influence other government departments and was largely ignored. And though the essence of British policy was social reform through welfare, the departments in the Caribbean were described by the first adviser to the Comptroller of Colonial Development and Welfare as "handy administrative dustbins in which to get rid of inconvenient governmental functions" . . . (Simey, 1946, pp. 92–3). Expenditure on welfare was drastically cut in the Budget of 1948. Probation services were attached to the Judiciary, public assistance was allowed to continue; and the eight Rural Welfare Officers were transferred to the Ministry of Education as the Education Extension Department.

One of the lessons to be learnt from the experience of "welfare" was, as Albert Gomes put it, that the country must "forget embroidered curtains and return to their own *te-le-le*".[5]

The policies of the 1950s

The orphan child. The fortunes of the community development apparatus after 1948 indicated the extent to which there was no clear conception of the importance of such activity. As one of its senior officers put it, the Department became the "orphan child" of the administration, shunted from Ministry to Ministry.

By 1955, the full complement of staff — field, clerical and supervisory — in Education Extension was twenty-one. There existed 170 village councils, 116 women's groups and 285 youth clubs with which the officers worked. Already thirty-one community centres had been built by voluntary labour and handicraft classes were conducted in sixty-six districts (*Administrative Report*, 1955, p. 2). In 1950, through the initiative of Carlton Ottley, the Department's Director, a biennial Arts Festival, which included folk arts, was

---

p. 2; Chanka Maharaj, questions nos 27 and 28, Trinidad and Tobago *Hansard*, 1947, p. 348; Albert Gomes, 1974, pp. 72–5.

5. Quoted in *Port of Spain Gazette*, 7 Mar. 1948, p. 5. "Te-le-le" was a cheap cotton fabric, commonly bought by working-class women for dressmaking. Freely translated, the warning was that the country could only develop by its own efforts, however humble these might be.

started; it was successful in gaining widespread popular support from all ethnic groups and from the schools.

In 1956, shortly after the PNM came to power, the Department was transferred to the Ministry of Health and Social Services. In 1958, the name of the service was changed to Community Development ànd it was placed under the Ministry of Labour, Co-operatives and Social Services. This first post-war attempt to bring the social services together was short-lived ànd the Department was moved again in 1959, this time to the Ministry of Home Affairs. In 1962 it was joined with the administration of Local Government. Finally, after the "Meet the People" tour by the Prime Minister, Dr Eric Williams, in 1963, it came to rest in 1964 as a Division of the Prime Minister's Office.

The neo-colonial context. In 1950, the passing of the Pioneer Industries Act began the promotion of a development strategy based on the importation of capital, technology and expertise in order to establish manufacturing industries which would create employment. After the PNM's accession to power in 1956, this strategy was extended on the advice of Teodoro Moscoso of Puerto Rico and Arthur Lewis, the distinguished development economist.

The major social consequences of this strategy have been analysed elsewhere (Craig, 1977; 1982). Suffice it to say that the local variant of the 'Puerto Rican model' had important implications for the practice of community development, since it reinforced features of the social order which were already present under the Crown Colony régime — high unemployment (after 1956, especially within the age cohort 15–24), over-centralisation, heavy urbanisation and an absolute and proportionate decline in the agricultural sector. Agrarian reform and rural development were never seriously emphasised, as the entire axis of the economy shifted to petroleum and urban industry. Once it had been decided that the basic orientation of the development strategy should be directed towards encouraging foreign enterprise, community development was allowed to remain a marginal activity. Indeed, the mobilisation of the resources of the local population was *not necessary* to such a strategy. By 1963, therefore, nearly all the items listed under Social and Community Development in the Second Five-Year Plan were concerned with recreation, the "crash" programmes in public works for unemployment relief being the outstanding exception.[6]

6. *Draft Second Five-Year Plan*, p. 43. In 1958–62, expenditure on Labour and Social Services was $2.3m.; that on "Special Works" was $6m. (*ibid.*, p. 34). The failure of the Puerto Rican model to provide permanent employment within

In 1957, the Depressed Areas Programme was started, first in sugar areas as an *ad hoc* measure to improve roads, privies etc., and later in districts east of Port of Spain to provide employment. It was also used for the "rehabilitation" of prisoners and inmates of Caura Sanatorium and the orphanages. Under the First Five-Year Plan, $1 million were allocated to the programme; $6m. were actually spent, most of it in the urban areas of the capital region. As unemployment was to become a more critical problem for the government, the compass of the programme became wider, and with it the disenchantment of the people. The "Meet the People" tour of 1963 was decisive in this.

The Prime Minister's 1963 tour and the "New" policies

The "Meet the People" tour: 1963. In March 1963, the Prime Minister began a series of tours of the various counties, an event which marked the crucial turning-point in the fortunes of the community development services.

Four major problems emerged from the tour. First, land hunger in the midst of land plenty was widespread (Counties Caroni, Tobago, St Patrick, St Andrew/St David). Secondly, there was high unemployment in both town and country. Thirdly, public services and amenities for health, recreation, transport, roads, and postal and other means of communication were poor. Farmers also complained of the lack of production, marketing and credit facilities. Finally, the people complained of the high degree of centralisation of the state machinery, and the inability of local institutions to affect the course of policy or to satisfy local needs. "I get the feeling", said the Prime Minister, "that there is a certain lack of liaison to link the government and the citizen . . ." (*Trinidad Guardian*, 28 Mar. 1963).

The official response was consistent with the tenor of the régime. A series of *ad hoc* committees was set up to inquire into the working of several government departments. Ten years later, similar investigations were being conducted anew. The answer to the landlessness of the farmers was a most unplanned and spontaneous distribution of Crown lands. In 1959 one application for Crown lands had been granted, and in 1960 three. But between March 1963 and February

---

Puerto Rico has led to a large-scale emigration to the eastern seaboard of the United States, and to an increasing disbursement of aid in the form of welfare. By 1978, the United States were granting $2 billion annually in direct welfare benefits and food stamps to Puerto Rico, and some 70% of the population were eligible for this "aid" (González Díaz, 1980, p. 43).

1964, no fewer than 7,700 applications were approved by Cabinet (*The Nation*, 7 Feb. 1964, p. 2). The hundreds of memoranda read to the Prime Minister had suggested that the planning machinery should embrace the people at the lowest levels in a continuous process. The action of the government thereafter negated any such possibility. During and after 1963, the Prime Minister displayed a penchant for "direct democracy", a personalist approach to communication with the population. This was pursued through tours — "Meet the Farmers", "Meet the Manufacturers" — along with national conferences and consultations. Such procedures are always *ad hoc*, by-pass existing institutions and seek to be a substitute for the normal democratic process (cf. Best, 1963).

Moreover, the new programmes were financed by the major transnational corporations operating in the country and were clearly an attempt to pacify the populace. In May 1963, the Prime Minister met Augustus Long of Texaco, David Rockefeller of Chase Manhattan Bank and other high-level company executives, and established what was called the "Better Village Programme". Texaco gave $8.5m. to Trinidad and Tobago for rural development; Chase Manhattan offered to provide two experts on agricultural credit, health services and tractor pools. A Better Village Programme Committee, comprising nominees of the government and representatives of the metropolitan companies, was formed and remained distinct from the Community Development Department.

The Second Five-Year Plan was published in August 1963, and did not embrace a conception of rural development based on the needs articulated to the Prime Minister. Instead, it expressed the hope ("It is expected . . .") that aid from the foreign firms would be forthcoming (p. 287) and cited possible areas of action. Further, no permanent machinery was established to involve the working people in decision-making for the localities. Significantly, the county councils, most of which were then controlled by the opposition, were ignored.

The net effect of the tour was to enhance the importance of the Prime Minister to the localities. It is not without irony that Dr Williams himself could say: "Most of all, we shall always remember the impact of the tour on the people themselves. No better medium could have been devised for bringing the Prime Minister close to the people and the people close to the Prime Minister" (*The Nation*, 7 Feb. 1964, p. 10). Finally, during the tour, the potential of the Village Councils for mobilising support and as a channel for benefits was clearly recognised. In May 1963 Dr Williams called on members of the ruling party, the PNM, at Couva to do what *The Nation* called "the follow-up work", by joining and influencing the village organizations (*ibid.*, 31 May 1963, p. 1). Similar messages were given at Arima in June, 1963, both by the Prime Minister and by Mr Thomasos, then Speaker of the House of Representatives. The latter is reported to have said: "Members [of the PNM] should get into these organizations and make the influence of the Party felt, so that they may win through the groups what was needed in the community" (*The Nation*, 28 June 1963, p. 10). Again, during the "Meet the Party" tour of 1964, the point was stressed to party groups around the country (cf. *The Nation*, 26 June 1964, p. 2).

Along with a new emphasis on Village Councils as the mouthpiece of the localities and the channels through which benefits to the people/party would be derived, the decision came to promote community development. This would consist of community centres, handicraft training and production, Prime Minister's Best Village Competitions, and the intensification of "crash" programmes, now designated Better Village Programmes. Under the Prime Minister's portfolio and patronage, the stage was set for Better Village and Best Village — bread (crumbs) and circuses.

The policies outlined (1971–1973)

Community Development Division. After 1963, the Department was no longer starved of funds. The complement of staff grew over the years, numbering in 1971 at least 84. Among the new posts created were those of community development aides, of whom there were 21 in 1971, and youth aides. The aides are all political appointees, whose duties include reporting to their political leader on local activities. In 1973, most of the aides were PNM members. The officers in the field were "bogged down", as one supervisor put it, with organizing the various competitions initiated by the Prime Minister: Best Village Trophy Competition, National Youth Arts and Craft Exhibition, Village Olympics, Food Fair. This left little time for what they understood by community development, and resulted in what a senior officer called the "malaise" of the Division.

By 1973, the Better Village Programme Committee had ceased to exist and Mr A.A. Thompson, its former Chairman, went so far as to describe it as "just old talk", having only established "good will" between the transnational companies and the government (interview with Mr A.A. Thompson, 21 Feb. 1973).

Handicraft and adult education classes. After 1968, there was an intensification of handicraft training and production. The staff, which in the late 1940s consisted of two persons, increased by 1972 to 4 senior officers, 12 manager–tutors and 212 part-time tutors in the field (*ibid.*) Several handicraft production and sales centres were provided but most are outside of the main shopping areas and are more useful for buying material than for selling finished products. Between 1967 and 1971, sales — whether of raw material or of finished products — never exceeded purchases in these centres (*Administrative Report*, 1971, App. VIII). And apart from two successful outlets in Tobago and the few privately-run co-operatives, handicraft is not a feasible economic proposition for most of the beneficiaries of the classes.

Adult education classes are undertaken throughout the country. Some are useful to housewives, but the courses offer no certificate, and it is difficult for the trainees to find jobs. CDOs complained that response to the courses was poor, that they were arbitrarily chosen and did not necessarily lead to employment. In Tobago in 1972, the situation was critical, for the Division of Labour was offering similar courses to those of the adult education programme. The duplication of effort served to underline the uselessness of the latter.

The Youth Development Programme. Much of the youth work of the Division is channelled through registered youth groups, and sporting and cultural clubs, the number of which exceeded 400 in 1973. In each county, there is an Assembly of Youth to which local youth groups send delegates, and the apex of the organizational structure is the National Youth Council (NYC).

Apart from the education classes, the major training schemes for young people are provided in the five youth camps, one of which is in Tobago, and the Kendal Farm School (Tobago). A comprehensive evaluation of these services is provided by the first and second interim reports of the National Task Force on Youth. The vocational training in the camps was found to be inadequate in view of the paucity of facilities and the lack of exposure to practical assignments. Task Force recommended a period of apprenticeship to skilled tradesmen as one way of overcoming this. The greatest disappointment was the teaching of agriculture in the youth camps. There was a lack of facilities for practical agriculture, no viable farm enterprises were attached to the camps, and the teaching facilities were poor. The placement service for graduates of the camps and the Kendal Farm School needed considerable improvement.

The reports of the Task Force convey a profound sense of dissatisfaction with the present involvement of youth in the 'development effort'. When we consider that the young bear the burden of much of the unemployment in the country, we can appreciate one of the factors contributing to the emergence of young people as political dissidents.

The Special Works Programme. After 1963, the designation of these public works projects was changed to 'Better Village' and 'Special Works' programmes, financed from the annual development budget. According to an official 'Appraisal of the Special Works Programme' (Ministry of Planning and Development, 1972, Appendix I), County St George, with the largest urban concentration, has dominated both the number of projects and the proportion of expenditure.

In 1970, at the height of the rebellion in the country, the Prime Minister announced that, in addition to the Prime Minister's Special Works Programme, there was to be the Prime Minister's Special Programme Works, financed from an Unemployment Levy which would be raised for that purpose (*Express*, 24 Mar. 1970, p. 1). The former is administered by the Community Development Division, and the latter, now renamed Development and Environmental Works Division (DEWD), by the Ministry of Works.

Between 1968 and 1971, $32 million was spent on these projects, of which 80% was on road maintenance and less than 5% on access roads for agriculture (Appraisal . . ., 1972). The official appraisal lists several fundamental problems with these projects (*ibid.*, pp. 7–8). Details of expenditure from the Community Development Division were not available because the relative costs of material and labour were not known. Recruitment was often through Members of Parliament (MPs), and labour was therefore difficult to discipline, since the workers believed that they owed their employment to contact and patronage. The policy of rotating labour ensured no continuous system of operations. Moreover, since deliveries of materials often occurred *outside* normal working hours and there was no proper checking or accounting system, the rate of supply of materials was not predictable. Payment was also made on the basis of delivery bills presented by the contractors, a system which invited irregularities in the absence of adequate checks.

The dramatic expansion of these programmes after 1963, and again after 1970, has to be seen partly as a palliative from above, and partly as a testimony to the quantitative and qualitative expansion of the unemployed from below. There have thus been constant tensions, at times overt and at times implicit, between the politicians' attempt at manipulation and the thrust for autonomy, away from state control, among the unemployed themselves. Up to 1973, the CDOs were usually oblivious of the decision-making whereby projects were located in the various districts, even though a part of the programme was administered by the Division. Even the PNM VCs had little control over either the location of the projects or recruitment to them, although they submitted lists of the unemployed and needy to the authorities.[7] The only persons interviewed who claimed knowledge of how projects and jobs were distributed were PNM County Councillors and leading activists, all of the latter being also leading VC members. It seems that the relative strength of the politicians and ardent supporters of the PNM over the administration was the critical factor.[8] However, in several areas attempts have been made by the unemployed to seize control over the projects and to initiate some form of development more relevant to their needs. The most articulate instances of this have been in East Dry River, as described by Howe and Rennie (1982), and in the occupation of the district office of the DEWD by residents of John John (*Express*, 12 July 1983, p. 3).

The Special Works have made very little impact on the problem of providing meaningful full-time employment. They have not been conceived as the short-term aspect of long-term programmes and have been subject to the caprice and power of individual politicians. In the context of the general administrative breakdown in the country, the beneficiaries regard the jobs as bribes and prolong the work as much as possible. The very arbitrariness of the arrangements for the projects allows them to become the spoils of party patronage; at the same time, it leads to poor planning, improper accounting, bribery, corruption, low productivity and waste of resources. Therefore, the lamentations of a former Minister of Labour about 'irregularities' and inadequate supervision in the programme reek of a kind of innocence that passes all understanding (*Trinidad Guardian*, 21 Dec. 1972, p. 1).

The policies in practice (1971–1973)

The Village Councils. In 1971, there were 457 village and community councils,[9] which are supposed to be voluntary, apolitical, advisory bodies of all individuals aged over eighteen within their boundaries.

7. Complaints about this were numerous and widespread: for example, at Parlatuvier, Indian Trail, Matelot, Felicity, John John.
8. The Prime Minister's Convention Address (1973, p. 29) supports this view: "To stop the improper practices and waste associated with selection of workers for the Special Works Programme, whether by village council, or worse still by Constituency Representatives, we have introduced the system of registration and recruitment by the Ministry of Labour. I have noticed the growing dissatisfaction with that decision by those who want to keep the patronage in their own hands. . . ." Political intervention did not cease with the system of registration.
9. *Administrative Report*, 1971, p. 3. This probably includes defunct VCs, since the election returns for VCs in 1971 mention the existence of only 287 councils. At any rate, the numbers are no indication of the level of activity in these organizations.

Each council's boundaries are often fixed by the people themselves, and often reflect local rivalries.

The most striking feature of the VCs is their composition. In all but two of the districts observed — Belle Garden (Tobago) and Felicity (Trinidad) — the core of the VC activists were also members of the PNM and aged over thirty-five. Where the population was predominantly African, women outnumbered men in the councils. In areas of mixed ethnic composition, even where Indians form the majority of the population, the VC members were usually Africans with few if any Indians (e.g. Rio Claro, Balmain, Couva — and when the VC existed, St Margaret's Village, Indian Trail). Young people stay away from these councils and there are generally disputes between them and the VC activists, especially over jobs and over the use of community centres which are controlled by the councils. In rare instances where substantial numbers of young people attended the VC meetings, they nonetheless referred to themselves as 'the Youth Group' as opposed to 'the Village Council' (e.g. at Red Hill, D'Abadie, where the young people had joined the VC only on the encouragement of the CDO [VC meetings, Red Hill, May and June 1972]).

The two non-PNM VCs deserve mention. In Felicity the Council, dormant since 1969, was revived in July 1972 by members of the Democratic Labour Party (DLP) because a Special Works project was being started in the area and they wished to ensure that not only PNM supporters would be employed (interviews with four VC members, Felicity, August 1972; *Express*, 20 Nov. 1972, p. 17). A leading member of the PNM in the village, herself a Special Works employee, reported that the project had been established through the influence of the PNM MPs for the area and that the *party group*, in deciding who would work, "tried to be fair, since we all live in Felicity. We gave jobs to some from the party group, some from the Village Council" (interview, 16 Aug. 1972).

In Belle Garden in 1972, the leading VC activists were members of the Democratic Action Congress who had ousted the PNM, including some of the founders of the Council. The VC was very militant and had been able to bring out the villagers in a boycott of the local school in 1970, so forcing the administration to remove the Principal. It had also intervened to prevent the recruitment of youths on the basis of party affiliation to the Kendal Farm School; it had caused another teacher to be removed (1971); and it had prevented a licence being given to operate a snackette near the school (1972). In 1972, it organized its own folk concerts in villages throughout Tobago, having since 1968 refused to participate in the Prime Minister's Best Village Competition "until the Prime Minister gets better" (interviews, Belle Garden, July and November, 1972).

The normal composition of the VC movement can be explained by three main factors. First, some of the people who formed the VCs in the 1940s and 1950s have remained in them over the years. These were·everywhere the people who later joined the PNM, many of them becoming important party activists and County Councillors. Men like Councillor Fuentes (Rio Claro), ex-Councillor Mylan Meschier (Mayaro), Luther Nelson (Fyzabad), Victor Barclay (Princes Town) and Councillor Desmond Baxter (Balmain) spring readily to mind. Secondly, PNM members have been explicitly urged from 1963 onwards to join and influence these organizations. Once they became identified with partisan interests in spite of their non-partisan constitution, those opposed to the PNM have kept away, or affiliated without becoming active in the VCs, in order to use amenities such as the community centres.

Thirdly, the abstention of all but a few party stalwarts from the VCs is due to the failure of these bodies to "deliver the goods" that are important to their localities. The fortunes of several VCs have risen and fallen with the Special Works projects, since these are the chief source of new employment, especially in the rural areas. The Supervisor for County Caroni asserted that throughout his district, VCs thrived with crash programmes and failed thereafter (interview, 31 July 1972). In Moruga as early as 1968, Hauofa's study revealed that the VC was regarded "almost entirely as an employment agency" (1968, p. 90). The capacity of the VCs to win work and amenities depends not on the councils *per se*, but on the influence of the *party activists* who are their leaders. It rests on the relative strength of these local power brokers within the party/state hierarchy. Often, this leadership is highly personalist, the villagers becoming clients of these local patrons. These services are a mixed blessing for the VCs. The supervisors of two counties complained of "undue" intrusion of party politics in the VCs. One of them remarked: "In all the councils, all the councils, you will find divisions because of politics" (interview, 26 May 1972).

The writings of several independent observers corroborate these findings in various ways. Hauofa (*ibid.*), Freilich (1960, pp. 90–100), the Niehoffs (1960, p. 70), all noted as early as the 1960s the African and PNM composition, the low membership and the ineffectiveness of the VCs in Moruga, Tamana and Penal respectively. Bason, a senior consultant on community development, observed the loss of support for the VCs in Counties Caroni and St David "because of what can be described as the subtle undertones of party politics discernible in the management of the councils" (1963, p. 12). A journalist, reporting on Cedros, whose villagers brought out a protest band in the 1970 Carnival to remind the authorities that they were a part of Trinidad, wrote of the 'ineffectiveness of the village council whose sole function . . . was to prepare for the Better Village Competition. The shell of a community centre, with heaps of bricks overrun with vines and grass, stands in mute testimony to the lack of community co-operation' (*Trinidad Guardian*, 25 Jan. 1973, p. 7.) Finally, the Prime Minister himself, echoing Pontius Pilate, asserted: 'I have frequently advised party members against operating in voluntary organisations of village councils as if they were spokesmen of a political party . . . and I have always been considerably upset by the extent to which a village divides on political lines, sometimes aggravated by racial distinctions" (1973, p. 31).

The VCs in the last decades have shown little sign of self-help and initiative in their activities. Their main thrust has been to provide the personnel for courses in handicraft and adult education classes, to participate in the Prime Minister's Best Village and other competitions and to make repeated requests for amenities. In Mafeking and several districts in Tobago, villagers refused to give voluntary labour for the building of community centres; and local initiative was usually confined to the organization of a few nursery schools (interview with Mr D.W. Rogers, consultant to the Prime Minister, 3 Jan. 1973). In a few cases, villagers, frustrated at the tardiness of the authorities, organized to repair the roads and drains in their area.

Social implications

The political control of the VC movement by the ruling party, whose supporters are largely of African descent, has generated, dialectically, political and cultural resistance from the local groups opposed to the PNM. The cases of Felicity and Belle Garden above illustrate this. In villages with large Indian populations, political and ethnic cleavages have tended to coincide, and this research revealed four modes of response to PNM hegemony.

In Balmain, the Indians accommodated to the PNM dominance of the VC by forming their own *"panchayati"* group to give members communal support in procuring materials and utensils for weddings and religious festivals. Theirs was a policy of *instrumental affiliation* to the VC only to ensure the use of the community centre by the group (discussion with six villagers, Balmain, 1 and 6 Aug. 1972).

In Rio Claro, Couva and Spring Village, the strategy was one of *withdrawal and self-reliance*. By 1972, the Rio Claro Maha Sabha temple had become the "Indian community centre", where independent classes were held (interview with Mr Sidney Dougdeen, retired County Councillor [DLP], 3 July 1972). The leader of the VC complained: "Nearly all [the VC members] are PNM. Only about three Indian members . . . Not for nothing at all, nothing, nothing, nothing, they [Indians] don't use the centre" (interview, 30 June 1972). A similar response was observed at Couva. In Spring Village, repeated attempts to revive the VC failed because the villagers refused to be co-opted into the services offered by the Department when their concerns were with land tenure, drainage, water and other amenities which the VC was powerless to provide. In 1972, they were building a community centre purely on their own resources.

A third response was *open conflict*. In Union Village near Rio Claro, shortly before the general elections of 1971, the VC became defunct because a dispute over jobs on the Special Works project broke out into physical violence between Indian and African factions. The leader of the African faction admitted: "We wanted everybody to be PNM and they didn't want to be. So . . ." (interview, 24 June 1972). Both factions agreed that the MP for the area had asked the PNM leader to suggest names for the Special Works project. No Indian was included and only PNM supporters were favoured. "It was not until the watchman (the husband of the PNM leader) was ambushed one night that jobs were given next day to a few East Indians." For "ambushed" read severely beaten. A young Indian was found guilty of assault in court for this incident; both factions perceived each other in racial terms (interviews, Union Village, 24 and 28 June 1972). After twelve years of existence, the VC had not managed to procure water, electricity, a school, a post office or a registrar of births and deaths for the area.

Finally, Navet is an example of *uneasy peace* between the ethnic groups in the VC. But at every general election, the VC would go into recess for three weeks before and two weeks after it. The village is predominantly Indian in composition and the impotence of the VC caused its members to consider forming a PNM group instead, although they did not support the PNM. The area CDO had discouraged this.[10]

Relations between the VCs and the young people were also affected adversely over the control and use of the community centres.[11] In 1971, there were 169 of these centres, built partly at

10. It is possible that these modes of resistance and accommodation to local cleavages occurred as well in villages which were homogeneously African. This research was more concerned with the implications of the policies for inter-ethnic relations.

11. Examples of these disputes were observed at Rio Claro, Rancho Quemado, Balmain, Indian Trail, Mayaro, John John; and at Black Rock and Les Coteaux

public expense, and under the control of a few VC activists or in some cases, a single individual. By 1972, government found it necessary to set up a committee to examine vandalism in community centres (*Express*, 24 Nov. 1972, p. 40).

The most popular aspect of the official policies since 1963 is, without doubt, the Prime Minister's Best Village Trophy Competition in which villagers compete in performances of local culture. Official support for this competition was matched by official neglect of the biennial Arts Festival, which folded after 1972 through lack of interest. The annual event organized by the Prime Minister has brought to the national stage and the television many aspects of the local folk tradition, giving entertainment to the audiences and a sense of importance to the participants. However, the competition has always reflected the politics of village life, and a low level of Indian participation led the Prime Minister to introduce "village integration" as a category in 1974. The authorities were asked "to instruct villages to integrate their music, dance and drama to include all ethnic groups" (*Trinidad Guardian*, 25 May 1974, p. 1). The Indian folk tradition in Trinidad lives on mainly through the independent activity of the "carriers" of that tradition.

Preparation for the competition has often taken precedence over economically useful pursuits. In 1972, forty out of the group of eighty-six who won the first prize for Mount St George were unemployed; no adult education class was offered in their village (*Trinidad Guardian*, 25 Nov. 1972, p. 6). Indian Trail received classes in folk dancing, but in nothing else. The VC president remarked: "It appears as if we have no voice" (interview, 23 Aug. 1973). The supreme irony was the case of Matelot, one of the most remote and neglected villages in the country. In 1972, villagers reported that the Special Works project was established to allow them to earn cash in order to participate in the competition (interviews, Matelot, 24 Sept. 1972). In September 1972, a delegation from the village went to the Prime Minister to inform him that they had no water supply, no electricity, no telephone; the post office opened irregularly; the health services were bad and the road appalling. One year later, the villagers travelled again the weary road to Whitehall to complain that their conditions had worsened in the interim. Still, they prepared $1,800 worth of produce, wild meat and

in Tobago. Both Dr C. Joseph when Minister of State for Community Development and Mr D.W. Rogers, former consultant to the Prime Minister, reported that such disputes were frequently brought to their notice (interviews with both officials, 3 Jan. 1973). See also National Task Force on Youth, First Interim Report, p. 5.

handicraft for the Prime Minister's Folk Fair in 1972 and were unable to participate because the bus reached the village late. For the Best Village competition, the bus went to another village by mistake (*Trinidad Guardian*, 10 November 1972). These examples form part of the chilling material context for the promotion of folk culture.

Conclusion

As defined by the United Nations and officially in Trinidad and Tobago, community development

connote(s) the processes by which the efforts of the people themselves are united with those of governmental authorities to improve the economic, social and cultural conditions of communities.[. . .] This complex of processes is then made up of two essential elements: the participation of the people themselves in efforts to improve their level of living with as much reliance as possible on their own initiative, and the provision of technical and other services in ways which encourage initiative, self-help and mutual aid . . . (quoted in *Our Community*. vol. I, no. 10, 1970).

By contrast, the practice of the state has emphasised brokerage politics through local leaders who perform personal and partisan services on behalf of clients, and has reduced emphasis on self-help and mutual aid in favour of programmes initiated by the central government. It should also be stressed that the strategy for development since 1956 has failed to satisfy the needs of the localities which were clearly identified to the Prime Minister during the Meet the People Tour of 1963. In so far as the community development apparatus has facilitated "the ways in which party politicians distribute public jobs or special favours in exchange for electoral support" (Weingrod, 1968, p. 379), it has to be seen as a system of patronage. As a corollary, it may well be that local initiative and autonomous participation from below are incompatible with the practices of the neo-colonial state (cf. Ngugi, 1981).

The community development machinery, while remaining within the mould of the colonial era, by a peculiar coincidence of factors, has served as a mechanism whereby the Prime Minister and the upper echelons of the ruling party have been able to maintain close contact with the party's rank and file, to mobilise support and expressions of loyalty, and to provide jobs and a limited number of amenities under the *de facto* control of the party. The emasculation of the Village Councils (VCs) and of county and municipal authorities has enhanced the importance of the central government and the Prime Minister in the political process.

Between 1973 and 1983, nothing has changed to warrant revision of this thesis. In 1981 a Ministry of Community Development and Local Government was established, thus removing the service from the Prime Minister's portfolio; but the programmes remained the same. In February 1983, the government published a 'Draft Policy Paper on Community Development and Local Government', stating: 'In many areas of Trinidad and Tobago, the village or community council is not representative of the people residing in that district'' (p. 14). The causes of this fact are not analysed; and nothing serious is proposed about the reorganization of the composition of the Village Councils, whose members overlap so greatly with the PNM party groups that it is impossible in many areas for the two to meet simultaneously.

Reform of the functions of these village bodies is once more under consideration. But to give greater powers and executive capacity to the VCs with their *present* composition would merely be to deepen the political, ethnic and inter-generational conflicts which this research describes. Yet the VCs represent an undeniable potential base for popular participation in decision making and policy implementation at the local level, although this possibility has so far been subverted by the politics of welfare and of patronage in which they have been enmeshed.

Provision of social welfare by the state carries within it a hidden potential for "regulating the poor" (Piven and Cloward, 1972). But it is gratifying to record, both from the official publications and the experience of the disaffected, the subtler aspects of the resistance from below to manipulation from above. It is this resistance which ensures that the Caribbean people are not victims but in the final analysis protagonists of their fate.

REFERENCES

Official documents

Government of Trinidad and Tobago

Achong, T., *The Mayor's Annual Report, 1942-43*, Port of Spain City Council, 1944.
Bason, G., "Report on a Survey of Village Councils and Community Centres", Ministry of Local Government and Community Development, mimeo, 1963.
Community Development Department, *Administrative Reports*, 1955, 1957, 1958, 1965, 1966, 1969, 1971.
——,*Our Community*, 1970-1.
Draft Second Five-Year Plan, Govt. Printery, Port of Spain, 1963.
Legislative Council, *Hansard*, 1947-8.
——,*Report of the Social Welfare Officer*, Paper no. 33, 1945.

Ministry of Local Government and Community Development, *A Draft Policy Paper on Community Development and Local Government*, Govt. Printery, Port of Spain, 1983.

Ministry of Planning and Development, *Budget Speeches*, Govt. Printery, Port of Spain, 1959–73.

"An Appraisal of the Special Works Programme and the Special Programme Works", mimeo, 1972.

National Task Force on Youth, "First and Second Interim Reports", mimeo, n.d.

Great Britain

Report of the Commission on the Trinidad and Tobago Disturbances, 1937 (Forster Report), HMSO, London, 1938.

Wells, A.F. & D., *Friendly Societies in the West Indies*, Colonial Research Publications, HMSO, London, 1953.

West India Royal Commission Report (Moyne Report), Cmd. 6607, HMSO, London, 1945.

Articles, pamphlets and monographs

Armstrong, E., "A Study of Community Development in Trinidad and Great Britain, with special reference to the work of women", presented for the Associateship of the University of London, Inst. of Education, unpub., 1955.

Bennett, L., *Jamaica Labrish*, Sangster's Bookstore, Kingston, 1966.

Best, L., "The Caribbean Today", series of articles in *Trinidad Guardian*, Sept. 1963.

Brown, W., *Angry Men, Laughing Men: The Caribbean Cauldron*, Greenberg, New York, 1947.

Craig, S., "The Germs of An Idea", afterword to Arthur Lewis, *Labour in the West Indies*, New Beacon Books, London, 1977.

—— "Background to the 1970 Confrontation in Trinidad and Tobago" in S. Craig (ed.), *Contemporary Caribbean: A Sociological Reader*, vol. II, Susan Craig, St Augustine, 1982.

Freilich, M., *Cultural Diversity Among Trinidadian Peasants*, Ann Arbor microfilm., 1960.

Gomes, A., *Through A Maze of Colour*, Key Publications, Port of Spain, 1974.

Gonzalez Diaz, E., "Las bases para el consenso político en la colonia: problema de la democracia en Puerto Rico", *Casa de las Américas*, no. 123, Nov.–Dec. 1980.

Hauofa, E., "Village-Government Communication: A Case Study in Trinidad", unpubl. MA thesis, McGill University, 1968.

Huggins, M., *Too Much To Tell*, Heinemann, London, 1967.

Lewis, G., *The Growth of the Modern West Indies*, McGibbon and Kee, London, 1968.

Lloyd, A. and E. Robertson, *Social Welfare in Trinidad and Tobago*, Antilles Research Associates, St Augustine., 1971.

Maynard, O., *The Briarend Pattern*, Busby's Printerie, Port of Spain, 1971.

Ngugi wa Thiong'o, *Detained: A Writer's Prison Diary*, Heinemann Educational Books, London, 1981.

Niehoff, A. and J., *East Indians in the West Indies*, Milwaukee Public Museum, Milwaukee, 1960.

Piven F.F. and R. Cloward, *Regulating the Poor: The Functions of Public Welfare*, Vintage Books, New York, 1972.

Simey, T. *Welfare and Planning in the West Indies*, Oxford University Press, 1946.

Weingrod, A., "Politics, Patronage and Political Parties", *Comparative Studies in Society and History*, vol. X, no. 4, July 1968.

Williams, E., *Address to the Annual Convention of the People's National Movement*, PNM Publishing House, Port of Spain, 1973.

Newspapers

Express, daily newspaper, Port of Spain, 1970–3.
Port of Spain Gazette, defunct daily newspaper, Port of Spain, 1947–9.
The Nation, organ of People's National Movement, Port of Spain, 1962–4.
Trinidad Guardian, daily newspaper, Port of Spain, 1948, 1963, 1972–3.

10

AGRICULTURAL EXTENSION FOR RURAL TRANSFORMATION: THE C.A.E.P.MODEL

Thomas H. Henderson and Michael Quinn Patton

Agricultural extension services exist in most parts of the world, but there is tremendous variation in their function, structure and effectiveness. This partly reflects differences in agricultural systems. Gunnar Myrdal comments on this diversity in his important book, *The Challenge of World Poverty*:

Perhaps in no other field of economic activity are there greater differences among the main underdeveloped regions in South Asia, Northeast Asia, West Asia, Africa and Latin America, as well as among individual countries in these regions and even between districts in the several countries, than in the field of agriculture. (Myrdal, 1970, p. 78).

In this article we trace briefly the development of agricultural extension services in the English-speaking Caribbean. Our review will make clear that there is substantial diversity across Caribbean islands in the nature and function of extension. After looking at the historical and cultural roots of extension diversity and tracing the changes over time, we present a model for adapting national extension systems to the unique conditions in each country so that extension can play a critical role in rural transformation and thereby realise its potential for contributing to the wellbeing of rural families. In this regard we believe that the worldwide observations made by Leagans and Loomis in their classic *Behavioral Change in Agriculture* can be applied to the Caribbean:

Extension education offers one of the primary inputs which has yet to be utilized to its potential in most of the developing countries. The emerging need to achieve wide use in the shortest possible time of the highly significant new technological break-throughs by agricultural scientists presents a new imperative to which a viable extension education system may, in fact, hold the key. . . . The lack of success of newly extablished extension systems in many countries stems not from the nature of the extension education process itself, but from default on such requisites as proper conceptualization of its role, administrative organization, staffing, adequate supplies of viable technology, and other conditions required for effectiveness (Leagans and Loomis, 1971, p. 77).

We share this view. This article, then, is an affirmation of the potential contribution extension services can make in the Caribbean if those services are appropriately organized and managed, if agents are properly trained and professionalised, and if sufficient resources are devoted to the extension process.

The historical context

Agricultural extension, in a formal sense, began in the Caribbean in the 1860s with the establishment of the Botanic Gardens. St Vincent, for example, was the first such in the Caribbean and one of the first in the world.[1] They were established in the latter half of the nineteenth century in many of these Caribbean territories. The Botanic Gardens, as the name implies, were mainly concerned with collecting and establishing museum plots of local and exotic plants. They also acted as centres for the propagation and distribution of economically and agriculturally important plants.

In those days, the emphasis in the Caribbean was on the production of sugar and other important export crops. In the last quarter of the century, the sugar industry experienced a serious depression. The sugar producers became alarmed, as did the British government, which was concerned about the welfare of its nationals who were agriculturalists in the region. That alarm led to the establishment of the Royal Commission of 1896, which recommended diversification from sugar into other economic crops, also that the Botanic Gardens system should be extended and, in fact, that each of the islands should have a Botanic Garden. The Royal Commission further recommended the establishment of what was called the Imperial Department of Agriculture which was to have responsibility for agricultural development, research and education in the Leeward Islands, the Windward Islands and Barbados, with its headquarters in Barbados.

There thus emerged at each of the Botanic stations the rudiments of an agriculture department with reduced emphasis on collection of plants and a new emphasis on economic plants, while also attempting to provide an educational and research service to the agricultural producers on how to grow diverse crops economically for export. Staffed by eminent scientists, many of whom had affiliation with British universities, a substantial body of highly useful research was developed by the Imperial Department of Agriculture. Interesting basic and applied work was done on soils, fertiliser trials,

---

1. Purseglove J.W., "History and Functions of Botanic Gardens with Special Reference to Singapore", *Tropical Agriculture*, 34,3, 1957.

varietal trials, and the introduction and testing of new crops.[2]

However, not long after the establishment of the Imperial Department of Agriculture in the early 1900s, it was recognised that although those Botanic Gardens were meant to have an educational influence on agriculture, they were not meeting the needs of small farmers. The latter were generally located on the remote and poor-quality lands while the better and more accessible lands were occupied by the plantations. With easy access to Botanic Gardens, the plantation and colonial producers benefitted from the work of the Gardens, but this did not significantly assist small farmers. In order to reach the latter, a service of agricultural instructors was created. Those instructors were appointed specifically to go out among the small farmers and educate them in the techniques of export farming, especially the various techniques of plant propagation for introducing and establishing new crops.

Agricultural instructors became very important people in the agricultural development of the Caribbean colonies. In those days of difficult communications, with hardly any roads and no mass media, the instructors were provided with the best horses available so that they could reach into the interior. The Botanic Gardens research staff made sure that the Extension Agricultural Instructors were properly trained and knew the appropriate techniques of farm operation. The reports produced in those times are of great interest. For example, in St Lucia one finds the Agricultural Instructor discussing new techniques with a group of farmers. He talked with them in the native patois which the local people understood and used the kinds of techniques still used today — method and result demonstrations. All of this was done right in the fields with the farmers. As a result, in the Leewards and Windwards the export trade in vegetables and other agricultural produce began to improve.

By the 1920s, extension was very active and was a respected element of the agricultural development sector; it was supported as a necessary and effective mechanism for increasing production. The need for training was recognised, not only training of the extension staff, but also of the farmers and the farmers' sons and daughters, in other words the potential farmers of the future. The specific agricultural departments, which were then still the Botanic Gardens, were given the responsibility under the Imperial Department of Agriculture to establish Agricultural Schools or Residential Farm Schools, which provided from six months to two years' training for the sons

2. Henderson T.H., and S. Mahabir, *Fifty Years of Research in Tropical Agriculture: A Bibliography 1922-1972*, Dept. of Agricultural Extension, Un. of the West Indies, St Augustine, 1974.

of farmers. These schools provided training for people who themselves went into farming, as well as training for those who would fill posts within the Agricultural Department.

Also recognised as being necessary and important was the organization of farmers. This was given more emphasis in the larger territories of Trinidad and Jamaica, where, for example, during the latter half of the nineteenth century, we saw the formation of agricultural societies, whose inspiration and leadership came from the large plantation owners.[3] These organizations did not wait for the establishment of extension services by the Imperial Department of Agriculture, but themselves established Advisory Services to provide necessary educational and service facilities to their members and to farmers generally. Throughout the region, there was realisation of the need for extension — an educational service for the farming sector. Today, two types of extension organizations continue to exist: (1) government services in the respective Ministries of Agriculture in each country, and (2) extension services operating as part of farmers' organizations and commodity groups.

Variations in extension approaches

The previous section reviewed the historical emergence of the recognition that extension was an important and needed agricultural service. We now review briefly some of the different forms that extension has taken over time in the Caribbean.

In the early part of this century, when the Botanic Gardens were the locus for extension education, a "generalist" model prevailed. This meant that each agricultural instructor was expected to be able to serve all the agricultural needs of farmers. The colonial officers in the Botanical Gardens would determine what farmers needed to be told, and agricultural instructors were trained to work with farmers to improve their farming generally. Of course, the emphasis was on export crops, but the generalist approach included attention to food crops and livestock.

The generalist model places great responsibility on each individual agent to promote agricultural development. However, agricultural development does not take place in isolation from other developments, e.g. roads, water supplies and markets. To increase the organizational connection between agricultural development and rural

---

3. Incorporated as a statutory authority by the colonial governments of the day, these organizations like the Agricultural Society of Trinidad and Tobago received financial grants from state funds.

development more generally, some alternative models of extension have been attempted in the Caribbean.

One such approach was the "co-ordinated services" model established in Jamaica. Co-ordination was attempted by bringing all the various extension-type organizations under one roof in a region of a country.[4] For example, co-operatives, community development, home economics, agricultural extension and other rural development organizations were provided with offices in one building. The hope was that when placed under one roof, the separate services would get together for planning purposes and would work together in the field. This did not work out too well because both co-ordination and co-operation requires more than physical proximity of civil servants under one roof. The co-ordinated extension services of Jamaica did not last very long.

A different model involved making all of these services the responsibility of one organization. This "multi-purpose" model was patterned to some extent on the Tennessee Valley Land Authority in the United States. Jamaica established the Yallahs Valley Land Authority, and this proved successful in bringing what had been an extremely denuded and non-productive hilly area back into economic agricultural production in a way that conserved the land. On the basis of this success, Jamaica established a second — the Christiana Area Land Authority — which again proved relatively successful. These two land authority systems defined the role of the extension officers as "multi-purpose" in that they dealt not only with agricultural problems but with all rural development problems, including roads, water supplies, and even co-ordination of the health needs of the area.

In the 1960s Jamaica, in common with the other Caribbean countries decided that extension officers who had to do everything spent so much of their time doing merely service-oriented tasks, i.e. providing fertiliser, preparing subsidy forms and so on for farmers that there was little time left to do any educational work, i.e. the main thrust of extension work. Hence, the multi-purpose model gave way to the idea of splitting the extension services into two sections — the so-called "development" section, to provide the service function, and a separate advisory information arm. This "advisory" arm was meant to do only educational work, e.g. farmer/group meetings providing motivation, technology transfer and related aspects of agricultural education. This "split-functions" model worked successfully in Jamaica for a while, particularly when

4. Miller, H.C. (ed.), *Report on The Caribbean Conference on Agricultural Extension*, Jamaica: Agricultural Information Service, 1966.

the advisory function was tied into co-operating with an agency dealing with marketing farmers' produce. For example, the Central Marketing Agency would provide a guaranteed price for a particular crop and the extension services would work to provide the motivation, skills and education for the farmers to produce the crop for that particular market.

Antigua, some years ago, briefly attempted to have a similar division of labour; a few officers were identified to do purely extension educational work while the others were left to do the service-work carried out by a Peasant Development Organisation. However, this did not last long, mainly because of staff shortages and other administrative problems, but also because it was necessary to separate the service and advisory functions to get agents focused on specific tasks.

More recently a new model has emerged, the "saturation" model. Where development needs are great but there is a shortage of staff and of resources, with the result that existing needs cannot be met, it is necessary to use resources as strategically as possible; in this way the concept of doing extension in stages emerged. Under the saturation approach to extension, the relative agricultural development potential of various regions of a country is first determined, and the government puts as much of its extension resources as possible into the region of highest potential. In this one area, then, extension is tied into marketing, credit, various services and educational functions. The area becomes a targeted and saturated development priority to motivate the farmers and maximise potential support. During saturation of one area, extension pays less attention to, other sections of the country but does not totally ignore them. In this way limited staff is used to the greatest advantage. After the development momentum has been firmly established in the first region, the extension "train" moves to a new area, having developed the farmers' capabilities to continue their work without continuous support from extension. This is the principal idea on which the development of the Caribbean Rural Development Advisory and Training Service Project (CARDATS) has been based.

The projects model of extension programming

The "saturation model" discussed above aims extension resources, staff and programmes at a particular geographical area. The projects model, by way of contrast, focuses extension resources, staff and programmes on particular crops or special problem areas. The projects model of extension work is largely being forced on Caribbean countries as a result of the nature of international aid. Because of the increasing prevalence of this approach and because of its implications for extension effectiveness, this model is worthy of special discussion.

During the late 1970s and early 1980s the efforts of extension, and of agriculture more generally, have become increasingly channeled through specific, highly focused projects. The project approach has several advantages which have contributed to this trend. First, international funding agencies are highly project-oriented, and funding a project, an international agency is able to make a specific and highly targeted contribution. This helps them to establish a clear identity for the project, and also to get credit and publicity for their contribution. In contrast, general contributions to agriculture, or to extension, are lost in the overall operations of the organization.

Secondly, projects are relatively easy to plan, implement and evaluate in comparison to a comprehensive extension effort. A project will typically have relatively narrow, highly focused and operational goals. The scale of activity is sufficiently delimited for allocation and supervision of staff to be relatively easy. Through concentration on a small number of specific objectives, it is much easier to evaluate projects than it would be if one attempted to evaluate the whole extension effort.

Thirdly, field staff typically prefer working on projects, as our interviews with field staff in the Caribbean made clear.[5] On a project, the job assignment is specific and visible; you know what you are supposed to do, and accomplishments are more easily identified and demonstrated than they are in general extension work. Moreover, projects usually include the provision of some specific service to farmers, to whom field staff prefer to have something to offer.

Fourthly, projects are good public relations and political instruments for the ministry because of their visibility and clear delivery of specific services. It is easier to account to the public by way of projects implemented than it is to explain and demonstrate such educational goals as "advising farmers on agricultural practices", "raising the farmer's confidence", and "increasing the farmer's self-sufficiency". Just as the global tasks of a comprehensive, educational approach to extension are often difficult for field staff to implement, such an approach is difficult to explain to the general public when an attempt is being made to demonstrate the government's accomplishments.

5. Survey of Agricultural Extension Officers of the Eastern Caribbean States and Belize. Caribbean Agricultural Extension Project (CAEP), working notes (unpubl.). 1982.

The predominance of the project approach in the Ministry of Agriculture is illustrated by the listing of Agricultural Projects published by the Commonwealth of Dominica in February 1981.[6] In this country of 80,000 people with about fifty technical agricultural staff, thirty-seven currently funded projects are listed with an additional twenty-one still in the proposal stage. There are also heavy staff commitments to projects. Three out of eight agricultural officers and four out of nine agricultural assistants have been seconded to projects.

The advantages of a project approach are balanced by certain disadvantages. First, projects are typically funded and staffed in such a way that they become relatively autonomous units. Communications with general extension can erode. Staff develop a primary allegiance to their own project, and they focus on accomplishing their own set of project-specific goals. This tendency means that they can lose sight of the general picture. As they become isolated, or simply intensely focused on their own efforts, they can sometimes become counter-productive to the more general aims of national agricultural development.

Secondly, projects often compete for scarce resources in such a way that the overall agricultural effort is hurt. The heavy secondments of key staff can contribute to specific project successes while eroding the ministry's capability to oversee the whole agricultural sector. Since most international projects now require local counterparts, the problem of secondments, and draining off other scarce resources, is likely to be a continuing one.

Thirdly, efforts to attain specific project goals can undermine more general agricultural policies. When project staff are narrowly focused on only one part of the picture, and when there is competition for scarce resources, it is possible for a project, in attaining its goals, to harm the overall state of agriculture. For example, critics of Dominica's tree crops programme have argued that in their commitment to plant the targeted number of trees, the staff of the project moved into lands that are among Dominica's best, lands which should be reserved for arable crops which cannot be efficiently grown in places where trees will do well (e.g. on the lower middle hill slopes). Thus by competing for scarce arable land, the tree crops programme could prejudice the overall efforts to make Dominica self-sufficient in foodstuffs, even though the project is exemplary in achieving its own planting targets.

Fourthly, the proliferation of projects often means that a farmer

6. See Raymond Austrie, CAEP, Phase I, Un. of the West Indies, 1983. "Institutional Analysis of the Agricultural Sector, Dominica".

has to deal with several specialists, each pushing a specific project. Sometimes technicians representing different projects or advocating differing objectives give farmers contradictory or incompatible advice. And fifthly, poorly trained junior staff latch on to projects as a way of making up for their general lack of expertise. The advantage here is that the project gives them at least one area of expertise; but the corresponding disadvantage is that this specialisation limits their development as general extension staff with broad expertise in farming.

Extension patterns across countries

Experimentation with different models of extension organization, function, and programming in the Caribbean has been aimed at making extension more effective. Yet, the evidence is that by the beginning of the 1980s, extension in the Caribbean was facing a major crisis. Ministers of Agriculture in the less developed Caribbean countries were openly complaining that their national extension services were ineffective. Farmers were likewise complaining of agents who lacked knowledge, training, and resources. The Department of Agricultural Extension of the University of the West Indies undertook a process of assisting eight Caribbean LDCs — Antigua, Belize, Dominica, Montserrat, Grenada, St Lucia, St Kitts/Nevis, and St Vincent — to analyse their extension services.[7] The results of that 18-month analysis showed that extension was poorly placed to facilitate rural transformation in the Caribbean. It was revealed that while each country has its own unique set of problems, certain common constraining patterns of extension services are observable throughout the region in varying degrees: (*a*) unclear roles and objectives; (*b*) technical inadequacies and inadequate backstopping services; (*c*) organizational and management weaknesses; and (*d*) inadequate support resources. There follows a brief synopsis of these common constraints:

(*a*) Unclear Roles and Objectives

(i) Extension staff lack direction and purpose; their work is unfocused and unsystematic; in short they are not sure what they are supposed to be doing, and why.
(ii) Frontline extension agents have been too involved in non-educational activities; great expenditures of staff time on regulatory duties and service

---

7. CAEP, Phase I, Un. of the West Indies, Project executed in collaboration with the Midwest Universities Consortium for International Activities (MUCIA) with funding by the United States Agency for International Development.

functions have interferred with advisory activities, although it is recognised that extension should be primarily an educational activity.

(iii) Extension agents reach few farmers; they tend to work exclusively one-to-one with individual farmers instead of using a more efficient group approach to reach more farmers more effectively.

(iv) Most extension agents are not well received by farmers; agents lack credibility, and agents do not work together with farmers to establish programme priorities and practical workplans.

(v) There is little co-ordination and collaboration with other ministry or private sector rural development staff; extension staff work in relative isolation.

(b) Technical inadequacies

(i) Frontline extension staff lack technical agricultural training. Only 43 of 106 frontline extension agents surveyed had a two year agriculture diploma, the level of training considered minimally desirable by all extension services.

(ii) Frontline extension staff lack knowledge of and skill in extension methods, i.e. they don't know how to effectively convey knowledge to farmers to bring about change.

(iii) The linkage between research and extension is weak. Research findings have not been translated into a form useable by and understandable to extension agents and farmers; research needs identified in the field are not being passed along to researchers.

(iv) Technical backstopping to frontline agents is either not sufficient to provide agents with necessary problem solving ability or they are left to make decisions which in many cases they are not qualified to make.

(v) Opportunities for ongoing staff development and in-service training at the national level are usually non-existent.

(vi) Professional role models of extension excellence have not been developed to enhance a sense of professionalism among staff.

(c) Organizational and managerial weaknesses

(i) Organizational structures are overly hierarchical, with poorly defined lines of authority, diffused assignment of responsibility and top-down communications.

(ii) Frontline field staff receive little supervision, support, or direction; district and senior officers lack supervisory and management training.

(iii) Most extension personnel do not have meaningful job descriptions or performance criteria.

(iv) Programme development, systematic planning and performance evaluation approaches are virtually non-existent in extension organizations.

(v) Equipment, budgets and other resources are poorly monitored and badly managed.

(vi) Staff vacancies, secondments, turnover, and dual assignments have resulted in many posts being left vacant while other posts are overburdened; staff morale was found to be quite low.

(vii) Political interference has contributed to organizational ineffectiveness and staff discontent, or confusion, in all extension services.

(d) Inadequate support resources for extension

(i) Mobility of agents is severely restricted.
(ii) Many field staff houses and district outreach posts have become dilapidated and have been abandoned, leaving some rural areas unserved.
(iii) Teaching and communications materials are not available to extension agents for working with farmers.
(iv) Demonstration and technical equipment are not available.
(v) Mass media systems (radio, printed matter, audio-visual materials) have not been used effectively to support extension programmes.

While the inadequacies in national extension services are substantial, it is important to recognise some of the more positive conditions revealed in the analysis. Just a few of these aspects follow:

(a) There is a great desire to improve extension effectiveness; this desire is expressed at all levels by farmers, field staff, district officers, senior staff, Chief Agricultural Officers, Permanent Secretaries and Ministers.
(b) In every country there exists a number of successful farmers (the top 10%) whose knowledge and skills can help point the way to profitable agricultural development.
(c) In every country there is one or more member of the extension staff with the technical agricultural training and effective extension methods experience to provide leadership to staff development efforts.
(d) National Agricultural Planning Committees have already been organized in every country as part of the analysis effort. These committees have demonstrated the viability of the extension planning process. The committees constitute a reservoir of commitment and knowledge that will provide a momentum and direction throughout a new rural transformation effort.
(e) National Extension Improvement Plans have been approved by the Cabinet in each country, usually with some ceremony and publicity, thereby alerting the national populace to government's commitment to improving extension effectiveness
(f) As a result of this analysis process, extension organization and systems have already begun to change.

The CAEP model of extension

The Caribbean Agricultural Extension project (CAEP) began with the analysis just reviewed. The analysis in each country was used to develop a National Extension Improvement Plan, the implementation of which is just beginning at the time of writing. The CAEP model of extension rests on several premises, which underlie the relationship of agricultural extension as an essential component of rural development, as discussed in the Introduction of this text. These premises are:

(*a*) Rural transformation processes will vary from locality to locality; therefore, an effective extension service must be adaptable to local needs.

(*b*) An effective extension organization will facilitate a two-way flow of communication from rural people to government, and from government to rural people.

(*c*) An effective extension organization needs broadly based support and planning participation from a variety of rural interest groups.

(*d*) Extension should play an educational role in mobilising rural people to make their own decisions so as to direct the rural transformation process through informed action.

(*e*) An effective extension service can play a leading role in rural transformation by building an integrated approach to rural development.

(*f*) An effective extension system requires clear agent roles and objectives; technical competence; a solid organizational and managerial foundation; adequate resources to reach rural peoples; and ongoing linkages to agricultural researchers.

Agricultural extension is a complex process through which farmers are educated, provided with appropriate knowledge and skills, and motivated to make decisions in the efficient utilisation of available resources for obtaining the optimum livelihood from their farming efforts. It therefore has the potential to become a major instrument of agricultural and rural development at the village and national level. However, the focus of agricultural extension should be the individual farmer and his family, and its ultimate objective is improvement in the level and style of living of the farm family.

An attempt to illustrate the fully functional agricultural extension process graphically is presented in Figure 1. The diagram shows that extension work is based on an agricultural policy which is arrived at from a consideration of national development goals and the consultation between the state and private agricultural organizations. The thrusts of programme priorities for extension are developed by a national planning committee with both public and private sector agriculture representation as well as representation from research, marketing, credit and other related organizations (e.g. agro-processing).

The "walls" of the extension process are composed of essential interlocking "bricks" or elements so organized as to facilitate the free flow of information, educational opportunities, and motivational influences to the extension target-group, the farmers of the nation. Of equal importance, this orderly organization and attention to the supportive position of each "brick" permits ease of feedback

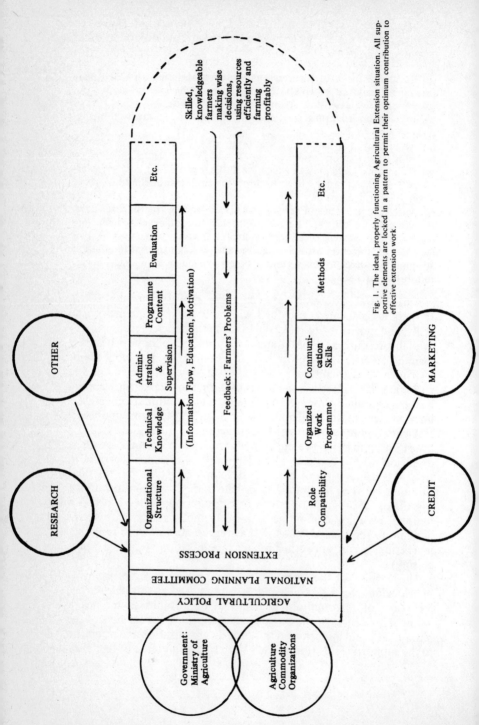

Fig. 1. The ideal, properly functioning Agricultural Extension situation. All supportive elements are locked in a pattern to permit their optimum contribution to effective extension work.

of farmers' concerns and problems which can then influence the degree of emphasis given by policy-makers to the various elements influencing or supporting the extension units.

Figure 2 illustrates the current situation existing in Caribbean countries. There is little co-ordination of public and private sector interests in determining agricultural policy on which to base extension efforts. There is no collaboration and integration of the efforts of the various agriculture-related segments in planning agricultural development action. All the major elements are present in some form, but their operations are such that more often than not they impede or totally block rather than enhance the flow of education, services and feedback.

CAEP will work to improve the existing situation in order to reach the position illustrated in Fig. 3. It will not be possible in a short time to transform the extension services of the participating countries to the ideal functioning model as shown in Fig. 1. What is realistically envisaged is that CAEP can have a significant streamlining effect on the extension process. All the "bricks" will not yet be bonded in place in the wall, but they will have been so shifted that they no longer constitute major blockages to the smooth forward and backward (feedback) flow of information and services, as in Fig. 2. Further, critical components of the extension system — i.e. technical knowledge, communication skills and extension methods — will be upgraded to provide the necessary inputs into the system, so that the output is more effective in attaining the system's goals.

A systems perspective

The CAEP model essentially encompasses a systems perspective, built on the processes of *analysis, planning, programme delivery*, and *evaluation*. These processes occur at the national level in each country through the National Extension Planning Committee established there. But they also occur at the regional and local level within each country. Frontline extension agents can be trained to adopt and consciously use a systems perspective to (*a*) *analyse* local needs in conjunction with local people, (*b*) *plan* an extension programme that is responsive to local needs, (*c*) *implement* the planned programme with local participation and collaboration, and (*d*) *evaluate* the programme strengths and weaknesses so as to improve future programmes.

The usual emphasis and concern when discussing agricultural extension is on the production decisions made as a result of the extension processes. However, the processes of extension planning,

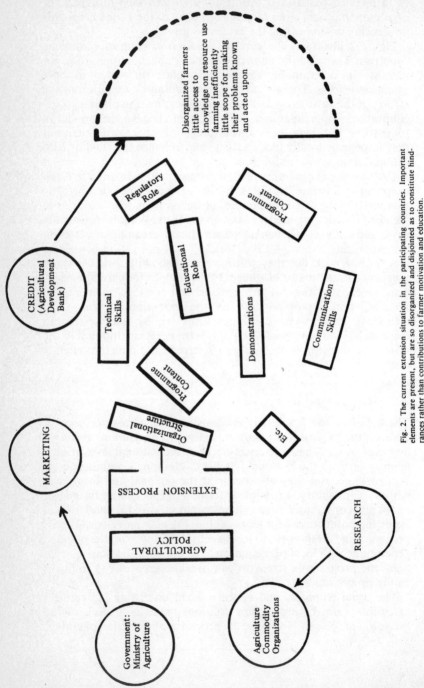

Fig. 2. The current extension situation in the participating countries. Important elements are present, but are so disorganized and disjointed as to constitute hindrances rather than contributions to farmer motivation and education.

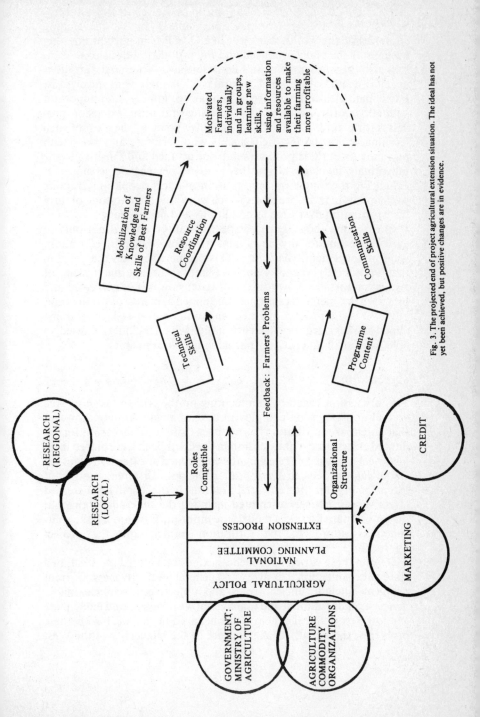

Fig. 3. The projected end of project agricultural extension situation. The ideal has not yet been achieved, but positive changes are in evidence.

programme delivery and evaluation can be viewed as ends in themselves. From this perspective, particularly in the developing countries of the world, a project like CAEP is important not only because of the plans produced and the production decisions taken, but also because of the self-consciousness generated, attitudes developed and skills learned by rural participants during the process. Participants learn the nature, potential, techniques, and important strengths and weaknesses of generating and using extension processes for planning and decision-making. To make the most of such learning opportunities, field agents who facilitate and work with participants in these processes must be attuned and sensitive to the individuals involved. Thus this systems perspective is aimed at enhancing the long-term mobilisation of rural peoples by training participants in those processes which will allow them to control rural transformation over time as conditions and needs change.

In this way, the systems perspective can be applied not only to agriculture but to any development sector — health, education, water management, roads, etc. This perspective takes the position that it is not only what is done that is important, but that it is also of critical importance how it is done. Extension is thus perceived and practised not merely as a programme aimed at increased production, but also as a process-oriented and outcomes-based programme aimed at integrated rural transformation which includes knowledgeable, confident and actively participating rural peoples.

Conclusion

This discussion began by commenting on the critical *potential* role agricultural extension can play in development. To date, however that potential contribution has not been realised. The reasons for the limited effectiveness of extension in the Caribbean were placed in an historical context by reviewing the emergence of extension from the Botanical Gardens in Caribbean countries. Different models of extension organization emerged over time in the search for increased effectiveness. Models attempted included the generalist approach; the co-ordinated services model; the multi-purpose model; the split-functions approach; the saturation model; and the project approach.

Despite these varied approaches, extension entered the 1980s in a state of organizational disarray and general ineffectiveness. Current problems include unclear roles and objectives; technical inadequacies; organizational and managerial weaknesses; and inadequate support resources. To help Caribbean countries deal with these problems, the Faculty of Agriculture of the University of the West

Indies is undertaking the Caribbean Agricultural Extension Project (CAEP) through its Department of Agricultural Extension. The premises of CAEP constitute a systems perspective based on analysis, planning, programme delivery and evaluation processes, which can be applied at both national and local levels. It is aimed at empowering rural people to participate fully in the rural transformation process, and is relevant to all sectors of development activities. The systems perspective of CAEP is built on the extension approach summarized in the timeless proverb: "Give a man a fish and he'll eat for a day; teach a man to fish and he'll eat for a lifetime." Effective extension is a lifetime process that contributes to the revitalisation and transformation of rural communities.

REFERENCES

Austrie, Raymond, "Institutional Analysis of the Agricultural Sector, Dominica", Caribbean Agricultural Extension Project, Un. of the West Indies, St Augustine, unpubl. report, 1983.

Henderson, T.H., "The University of the West Indies and Agricultural Extension Work in the Caribbean", *Agricultural Progress* vol. 48.

Henderson, T.H. and S. Mahabir, *Fifty Years of Research in Tropical Agriculture: A Bibliography 1922-1972*. Dept. of Agricultural Extension, Un. of the West Indies St Augustine, 1974.

Leagans, J. Paul and Charles P. Loomis, *Behavioral Change in Agriculture*. Ithaca: Cornell University Press, 1971.

Miller, H.C. (ed.), *Report on the The Caribbean Conference on Agricultural Extension*, Jamaica: Agricultural Information Service, 1966.

Myrdal, Gunnar, *The Challenge of World Poverty*, New York: Vintage Press, 1970.

Purseglove, J.W., "History and Functions of Botanic Gardens with Special Reference to Singapore", *Tropical Agriculture, 1957*, 34:3.

11

NUTRITIONAL NEEDS, FOOD AVAILABILITY AND THE REALISM OF SELF-SUFFICIENCY

Curtis E. McIntosh and Patricia Manchew

Introduction

Despite the efforts of Caribbean governments and their institutions, a relatively large segment of the population remains in a chronic state of undernutrition. But co-existing with these is a growing mass of obese individuals, primarily women. The consequence is a constraint on the total development process in that a large segment of the population is destined to lead a less than optimum productive life. Analysis of this problem points to the cause being not an insufficiency in food available but inequity in its distribution, associated with income inequalities and injudicious food choices both in quantity and quality in relation to nutritional requirements. There is, however, an associated food availability problem relating to the high dependence on imports to meet basic energy and protein requirements.

It is suggested that these problems of food and nutrition could be solved by implementing unified multi-sectoral food and nutrition programmes which seek to address the problem of dependence through greater regional self-sufficiency. However, even with the best efforts there would remain significant shortfalls particularly in legumes, vegetables and cereals at the end of the twentieth century.

In their quest to attain a better standard of living for the populations of states which were once colonies of European powers, governments in the Caribbean region embarked on a series of development plans beginning in the late 1950s and early '60s. This period of development planning coincided with political movements towards self-government and independence, as well as efforts towards integration. These development plans focussed heavily on four major objectives: the achievement of a rapid rate of growth in the gross domestic product; the attainment of 'full' employment; the control of inflation or relative price stability; and the generation of a trading surplus or a positive balance of payments. Little emphasis was given to such matters as nutrition and health as explicit development goals.

Indeed, the preoccupation with rapid economic growth led to the choice of strategies comprising a continued emphasis on export agriculture, tourism and 'industrialisation by invitation' (inviting foreign investment into the country and providing tax holidays for investors) with external backward and forward linkages. These strategies have led to varying degrees of success and failure in the achievement of the stated objectives.

While most countries achieved reasonable to impressive rates of growth in Gross Domestic Product in the 1960s, they were at the same time plagued by problems of creeping inflation, unemployment, balance of payments deficits and increasing dependence on imported food. With few exceptions, Caribbean countries experienced phenomenal increases in all these variables resulting primarily from increases in oil prices in the early 1970s. Increased balance of payments problems, galloping inflation in food, fuel and other oil-based products, and the inability to obtain loan funds for investment and debt-servicing led to lower productivity, unemployment and a worsening of the socio-economic conditions of the population.

The consequences of the "oil crisis", as it came to be called by non oil-producing countries, brought into sharp focus the need for a change in development objectives and strategies. The "basic needs" approach to development planning with its focus on such items as food, clothes, shelter, nutrition and health has been receiving greater attention, as is the increasing concern for multi-sectoral co-ordination and peoples' participation.

In the 1970s there has been renewed effort to develop strategies for the redress of, among other things, nutrition and health problems as well as the increasing dependence on imported foodstuffs. Our purpose here is to provide information and ideas that will contribute to a better understanding of the food and nutrition problems and to the development of more effective strategies for their solution. We examine the chronic state of undernutrition affecting a relatively large segment of the population, and the obesity which exists simultaneously among an equally large proportion. Matters of food availability and import dependence are analysed. Nutritional needs are examined in relation to adequate diets as well as the levels of self-sufficiency that are likely to be achieved by the end of the century.

The nutrition problems analysed

The major current nutritional problems in the English speaking Caribbean are Energy-protein malnutrition, Anaemia and Obesity and related diseases such as Diabetes and Hypertension. Evidence

214   *Curtis E. McIntosh and Patricia Manchew*

also exists for possible vitamin and mineral deficiencies, particularly Vitamin B_{12} and Vitamin A.

Energy-protein malnutrition. In the Caribbean, there is no plain starvation of the kind found in parts of Asia and Africa. There is almost no undernutrition of public magnitude in children 0–5 years of age in some of the countries of the Region. In others it is mostly Gomez Grade II (moderately malnourished) and Gomez Grade I (borderline) with approximately 5–10% of children under 5 years moderately malnourished and about 30–40% borderline. Third-degree malnutrition or Gomez Grade III (severely underweight) varies from 0 to 1.5% in this age group.[1] Groups affected include pregnant and lactating women, children over 5 years, labourers and the elderly.

Energy-protein malnutrition (EPM) is the result of insufficient energy (calories) as well as protein. National food supply data do not seem to influence EPM in the countries studied. This suggests a maldistribution of available foodstuffs both quantitatively among various segments of the population, and in the form of maldistribution within households. Studies conducted in St Lucia (Food and Nutrition Survey, 1976) showed a wide difference between satisfaction of their nutrient requirements by individual small children and that of households to which they belonged. Some children were being well-fed despite inadequate food availability to the household while others were undernourished even though household supplies were adequate.[2]

Overnutrition (obesity) and related diseases. Prevalence data on overnutrition and related diseases in the Caribbean are scarce. Many of those available lack both reliability and a common denominator to make figures comparable. Despite this, it is evident that overnutrition and related diseases such as diabetes, hypertension and coronary heart disease are major public health problems in the Region. These diseases affect not only old people; they are also important causes of premature deaths and disabilities and consequent loss in productivity in the middle years (45–64)

A very large proportion of the adult population, particularly females, suffer from obesity. Data obtained from national food and nutrition surveys show that in Barbados (1969) 32% of females and 7% of males (45 years and over) were 20% or more above standard

1. Sinha, D.P., *"Overnutrition and Related Diseases"* (Diabetes and Cardio-vascular Diseases), CFNI-J-71–80.
2. CFNI, *Food and Nutrition Survey of Saint Lucia*, 1976.

weight for height. A similar proportion was found to be obese by skinfold measurements. Data from a similar survey in Guyana in 1971 and St Lucia in 1974 show that obesity was more pronounced after thirty-five years of age. In both St Lucia and Guyana, far more women than men were obese. The household food consumption survey in Trinidad (1970) suggested that 28% of females and 12% males were obese.

Obesity is found consistently in a large percentage of babies in the first six months of life in all countries of the Caribbean where undernutrition is also a problem in the 6–59 month age group. The cause may be genetic, environmental, psychological, endocrine or neurological, or obesity may result from taking certain drugs. It must be emphasised, however, that by far the commonest and most important cause is environmental, i.e. a simple excess of energy (calorie) intake over utilisation.

Studies have shown a relationship between obesity and increased mortality and morbidity from ischaemic heart disease and prevalence of hypertension. Other effects include decreased work capacity, and reduced physical fitness and sense of wellbeing, all of which have social and economic implications.

Anaemia. Available data in most of the member-countries of CFNI show that there is a moderate to high prevalence of anaemia. It is widespread in children under five years (especially 0–18 month age group) and in pregnant and lactating women. One out of every three children in the 5–12 year age group is anaemic. This is essentially an iron deficiency, anaemia resulting from poor absorption and/or inadequate intake, possibly aggravated by folic acid deficiency.

The level of Hb (haemoglobin level) used to determine the existence of anaemia varies from 10 g/dl (grams per decilitre) in some countries to 11 g/dl in others (11 g for women and 12 g for men). The World Health Organisation has recommended Hb values below which anaemia is likely to be present as 11 g/dl for pre-school age children and pregnant women, 12 g/dl for school children and non-pregnant women and 13 g/dl for adult males. (See Table 1.)

Based on these criteria, anaemia does exist in the Commonwealth Caribbean. Evidence to date indicates that blacks normally have a Hb concentration about 0.5 g/dl below that of whites at all ages, except perhaps in the peri-natal period.[3]

Research conducted among female blacks in the United States

3. Dallman, P.R., *et al.*, "Haemoglobin Concentrations in White, Black and Oriental Children. Is there a need for separate criteria in screening for anaemia?", *American J. of Clinical Nutrition*, vol. 31, p. 377, 1978.

Table 1. W.H.O. CRITERIA FOR THE
DIAGNOSIS OF ANAEMIA

*(Hb concentrations below which anaemia is
likely to be present at sea level according to
different age, sex and physiological status)*

	g/dl
Children (6 months — 6 years)	11.0
Children (6–14 years)	12.0
Adult males	13.0
Adult females, non-pregnant	12.0
Adult females, pregnant	11.0

Source: World Health Organisation, *Nutritional Anaemia*. Report of WHO Scientific Group Technical Report Series no. 405. WHO, Geneva, 1968. World Health Organisation, *Nutritional Anaemia*. Report of a WHO Group of Experts. Technical Report Series no. 503. WHO, Geneva, 1972.

suggests race adaptability since the population studied did not demonstrate the usual clinical symptoms of lassitude, dizziness, breathlessness or pallor at Hb levels 10 g/dl. Surveys have not been conducted to determine whether similar levels of adaptability exist within the Caribbean. Indications are that, based on criteria for lower levels of Hb, much of the population formerly classified as being at risk of becoming anaemic will not now be so classified. Urgent research is needed in this area.

Of crucial importance, however, is the fact that anaemia remains a preventable public health problem. The nature of the Caribbean diet may well be a contributing factor. It has now been documented experimentally that certain foods enhance iron absorption while others inhibit absorption. Among the enhancers are ascorbic acid and the protein of meat, fish and poultry. Sources of ascorbic acid are widespread in the Caribbean, and Food Balance Sheets for Jamaica, Barbados, Guyana, Trinidad and Tobago and St Lucia indicate that between 14% and 20% of the food energy is of animal origin. Inhibitors to iron absorption include phytates found in cereals, spinach and cocoa and tannins found in tea, coffee and cocoa. Food Balance Sheets for the above countries indicated that 31% of total dietary energy and 38% of protein come from all cereal products, and that 22% of energy and 30% of protein come from wheat products. Many Caribbean diets have a high level of phytates, which inhibit iron absorption. Nutritional anaemia is therefore probably a problem both of inadequate iron intake and low absorption.

Anaemia reduces productivity and work capacity, diminishes the sense of individual's wellbeing, contributes to the overall mortality associated with malnutrition and, when it occurs in pregnant women, threatens the life and health of the mother and contributes to low birth weight of the infant.

Vitamins and Minerals. Problems of vitamin and mineral imbalances in the Region have not been fully investigated. However, in the light of the prevalence of undernutrition, anaemia and obesity, it is assumed that such imbalances exist. Vitamin B_{12} deficiency is likely to occur in vegans (strict vegetarians) who do not eat any animal products. (Vitamin B_{12} is not found in foods of vegetable origin.) Indeed, Vitamin B_{12} deficiency has been documented in some vegans in Jamaica.[4]

Problems of food availability

The assessment of food availability on a quantity basis is useful, but far more meaningful estimates could be obtained by conversion of food quantities to nutrients available per head of population. The basic limitation of this data is that the actual distribution of the food per person and over time (seasons) is unknown.

The tool for assessing food availability for a country for a particular time period (usually a year) is the food balance sheet. This shows for each foodstuff the supply sources — domestic production, imports or from stocks of a previous period — and its utilisation either for exports, feed, seed, manufacture, stocks for a future period, or consumption. In each case, adjustments are made for losses during storage, transport and manufacture.[5] The quantities available for human consumption are converted to nutrients available per head of population, given the population estimate and appropriate food composition tables. Bearing in mind the above limitations of distribution over time and by socio-economic groups, the nutrient availabilities per person are compared with theoretical estimates of nutrient requirements per person of the population to give some indication of the national sufficiency of the food supply. The relative contribution of local production *vis-à-vis* imports gives the degree of self-sufficiency or import dependence.

Based on the age and sex distribution and other characteristics of Caribbean populations, it has been estimated that an overall allowance of 2,250 kilocalories (kcal.) per person per day is

4. Campbell *et al.*, "The Vegan Syndrome in Jamaica". 22nd Scientific Meeting, Caribbean Medical Research Council, Belize, 1977, p. 5.
5. FAO, *Provisional Food Balance Sheets*. FAO, Rome, vol. VII, 1977.

adequate. Correspondingly, a daily allowance of 43 grammes of protein per person is satisfactory.[6] These estimates assume equity in the distribution according to estimated requirements per person. Other nutrient allowances could be estimated using the Recommended Dietary Allowances for the Caribbean.[7]

Several agencies and persons have computed food balance sheets for various Caribbean countries. As expected, varying estimates for the same time period exist, and lack of continuity in the data precludes in-depth analysis and inference from the data. Applying the above allowances for energy and protein deemed to be satisfactory, the available data on food supply for consumption suggest an adequacy for both energy and protein, with protein reaching a higher level of satisfaction than energy (Table 2). Recent evidence

Table 2. ENERGY AND PROTEIN AVAILABLE FOR
CONSUMPTION FOR SELECTED COUNTRIES

		Energy *Kcal/Caput/Day*	*Protein* *g/Caput/Day*
Barbados	1971	2,927	75.4
Guyana	1970	2,819	63.4
Jamaica	1972	2,687	74.5
Trinidad and Tobago*	1972–4	2,530	64.8
St Lucia	1970	2,271	53.5

Source: Food Balance Sheets for the Caribbean, CFNI, 1976; *Provisional Food Balance Sheets, FAO, Rome, 1977.

suggests that the current protein allowances on which recommended dietary allowances for the Caribbean are based may be too low for long-term adequacy. The recommended allowances allow for approximately 8% of the energy to be in the form of protein. This level is deemed satisfactory only when the equivalent protein calories are in the form of high quality protein (milk or eggs). When this condition does not hold, the protein/energy ratio requirement is expected to be somewhat higher.[8] As is indicated in Table 3, a rather high percentage of the protein comes from crop products, suggesting that the over-supply of protein is perhaps more apparent than real. The

6. Gurney, J.M., *Available Data on the State of Food and Nutrition of the Peoples of the Commonwealth Caribbean* (1975).
7. CFNI, *Recommended Dietary Allowances for the Caribbean* (1976).
8. Scrimshaw, N.S. and R. Lockwood, "Interpretation of Data on Human Food Availability and Nutrient Consumption", *Food and Nutrition Bulletin* 2(1), 1980, pp. 29–37.

Table 3. PERCENTAGE CONTRIBUTIONS TO ENERGY AND PROTEIN BY VARIOUS FOOD GROUPS IN SELECTED COUNTRIES

Food group	ENERGY						PROTEIN					
	Jamaica 1972	Guyana 1970	Trinidad & Tobago 1970	Barbados 1971	St Lucia 1970	Simple Average	Jamaica 1972	Guyana 1970	Trinidad & Tobago 1970	Barbados 1971	St Lucia 1970	Simple Average
Cereal products	34.5	53.5	39.6	30.6	27.8	37.2	38.5	49.8	42.8	30.0	33.1	38.8
Starchy fruits, roots & tubers	16.4	5.3	2.7	8.4	16.5	9.9	9.5	3.0	2.1	6.1	11.0	6.3
Sugars & syrups	12.7	13.9	17.1	14.1	14.7	14.5	0.0	0.2	0.0	0.3	0.0	0.1
Pulses, nuts & seeds	2.1	3.9	4.5	4.5	1.6	3.3	3.5	8.0	11.9	8.9	3.7	7.2
Vegetables	1.0	0.4	0.5	0.7	0.4	0.6	1.1	0.3	1.2	1.2	0.6	0.9
Fruits	2.5	1.2	1.7	1.2	6.7	2.7	1.5	0.8	0.7	0.3	2.8	1.2
Animal products	18.9	12.1	13.7	23.2	16.8	16.9	44.3	37.1	39.1	51.6	45.2	43.5
Oils & fats	9.8	6.5	16.7	12.0	11.2	11.2	0.1	0.0	0.2	0.3	0.2	0.2

Source: Calculated from CFNI, Food Balance Sheets for the Caribbean, 1976 and Y.H. Yang, "Food Balance Sheets of Trinidad and Tobago" in J.M. Gurney (ed.), *Food and Economic Planning in Trinidad and Tobago,* 1975.

table also shows the dominance of cereal products (mainly wheat) in the diet of Caribbean peoples.

Food consumption surveys have been conducted by CFNI in member-countries. The data indicate that among some households there is a significant deficit in dietary intake — primarily of energy, protein and iron and to a less extent calcium, thiamine, riboflavine, niacin and Vitamin A. Others, on the otherhand, receive more than their requirements. Thus, approximately 56% of households in the region fail to meet recommended dietary allowances. The corresponding figure for protein is 44%. While it cannot be concluded that these deficits correspond to a similar proportion having dietary deficiencies, the evidence certainly points to a rather high risk of deficiency among Caribbean peoples.

The inescapable conclusion from this analysis is that the problem of food availability at household level is a problem of distribution rather than of aggregate supply. A search for factors that affect distribution would reveal that maldistribution of income and a high dependence ratio within the population are implicated — the poor and the large families being the most underfed and at the greatest risk of malnutrition.

The high import dependence for most of the protein and a substantial part of the energy requirements is shown in Table 4. The historical pattern of agricultural development and food distribution makes this a predictable discovery. The conquest and eventual colonisation of Caribbean countries by Europeans led to the development of an agricultural production system based on cheap labour, extensive acreages and monoculture; individual countries became one-crop economies. In sum total, however, there was tremendous diversity. Thus the monoculture of sugar-cane in Barbados and St Kitts, for example, complements the banana monoculture in St Lucia and Dominica. Exceptions to this system of monoculture are to be found in Grenada (cocoa, bananas and nutmegs) and Guyana (sugar-cane and rice), indicating changes in cropping systems over time. The plantation economy, which developed in the colonial era, persists to a large extent even today. Caribbean countries remain, first, sources of agricultural raw materials — sugar, cocoa, bananas, spices — for processing, consumption or export by foreign countries; and, secondly, markets for agricultural inputs and foodstuffs originating from external sources.[9]

9. McIntosh, C.E. and M. Limchoy, *The Performance of Selected Agricultural Marketing Agencies*, Dept. of Agricultural Economics and Farm Management, Un. of the West Indies, St Augustine, 1975.

Table 4. IMPORT DEPENDENCE OF SELECTED
CARIBBEAN COUNTRIES

	% of nutrients from external sources	
	energy	protein
Guyana (1970)	34	42
Trinidad and Tobago (1970)	49	71
Barbados (1971)	58	76
St Lucia (1970)	65	67
Grenada (1975)*	78	70
Montserrat (1978)*	90	79
Jamaica (1972)	46	62

Sources: Gurney (1975); Weir* (1979, 1980).

The production and trade patterns which developed have important implications for the food situation. Since the best lands were used in the production of export crops, the production of other foodstuffs for local consumption was relegated to poorer lands in small parcels which were highly dispersed. The consequences were low production at high cost, and high marketing costs occasioned by the low volumes moved over long distances. Despite the longer distances travelled by foodstuffs from European and North American markets, the high volumes and transport systems (water transportation), together with low-cost production in the originating country, made for relatively cheaper imported foodstuffs.

The application of price controls and subsidies to a number of these imported foodstuffs often widened the gap in prices between them and locally-grown foodstuffs and thus lowered the competitiveness of the latter, with the obvious sequel of lack of expansion, if not decline, of local production. Export crops provide the foreign exchange for the purchase of inputs and foodstuffs, and the strengthening of trade relations provides reasonably good assurances of obtaining foodstuffs of good quality in appropriate quantities. These factors among others are responsible for the high dependence of Caribbean countries on external sources for food supplies.

Addressing the food and nutrition problems

The English-speaking Caribbean countries with a population of approximately 5 million are expected to maintain a population of just above 7 million in 1990 and nearly 8 million by the year 2000.[10]

10. PAHO (1980), *Health for All by the Year 2000-Strategies*, p. 25.

Life expectancy for births during the 1980s and 1990s are not dissimilar from those for the United States of America and Canada (Table 5). However, a look at the *per caput* food production for

Table 5. ESTIMATED LIFE EXPECTANCY AT BIRTH:
SELECTED CARIBBEAN COUNTRIES AND
NORTH AMERICA, 1970-2000

	1975-80	1985-90	1995-2000
Barbados	70.5	72.6	73.7
Guyana	69.1	72.0	73.2
Jamaica	70.6	72.2	73.1
Suriname	67.2	70.2	72.3
Trinidad and Tobago	70.8	72.7	73.9
Windward Is.	67.4	70.4	72.5
Canada	72.5	72.7	72.7
U.S.A.	71.6	72.2	72.5

Source: PAHO (1980), *Health for All by the Year 2000/Strategies*, p. 30.

countries of the Region tells a sad story of increasing dependence on imported food supply for basic sustenance (Table 6), which has far-reaching consequences. No independent country could be satisfied if it is being fed by another.

Table 6. PER CAPUT FOOD PRODUCTION INDICES FOR
JAMAICA AND TRINIDAD AND TOBAGO
(1961-65 = 100)

	1970	1971	1972	1973	1974	1975	1976	1977*
Jamaica	76	78	77	73	75	69	71	66
Trinidad and Tobago	82	79	81	70	74	63	75	72

* Provisional figures.

Source: PAHO, *op. cit.*, p. 71.

Many Caribbean countries are plagued by disasters of one kind or another arising from hurricanes, volcanic activity, earthquakes and floods, and to meet shortfalls brought about by these catastrophes basic food reserves are necessary. Failure to achieve a reasonable level of food reserves could lead to a serious worsening of the nutritional status in times of disaster as well as prolonging the period required for complete rehabilitation.

The sizeable balance of payments deficits which are largely accounted for by food imports could be reduced by a reversal of the downward trend in per person production accompanied by a shift from export crops to the production of local food crops. Most of the exports are in raw form — sugar, cocoa, coffee, nutmegs, bananas, citrus fruits etc. While some exports in this form are inevitable, there is a need to bring about changes in the market mix which would lead to additional gains from the basic raw materials produced. For example, a study on an economic assessment of an alternative marketing strategy for nutmegs from Grenada indicated that a change in product mix from whole nutmegs to nutmegs with shelled kernels and nutmeg oil and butter could increase net returns by 66%.[11] Studies such as these lead to the conclusion that foreign exchange earnings could be greatly increased through processing some of the major export crops — e.g. cocoa and nutmegs — thus achieving diversification at a different level, namely in end-products.[12]

Effective use of such foreign exchange earnings implies that leakages through food imports must be curtailed. Increased food production for domestic consumption must be a reality if increased demands are to be satisfied. Where foreign exchange earnings are minimal, the problem is magnified in that effective demand is reduced as well as the capacity for further investment in food production.

The crucial problem to be resolved is how to ensure an optimum balance between nutritional needs and food availability while increasing efforts are made towards self-sufficiency; and, subsidiary to that, how realistic the aim of self-sufficiency actually is, and what levels of self-sufficiency can be aimed at and maintained without jeopardising the nutritional status of Caribbean peoples. Table 7 portrays clearly the varying degrees of self-sufficiency in various foods of selected member-countries, given their present consumption patterns, and highlights the need for regional co-operation in attempts to solve problems of food availability and extra-regional dependence for food supply. The resolution of these problems could best be achieved through the formulation and implementation of multisectoral food and nutrition programmes at the national level, with cognisance being taken of comparative advantages within the Region and the benefits of regional co-operation in intra-regional trade.

11. Regis, V., "An Economic Assessment of An Alternative Marketing Strategy for Grenada Nutmegs", unpubl. M.Sc. thesis, Dept. of Agricultural Economics and Farm Management, Un. of the West Indies, St Augustine, 1975.
12. McIntosh, C.E. and P.O. Osuji, "Economic Aspects of Food Production in Grenada", *Grenada's Independence, Myth or Reality*, ISER, 1975.

Table 7. SELF-SUFFICIENCY LEVELS IN VARIOUS FOOD
GROUPS FOR SELECTED CARIBBEAN COUNTRIES (%)

	Barbados 1971	Guyana 1970	Jamaica 1972	Trinidad & Tobago* 1972–4	St Lucia 1970
Staples:					
Cereals	3	111	5	11	0
Starchy fruits, roots and tubers	84	85	121	72	198
Sugar	945	570	88	502	0
Legumes, nuts, seeds	39	47	72	28	20
Vegetables	51	49	69	60	22
Foods from animals	25	45	53	37	36
Fruits	10	85	106	88	95
Oils and fats	68	76	72	68	173

Source: CFNI, *Food Balance Sheets for the Caribbean*, 1976; *Provisional Food Balance Sheets, FAO, Rome, 1977.

Strategy for meeting nutritional needs. The nutritional needs of Caribbean peoples are not dissimilar to those of most other world populations. Based on the particular characteristics of the Region, dietary allowances to meet the needs of most healthy individuals have been recommended.[13]

In the context of planning to meet nutrient requirements for the Region's population, it is felt that the aim should be the achievement of a 20% level of availability over the estimated requirement. This level should allow for an adequate level of foodstuffs in storage at all times in order to meet requirements during natural disasters to which the Region is subject and to take care of production shortfalls. The recommended energy requirement per person is therefore 2,700 kilocalories. In the case of protein, a further allowance has been made to ensure that the Protein/Energy (P/E) ratio approximates 11%. This is in keeping with recent views that the Recommended Dietary Allowances for protein are somewhat low, given the high contribution of crop products to total protein intake in the Region. This gives a total recommended allowance of protein as 75 grammes per person per day.

A simple approach to ensuring that all segments of a population consume nutritionally well-balanced meals on a daily basis is through the application of the 'multimix' principle, according to which the consumer makes a judicious selection of foods from predetermined food groups, namely staples (cereals, starchy fruits,

13. CFNI, "Recommended Dietary Allowances for the Caribbean" (1976).

roots and tubers), legumes, vegetables and foods from animals with appropriate additions of fats and fruits. Adoption of this approach reduces the problem of computing balanced meals essentially to one of energy, which ranks as the number one nutrition problem in the Region — both as a shortfall on the one hand, leading to protein-energy malnutrition, and an oversupply leading to obesity. Table 8 shows an appropriate combination of these food groups with respect to energy and protein and from contributions based on specific foods called 'food equivalents'. The estimated quantities per person per year from the various food groups in terms of food equivalents are also shown. Substantial increases in the percentage contributions of legumes and vegetables have been recommended. To a less extent, increases have been recommended for starchy roots, starchy fruits and tubers and fruits. Reductions in the contributions of foods from animals and imported cereals (flour and by-products), and oil to a smaller extent, have also been recommended.

It is possible to make conversions from one equivalent to another by multiplying the estimated quantity per year by the energy value for the reference equivalent, divided by the energy value for the desired equivalent. For example, to determine the amount of beef that is equivalent to 263.3 lb. of chicken per year, the formula is:

$$\frac{263.3 \text{ lb chicken} \times 524 \text{ kcals (in 1 lb chicken)}}{1,021 \text{ kcals (in 1 lb beef)}} = 135 \text{ lb beef}$$

The challenges of the food sector. For most Caribbean countries the Food and Agriculture sector has played a significant role in the development process through employment creation, foreign exchange earnings, food provision, provision of raw materials for industrialization, and markets for agricultural inputs and industrial goods and services. The nature of these contributions is such that when an assessment is made of the performance of the sector, some serious shortcomings become clear.

The high employment level within the food and agriculture sector is symptomatic of declining agricultural productivity and a failure of the sector to industrialize, thus making use of the basic raw materials of the sector. With no opportunities for employment elsewhere within the economy, the populations of these agricultural economies are forced to engage in basic agricultural production in a mixed subsistence/cash farming system. The industrialization efforts by governments in which food processing plants with little or no backward or forward linkages with the rest of the economy aggravated the unemployment situation and created even greater problems for the agricultural sector.

Table 8. PROPOSED CONTRIBUTION OF FOOD GROUPS TO TOTAL ENERGY AND PROTEIN IN THE DIET AND ESTIMATED QUANTITIES PER PERSON PER ANNUM

	% contribution to dietary Energy	Energy (kcal.)	Food equivalent	Protein (g)	Iron (mg)	lb. per person/annum
Staples:						
Cereals	30	810	Rice	16.3	6.3	176.6
Starchy roots, fruits & tubers	15	405	Sweet potato	4.5	3.5	336.0
Sugar	15	405	Brown sugar	0.0	3.7	88.0
Legumes	10	270	Pigeon peas	15.4	4.0	64.5
Vegetables	2	54	Pumpkin	1.1	0.9	278.8
Foods from animals	14	378	Chicken	40.5	3.3	265.3
Fruits	4	108	Ripe bananas	1.3	0.7	140.0
Oils	10	270	Oil	0.0	0.0	24.6
Total	100	2700		79.1	22.4	–

N.B. The energy values are calculated using specified % contributions of various food groups based on past consumption patterns in the Region, with appropriate modifications utilising the 'multimix' principle (see Table 3). The protein and iron values are those associated with that level of energy from the designated foods called 'food equivalents'.

Source: CFNI, *Recommended Dietary Allowances for the Caribbean* (1976).

As indicated earlier, foreign exchange earnings from raw material exports could increase tremendously through further processing and changes in marketing strategy. The related employment generating benefits have also been alluded to. Unless the sector is transformed to give a strong emphasis to an industrialized component, the foreign exchange earnings will remain minimal.

In the area of food production, the sector has failed to generate food surpluses so distributed as to ensure that every segment of the population receives their basic nutrient requirement for dietary well-being. Instead, the agricultural economies of the Caribbean remain heavily dependent on food imports. Despite the fact that colonial agricultural policy laid the foundations for this dependence, the agricultural policies of self-governing and independent governments in the post-colonial era have not changed significantly the dominant institutional constraints that block the transformation of the development process from external stagnation to internal propulsion.

The supply of raw materials as well as markets for agricultural inputs are clearly in evidence. The disturbing feature is that the agricultural inputs originate principally from external sources and the raw materials are destined for processing in foreign countries. Leakages and minimal gains in foreign exchange result in negligible development benefits.

The challenges of the food sector, therefore, can be summarised as follows:

(1) the generation of an adequate supply of a wide variety of foods to meet most of the nutritional requirements of all segments of the population;
(2) the transformation of the production/distribution pattern to ensure (*a*) and to create an industrialized food sector;
(3) the generation of foreign exchange consistent with development needs;
(4) the maintenance of a level of employment consistent with increasing productivity within the sector; and
(5) the reorganization of the rural setting to ensure the economic viability of the food sector and the continuity in food supplies.

The mechanics for these challenges require in-depth analysis of the various factors which now interact to determine the current situation. We devote the rest of our paper primarily to the first challenge above.

The realism of self-sufficiency. With the exception of sugar, there are production shortfalls in all the basic food groups, ranging from a

Table 9. SELF-SUFFICIENCY LEVELS ADJUSTED TO CONSUMPTION LEVELS
PROPOSED IN TABLE 8 (%)

	Barbados 1971	Guyana 1970	Jamaica 1972	Trinidad & Tobago 1970	St Lucia 1970	Weighted average
Staples:						
Cereals	4	206	5	14	0	42
Starchy fruits, roots and tubers	51	31	131	12	183	82
Sugar	964	552	74	534	0	322
Legumes, nuts and seeds	19	9	36	26	4	27
Vegetables	19	19	17	18	3	17
Foods from animals	44	41	71	31	36	49
Fruits	3	27	67	33	135	50
Oils and fats	68	52	70	60	107	66

level of just 17% self-sufficiency in legumes to 82% in starchy fruits, roots and tubers (Table 9). In this latter group, substantial extra-regional export quantities of bananas are included. The need for foreign exchange via food exports for development purposes thus lowers the levels of self-sufficiency that are actually achievable.

It has already been noted previously that food production per head of population in the two most populous Caribbean countries, Jamaica and Trinidad and Tobago, declined during the 1970s — minus 1.7% per annum for Jamaica and 1.7% per annum for Trinidad and Tobago during 1970–6. The levels of self-sufficiency estimated from food balance sheets for the early 1970s could be assumed to approximate current levels. The desire to achieve greater self-sufficiency in the 1980s and '90s requires well-planned food production programmes supported by finance and approximate changes in the institutional infrastructure to allow for successful implementation of the programmes. With appropriate incentives, Caribbean agricultural economies should be able to halt the decline in productivity per head of population in food production and achieve approximately 1–1.25% increase during the '80s and '90s. At these rates, the levels of self-sufficiency that could be achieved by 1990 and 2000 are shown in Table 10. It is expected that sugar and bananas will remain export commodities. When export bananas are excluded from the group "starchy fruits and tubers". Table 10 shows that the region will experience shortfalls in the levels of self-sufficiency in all food groups even by the year 2000; legumes, vegetables and cereals in that order show the worst shortfalls. Achieving greater levels of self-sufficiency is possible, but these are highly improbable, given past trends.

Table 10. ESTIMATED LEVELS OF SELF-SUFFICIENCY
ACHIEVABLE BY 1990 AND 2000 IN THE CARIBBEAN
REGION (%)

	Current	1990	2000
Staples:			
Cereals	42	45–46	50–52
Starchy fruits, roots and tubers	82	89–90	97–101
Legumes	17	18–19	20–21
Vegetables	27	29–30	32–33
Foods from animals	49	53–54	59–61
Fruits	50	54–55	59–61
Oils and fats	66	71–73	78–81

Even if these levels of self-sufficiency in food supplies are achieved, there still remains the question of self-sufficiency with respect to the levels of production inputs. Livestock production, particularly poultry and pigs, depends heavily on the importation of feedstuffs, and these inputs contribute significantly to the import dependence in food supply and represent another problem area that must be addressed. Recent developments in Trinidad and Tobago in fertiliser production and the use of sugar-cane pulp in feeding ruminants are steps in the right direction but much needs to be done.

We have attempted above to describe the food and nutrition problems and their causes in the English-speaking Caribbean region, using data from selected countries. Problems of undernutrition, overnutrition, anaemia and possible vitamin and mineral imbalances have been discussed. Distribution of the available food supply and the high import dependence of Caribbean countries were highlighted as crucial problems. A simple model based on the 'multimix' principle was proposed for the incorporation of nutritional consideration in food production programmes on a regional basis. The poor performance of agricultural economies in the area of food production indicates that the chances of an increase in self-sufficiency by the year 2000 are slim unless more intensive efforts are made by governments and their institutions, particularly in the areas of legumes, vegetables, cereals and agricultural inputs.

REFERENCES

Bruce, C., *et al., A Model for the Development and Implementation of the Caribbean Food and Nutrition Plan*. CFNI, Kingston, 1979 (*CFNI-J-28–79*).

Campbell, V.C., et al., "The Vegan Syndrome in Jamaica," presented at 22nd Scientific Meeting, Caribbean Medical Research Council, Belize, 1977, p. 5.

Caribbean Food and Nutrition Institute, *Household Food Consumption Survey of Trinidad and Tobago*. CFNI, Kingston, 1970.

——, *Recommended Dietary Allowances for the Caribbean*. CFNI, Kingston, 1976.

——, *The Caribbean Food and Nutrition Plan — an economic framework*. Prepared for the Caribbean Community Secretariat. CFNI, Kingston, 1978 (*CFNI-J-32–78*).

CARICOM, *CARICOM Feeds Itself. A regional food and nutrition strategy; A strategy for the 80s*. CARICOM Secretariat, Georgetown, Guyana, 1980.

Dallman, P.R., *et al.* "Haemoglobin Concentrations in White, Black and Oriental Children. Is there a need for separate criteria in screening for anaemia?", *Am. J. Clin. Nut.*, vol. 31, 1978, p. 377.

FAO, *Provisional Food Balance Sheets*. FAO, Rome, 1977, vol. VII.

Government of Saint Lucia and Caribbean Food and Nutrition Institute, *The National Food and Nutrition Survey of Saint Lucia*. CFNI, Kingston, 1976.

Gurney, J.M., "Available Data on the State of Food and Nutrition of the Peoples of the Commonwealth Caribbean", *Cajanus*, 8(3) (1975), 150.

Marx, Herbert L. (ed.), *The World Food Crisis*. H.W. Wilson, New York, 1975.
Marei, Sayed Ahmed, *The World Food Crisis*. Harlow: Longman, 1978.
McIntosh, C.E., and P.O. Osuji, "Economic Aspects of Food Production in Grenada", *Grenada's Independence, Myth or Reality*? ISER, 1975.
PAHO, *Health For All by the Year 2000 — Strategies*. PAHO, Washington, 1980, pp. 25 and 30 (*RA427.P.32*).
——, The National Food and Nutrition Survey of Barbados. PAHO Scientific Publications, 237, 1972.
——, The National Food and Nutrition Survey of Guyana. PAHO Scientific Publications, 323, 1976.
Regis, V., "An Economic Assessment of an Alternative Marketing Strategy for Grenada Nutmegs". Unpubl. M.Sc. thesis, Dept. of Agricultural Economics and Farm Management, Un. of the West Indies, St Augustine, 1975.
Scrimshaw, N.S., and R. Lockwood, "Interpretation of Data on Human Food Availability and Nutrient Consumption", *Food and Nutrition Bulletin* 2(1), 1980, pp. 29-37.
Sinha, D.P., *Overnutrition and Related Diseases (diabetes and cardiovascular diseases), a Major Health Problem in the English-speaking Caribbean*. CFNI, Kingston, 1980. (*CFNI-J-71-80*).
World Health Organization, *Nutritional Anaemia: Report of a WHO Scientific Group*. WHO, Geneva. Technical Report Series no. 405, 1968.
——, *Nutritional Anaemia: Report of a WHO Group of Experts*. WHO, Geneva. Technical Report Series no. 503, 1972.
Weir, C., *Food Production and Availability in Grenada*. CFNI, Trinidad, 1979 (*CFNI-T-72-79*).
——, *Food Production and Availability in Montserrat, with some suggested programmes for improving the food and nutrition situation*. CFNI, Kingston, 1980 (*CFNI-J-18-80*).
Willett, J.W., *The World Food Situation: Problems and Prospects to 1985*. vols. I & II, Oceana Publications, Dobbs Ferry, New York, 1976.

12
POSTSCRIPT: CONCLUSIONS AND POLICY IMPLICATIONS
P.I. Gomes

In the preceding essays, having regard to both the historical and the contemporary context, the hypothesis that the causes of rural poverty are inter-related has been explicitly elaborated. This point of departure in our understanding of the problems of rural under-development should allow readers to grasp practical implications that bear on effective policies aimed at overcoming rural poverty. It follows from this hypothesis that adoption of a mono-causal approach or exclusive consideration of one or other factor, at the expense of others, will be futile as a comprehensive strategy for achieving the objectives of rural development. This awareness underlies what is commonly known as an 'integrated approach' to rural development. Moreover, since the basic human needs of the rural populations and their demand for services are interdependent, the likelihood of responding to those needs by common strategies can help to reinforce the notion that development is not merely an economic issue, but must also include their meaningful satisfaction.

The widely circulated World Bank Publication (1975) has been one of the most influential documents propagating this approach. Indeed, that publication has been recognised virtually as a standard handbook on integrated rural development. In it is the clear statement that 'the objectives of rural development' are understood as extending 'beyond any particular sector', so that these 'encompass improved productivity, increased employment and thus higher incomes for target groups, as well as minimum acceptable levels of food, shelter, education and health'.[1] It is further stated that 'a national program of rural development should include a mix of activities, including projects to raise agricultural output, create new employment, improve health and education, expand communications and improve housing. Such a program might be made up of single-sector or multisectoral projects, with components

---

1. "Summary and Recommendations" in The World Bank, *The Assault on World Poverty: Problems of rural development, education and health*, Baltimore, Johns Hopkins University Press, 1975, pp. 3–15.

232

implemented concurrently or in sequence. The components and phasing must be formulated both to remove constraints and to support those forces prevailing in the target area which are favourable to development' (*ibid.*, p. 4).

Several comments need to be made on the underlying insights and assumptions expressed in that concise summary of an integrated approach to rural development. At the outset it is recognised that rural development must be situated within the context of a national programme. The mix of activities referred to are *economic*, in the sense of aiming at the production of agricultural commodities and creating employment, as well as improving *social services* such as health, housing and education while expanding the *infrastructure* of communications and, obviously, utilities such as water and electricity. Reference to these economic, social and infrastructural needs as part of a mix of activities is certainly a basic requirement for an 'integrated' approach. But in addition to this discussion, there is even more significance and urgency for policy-makers to understand that rural development has to be 'integral' to national development. Hence, in the introduction to this reader we have elaborated on an 'integrated and integral approach' to rural development.

Useful as the World Bank has been in propagating the notion of 'integrated' strategies, there has arisen in the last decade, since the so-called shift in emphasis to the 'rural poor', a growing misconception whereby rural development projects are seen as alternatives to what were conventional 'industrial' development programmes. This partly occurred with the extensive pronouncements by the former World Bank President that development strategies were to be reshaped in ways that emphasise the needs of the largest number of the poor, who live in the rural areas of the developing world. The so-called 'aid schemes' of the developed countries expressed a faddish predilection for programmes targeted primarily on 'the rural poor'.

By the mid-1970s, it was evident that industrial development of Third World societies, premised on import substitution policies, amounted to little more than a facile modernisation of a semi-urban industrial sector.[2] Not only was there economic 'growth without development', but this 'growth' was of an unbalanced and unequal kind, in which rural stagnation was the other side of an urban explosion of slums, crimes and unemployed masses. The inadequacies of

---

2. An interesting critical appraisal of Puerto Rico's development policies is provided by Angel Quintero Rivera, "The Socio-Political Background to the Emergence of 'The Puerto Rican Model' as a Strategy of Development" in S. Craig (ed.), *Contemporary Caribbean: A sociological reader*, vol. 2 (St Augustine, 1982), pp. 9–57.

these policies in dealing with the required structural changes in the dominant control of the resources of underdeveloped societies were used as rationalisations· in concealing the neglect of the agrarian question and the rural sector. As a result, the basis was laid for a 'reshaping' of policy by development agencies favouring rural development, as if unrelated to the issues of structural change in general, and without an integral connection to the wider demands of national development. To be fully conscious of the consequences of these dangers is especially important at the level of national planning.

Forcefully and lucidly, Julius Nyerere reminded the 1979 World Conference on Agrarian Reform and Rural Development of this issue, as follows:

There is now a widespread tendency for any proposal to build a modern factory to be condemned as contrary to the priority needed for rural development. An example of this attitude is that when developing countries ask for external aid to finance a new trunk road, a railway, an airport, or a consultant hospital, they are at present liable to be told that prospective donors want to support rural development, not industrialisation, communication systems or sophisticated medical services. We must keep in mind that the rural economy and society are subsectors of the wider society. National goals of 'balanced and even' development aimed at abolishing domination of one sector, region or class by another constitute the total framework within which rural development should occur.

The essays in this volume fit within this holistic framework of rural development. The goal is ultimately the abolition of economic, social, cultural and psychological domination as these forces are manifested in the rural sector, primarily among small and poor farmers, landless labourers, and the many deprived and disadvantaged households of the Caribbean countryside. Readers will readily acknowledge that the essays move between micro, location-specific studies or issues on the one side, and the macro-historical and structural context on the other, in which a struggle to resist or overcome domination continues to be enacted.

The creativity and resilience of the rural inhabitants, who were part-subsistence, cash-crop cultivators and at the same time wage-labourers of the plantations, were manifested in the institutional innovations they displayed immediately after the abolition of slavery in 1838. Chapter 1 highlighted this intrinsic characteristic of Caribbean rural society. Whether it is the plantocracy of the nineteenth century, or the emergent nationalism of the neo-colonial politicians in the twentieth, as manifested in the manipulation of village councils described in Chapter 9, there is a conscious resistance to domination by those classes and groups which attempt to satisfy their own interests at the expense of the rural poor. In our view it is important that persons studying or designing rural development strategies should recognise this resistance, not as a constraint on change but as a positive force favourable to development. This presupposes acknowledgement that there are conflicting interests among the various social groups involved in the rural sector. It is in this regard that the land question, as the basic resource for productive economic activities, remains of fundamental importance.

Chapters 2 and 3 gave this question explicit attention in connection with Barbados, Martinique and St Lucia. Of course, the land reforms in Cuba after 1959, as discussed in Chapter 8, illustrate the way that attempts at socialist policies have resulted in significant changes. By drawing attention to the way the Cuban reforms were conceived and executed within the framework of a socialist political system, the question of ideological factors, as part of a development strategy, is inevitably raised. It is both self-deceptive and totally irresponsible for scholars to pretend that issues of development can be addressed without reference to ideological considerations. One regrets that it is still common to hear it said that we must "get on" with the questions of agricultural development, which is usually seen as increasing agricultural production and productivity, which is a merely scientific and technical matter, while ideological factors are forgotten.

Whether we are considering priorities or goals, or the forms of social organization by which production will be pursued and goods distributed, the questions of choice, of values and desirable criteria, arise. Thus ideological factors have to be reckoned with. The "sociology of development" literature came to grips with the various conflicting viewpoints on these questions some time ago.[3] As is often the case, those who protest most forcibly in favour of "ideological neutrality" themselves unwittingly support the ideologies by which underdevelopment, as domination and dependence in the Third World, has been justified and maintained. In the view of this writer, no systematic or comprehensive effort to achieve the authentic development of the rural sector will be possible without a process of total transformation of the social relations accompanying the present conditions of rural poverty and exploitation. In this sense, how one views the world and explains the ideas, attitudes and values used to justify the way in which agricultural production is organized, must inevitably inform the strategies by which

---

3. Cf. Gail Omvedt, "Modernisation Theories: The Ideology of Empire" in A.R. Desai (ed.), *Essays on the Modernisation of Underdeveloped Societies*, New York: Humanities Press, 1972.

policy decisions are formulated and executed. This requires recognition of the ideological factors as an element in the forces favouring
or preventing development. This leads us to conclude that the constituent elements of rural underdevelopment form a systemic whole
composed of: the resource base and kinds of activities engaged in for
the production of goods and services; the institutional mechanisms
or forms of social organization within which human interactions
take place in association with productive activities; the group and
class relations by which competing or conflicting economic and
political interests are pursued; and the prevailing values, social
norms, manifest or latent attitudes by which behaviour is guided and
justified.

Within the conceptual categories and the experiences presented
in this volume, readers will see that a comprehensive approach
aimed at overcoming the problems of rural development ought to be
developed with regard to at least the following four kinds of
issues:

1. *Regional Planning.* In addition to national and sector plans,
there ought to be regional plans for groupings of rural communities
based not on administrative criteria but rather in relation to
ecological zones such as water catchment areas, land capability
and/or traditional community boundaries. Implicit to the use of
regions or sub-regions for planning purposes are political considerations for effective decision–making at community levels.

2. *Resource Expansion.* In any effort of comprehensive agricultural planning, the bringing of 'idle' land into productive use must
play a significant part. This is one aspect of *agrarian reform.*
Similarly effective conservation measures can be adopted for better
use of land resources. Various other aspects for the control, use and
allocation of resources will require detailed consideration.

3. *Institutional Adaptations.* All human activities are grounded in
institutions. They operate to satisfy goals of those who control their
functioning. The entire *institutional framework* within which agricultural activities and rural life occur must be *re-examined* and
modified, where necessary, so as to achieve the stated objectives of
development. Whether these institutions function for administrative
or research purposes (Ministries of Agriculture), for the provision of
services (marketing boards etc.) or to pursue the interests of rural
groups (e.g. farmers' associations), critical appraisals are necessary
to determine their effectiveness and how they relate to the goals of
development. Attention will need to be directed at building or reinforcing rural community-based groups and organizations to facilitate control in the interest of the rural communities. Adaptation

and diffusion of improved technologies and services for rural situations will require changes in research policies.[4]

4. *Education and Training.* For this to be meaningful, the above will require wide participation of the rural populations, and such a momentous change entails *education and training* by both *formal and informal* means. The design of education and training programmes for specific objectives must be related to precise needs. Farmer Training Centres and efforts at public education on the importance of land reform, for instance, might be beneficially complemented by the training and deployment of cadres at para-professional levels and based in rural communities. Outside of the formal educational curricula, there is still urgent need for growth in awareness of development involving economic as well as non-economic factors.

In the light of this discussion, it seems reasonable to argue that the following five propositions underlie a basic orientation to "integrated and integral" rural development:

1. The causes of rural poverty in the Caribbean are rooted in the colonial socio-economic systems which have been perpetuated by current modernisation.
2. Any system of social relations can be analysed into its constituent elements. In such an analysis a distinction can be made between *structural factors*, which interact to produce a given outcome at a macro-level, and *location-specific factors* which are of peculiar importance at micro-level.
3. Rural development is an integral aspect of the national development of the people in a society.
4. Integrated rural development implies that the structural causes of rural underdevelopment are interrelated. It also implies that the subjects of rural development are not merely 'elements' of a labour force who may be farmers, labourers or fishermen, but they are living human beings with a wide spectrum of needs. The means to fulfil these needs must be integrated or co-ordinated from various sources, whether these be for employment, education, nutrition, health or recreation. To satisfy these in both material and non-material terms comprises the goals of development.
5. Optimum social and economic development cannot be achieved without securing the active participation of those persons whose needs are to be satisfied as the successful outcome of rural develop-

4. Cf. N. Girvan (ed.), "Essays on Science and Technology Policy in the Caribbean", *Soc. & Econ. Studies*, March 1979.

ment projects. Such participation not only acknowledges the dignity of the human being but is essential to genuine democracy.

We readily acknowledge that success stories manifesting a tangible expression of these propositions are rarely found. Perhaps in the Caribbean, the Castle Bruce Co-operative experiment in Dominica was a glimmer of what may have been possible.[5] Certainly Cuba, in the first decade after the 1959 Revolution, made rapid strides toward establishing the structural prerequisites for such authentic development.[6] But the struggle to make an overall vision into a permanent social reality is one that has to be waged continually. There is no doubt that more refined and rigorous formulations will be needed to enhance the awareness of development and underdevelopment as two sides of the same coin of domination and dependence. It is hoped that this volume will help to guide better-informed policies for the attainment of social transformations in the Caribbean countryside.

5. Cf. G. Draper and F. Nunes, *Notes on Organisation and Change*, Mona: I.S.E.R. Working Paper, 1974.
6. E. Boorstein, *The Economic Transformation of Cuba*, New York: Monthly Review Press, 1968.

SELECT BIBLIOGRAPHY

Adamson, A.H., *Sugar Without Slaves: The Political Economy of British Guiana 1838-1904*, New Haven, Conn., 1972.
Ambursley, F. and R. Cohen, *Crisis in the Caribbean*, New York, 1983.
Beachey, R.W., *The British West Indies Sugar Industry in the Late Nineteenth Century*, Oxford, 1957.
Beckford, G., *Persistent Poverty: Underdevelopment in Plantation Economies of the Third World*, New York, 1972.
Bengtsson, B., *Rural Development Research and Agricultural Innovations*, Uppsala, 1983.
Best L.A., "Outlines of a Model of Pure Plantation Economy" in *Selected Papers from the Third West Indian Agricultural Economics Conference*, Mona, Jamaica, 1968.
Buttel, F.H., *The Rural Sociology of the Advanced Industrial Societies*, Montclair, NJ, 1979.
Campbell, Peter, *Commercial Hall*, Bridgetown, 1969.
Casimir, Jean, *La Cultura Oprimida*, Mexico, 1980.
Clarke, E., *My Mother Who Fathered Me*, London (1957), 1972.
Craig, S., *The Contemporary Caribbean: A Sociological Reader*, vols I and II, Port of Spain, 1981.
Crusol, J., "La Martinique, Economie de Plantation" in *Les Cahiers de Cerag*, Fort-de-France, 1972.

De Croze, F., *La Martinique: Catastrophe de Saint-Pierre*, Limoges, 1903.
Durant-Gonzalez, V., "Role and Status of Rural Jamaican Women: Higglering and Mothering", unpubl. Ph.D. thesis, University of California, Berkeley, 1976.
Galli, R.E., *The Political Economy of Rural Development: Peasants International Capital and the State*, Albany, NY, 1981.
George, S., *How the Other Half Dies*, Middlesex, (1976) 1980.
Griffin, Keith B., *Land Concentration and Rural Poverty*, New York, 1976.
Harrison, P.D. and B.L. Turner, *Pre-Hispanic Maya Agriculture*, Albuquerque, NM, 1978.
International Labour Organisation, *Poverty and Landlessness in Rural Asia*, Geneva, 1977.
Katzim, M.F., "The Business of Higglering in Jamaica", *Soc. and Econ. Studies*, vol. 9, no. 3, 1960, pp. 297–331.
Kerr, M., *Personality and Conflict in Jamaica*, London, 1963.
Kovats, E., "Une Minorité Dominante: Les Blancs Créoles de La Martinique", unpubl. Ph.D. thesis, University of Paris, 1969.
Leyburn, J.G., *The Haitian People*, New Haven (1941), 1966.
Leiris, M., *Contracts de Civilisations en Martinique et en Guadeloupe*, Paris, 1975.
Mintz, S., *Caribbean Transformations*, Chicago, 1974.
Newby, H., *International Perspectives in Rural Sociology*, London, 1978.
Pares, R., "Merchants and Planters", *Econ. Hist. Rev.*, 1960.
Revert, E., *La Martinique: Etude de Géographie Humaine*, Paris, 1949.
Riley, J.J., *Land, Water and Man as Determinants in Small Farm Production Systems*, Rockefeller Foundation, New York, 1980.
Sheppard, J., *The Redlegs of Barbados*, New York, 1977.
Smith, M.G., *The Plural Society in the British West Indies*, Berkeley, 1965.
Trollope, A., *The West Indies and the Spanish Main*, London, 1859.
Whyte, William F., and G. Alberti, *Power, Politics and Progress: Social Change in Rural Peru*, Amsterdam, 1976.
—— and D. Boynton, *Higher-Yielding Human Systems of Agriculture*, Ithaca, NY, 1983.
Zandstra, H., K. Swanberg, C. Zulberti and B. Nestel, *Caqueza: Living Rural Development*, Ottawa, 1983.
Zuvekas, C., *A Profile of Small Farmers in the Caribbean Region*, Working Document, no. 2, USDA, Washington, D.C., 1978.

NOTES ON THE CONTRIBUTORS

Yvonne Acosta teaches Sociology in the Faculty of Social Sciences at the University of the West Indies, St Augustine. Formerly a Research Associate with the Caribbean Office of the United Nations Economic Commission for Latin America (UNECLA), she has conducted field research on the social history of rural communities in St Lucia and Dominica.

Jean Casimir, Senior Social Affairs Officer with the United Nations Economic Commission for Latin America (UNECLA) based in Port of Spain, Trinidad and Tobago, has published *De la Sociologia Regional a la Acción Política* (Unam, Mexico, 1978) based on field research in North-East Brazil. His widely-known *La Cultura Oprimida* (Mexico, 1980) is a study of Haiti's historical experience. He is currently completing monographs on social structural changes in Dominica and St Lucia.

Susan Craig is Senior Lecturer in Sociology at the University of the West Indies, St Augustine. As a specialist in Caribbean society and culture, she has written extensively on race and class in Caribbean social history, and has recently edited a two-volume compendium on *The Contemporary Caribbean* (1980).

Victoria Durant-Gonzalez is Associate Professor of Anthropology in the Division of Social Sciences at the Georgia Institute of Technology, USA. Her anthropological research has been concentrated on the roles of rural women in both the formal and informal sectors of underdeveloped economies.

P.I. Gomes teaches Rural Sociology in the Faculty of Agriculture at the University of the West Indies, St Augustine. He has conducted research on the socio-economic and cultural aspects of small farmers in the Caribbean and has served as a consultant to UNESCO and the FAO on farmer-training programmes in pursuit of integrated rural development.

T.H. Henderson is Professor of Agricultural Extension in the University of the West Indies, St Augustine. With wide experience throughout the Caribbean, Professor Henderson has designed and conducted training courses for extension field workers over the last two decades. He is presently Director of the Caribbean Agricultural

Extension Project which includes Belize and seven member-territories of the Organization of Eastern Caribbean States (OECS).

Patricia Manchew is a public health nutritionist based in Trinidad and Tobago with the Caribbean Food and Nutrition Institute (CFNI). By regular and extensive travel in the Caribbean region, notably to remote rural communities, she has directed comprehensive surveys on the food and nutritional status of Caribbean populations and has conducted training courses for nutrition and allied health workers.

Woodville K. Marshall, Professor of History at the University of the West Indies, Cave Hill, Barbados, has for the last 25 years been studying aspects of post-slavery social adjustments in the Commonwealth Caribbean. He has published several articles, and edited *The Colthurst Journal* (KTO Press, 1978). He is currently completing research on the establishment of post-slavery villages in Barbados.

Curtis McIntosh, Agricultural Economist with the Pan American Health Organisation, is attached to the Caribbean Food and Nutrition Institute. Dr McIntosh was formerly a Research Fellow in Agricultural Marketing at the University of the West Indies, St Augustine. He has conducted extensive research on food and nutrition surveillance and assisted in the development of food and nutrition policies for Dominica, Antigua and Barbuda, Grenada, St Vincent and the Grenadines, Montserrat and St Kitts-Nevis. He has published several scientific papers on food marketing and human nutrition.

Michael Quinn Patton is a former Director of the Institute for Social Research at the University of Minnesota, Minneapolis, and is currently a Co-ordinator in the International Agricultural Programmes of that University. As a specialist in evaluation methodologies and policy analysis techniques, Dr Patton is well known for his books, *Utilization-Focused Evaluation* (Sage, 1978), *Qualitative Evaluation Methods* (Sage, 1980), *Creative Evaluation* (Sage, 1981) and *Practical Evaluation* (Sage, 1982).

Carlisle Pemberton teaches Agricultural Economics in the Faculty of Agriculture at the University of the West Indies, St Augustine. He has a special interest in survey research methods and the application of linear programming models in the study of farmers' decision-making. Dr Pemberton is currently President of the Caribbean Agro-Economic Society.

242   *Notes on the Contributors*

Brian Pollitt, lecturer at the Institute of Latin American Studies at the University of Glasgow, Scotland, specialises in the area of the Cuban agrarian economy. He conducted fieldwork in rural Cuba in 1963–8 and revisited the island periodically in 1978–83. He has been a Visiting Professor at universities in the United States, Chile and Australia, and is at present editing the papers of the late Maurice Dobb of Cambridge.

Michael J. Sleeman has specialised in Contemporary Sociological Theory and Caribbean Area Studies. He has conducted fieldwork in the Caribbean studying white creole planter/mercantile élites in Barbados and Martinique. In addition to extensive teaching experience in higher education, Dr Sleeman has worked as a research officer on race relations in Britain. He is an editorial adviser to Longmans Caribbean, and is currently teaching in North West Jamaica.

Robert Thompson is an Ottawa-based researcher who has acted as a consultant, resource and staff person for Canadian non-governmental aid agencies and the Canadian government on development projects and management. He was the Eastern Caribbean field representative of CUSO from 1976 to 1979.

INDEX

ackee, 104
agrarian proletariat, xvi, 22, 36, 42, 51, 53, 70, 160, 162–3
Agricultural Aids Act, 17
agricultural extension: 194–211;CAEP, 204–11; Imperial Department and, 195–6; various models, 197–202
Amin, Samir, 123, 125–7
Antigua, 4, 8, 17
Appley, M.H., 87
Armstrong, Eileen, 175
arrowroot, 7, 11
Austin & Co., Gardiner, 19

bananas, 7, 33, 35, 42, 47–51, 53, 142, 145, 220; see also Dominica, St Lucia
Barbados: 4, 15–23, 214; Agricultural Aids Act, 17; Chancery Court System, 17, 18, 28; Encumbered Estates Act, 17; House of Assembly, 32; Mutual Life Assurance Society (BMLA), 18, 28, 30; new merchandise class, 21; Savings Bank, 18; Shipping and Trading Co., 22; Sugar Industry Agricultural Bank, 28; West India Bank of, 18; white oligarchy, 23
Beckford, G, xiv, 39; Land Reform Commission, 44, 58
beet sugar, 16, 22; see also sugar industry
Béké, Grand, 24, 26–8, 29, 30, 32; ——, Moyen, 31, 33; see also Martinique
Belle Garden, 185, 186, 187, 189
Berekua Farmers' Cooperative, 73
Berricoa, 62, 65, 67, 68; see also Dominica
Best, L., viii, 76
Booker-McConnell, 16
bourgeois de couleur, 30
Braithwaite, L., viii, 87, 100, 101
breadfruit, 105, 111
Bryden, Arthur Sydney, 20; see also Barbados

Cail, Jean-Francois, 26
Cameron & Co., A., 19
Caribbean Agricultural Extension Project (CAEP), 204–11
Caribbean Agro-Economic Society, 60
Caribbean Rural Development Advisory

and Training Service Project (CARDATS), 199
Cavan, Michael, 19
centres agricoles, 27–8; see also sugar industry
Challenor Ltd., R. & G., 21, 22
children, see pickney
class consolidation: 28–30; and "caste" solidarity, 31; alliances, 131–2; class and food, 149
cocoa, 36, 42, 68, 77, 79–81, 83–5, 93, 131, 142, 216, 270
coconut, 63, 64, 77, 82, 83
coffee, 5, 11, 82, 83
Commission Merchants' Association, 22, 30
commissionaires, 23, 24, 25
Commonwealth Caribbean, viii, xiv
community development, 173, 190
community property system, 39, 40
Conseil General, 32
consignee system, 17, 24
cooperatives, 5, 12, 73, 173, 175
cooperative farming, 162
Coronation Market, 106; see also higglering
Coterie of Social Workers, 165, 168
Crédit Colonial, 25, 27
Crédit Foncier Colonial, 27, 29
Cuba: 154–72, 235; First Agrarian Reform Law, 154; labour shortages, 162, 167; mechanization, 167–8; private ownership, 166–72; Second Agrarian Reform Law, 161, 166–7; Soviet-Cuban trade, 166; sugar production, 154, 161
cultural dualism, 39
Cumper, G., 44

Da Costa & Co. Ltd., 20
Dellimore, J., 136–7
Demas, W.G., 76, 86, 101
Dominica: 9, 17, 60–75; family lands, 67; Geneva Estate, 62–9; Land Management Authority, 63, 65, 74; unemployment, 68; Village Improvement Committee, 71

emancipation, 34, 36
ethnic conflict, 176, 179, 182
Eustache, Eugène, 25

243

Paget, H., 2, 4
panchayati, 187
Pares,R., 18, 239
patois, 39–40
patronage, xvii, 31
peasantry: 1, 2, 8, 35, 76, 131: as counter-plantation system, 35, 39, 59; as innovators, 10–12, 39–40; government policy towards, 12–14; growth of, 3–10; motivational structure of, 76, 88, 100; off-farm employment, 88–9, 91, 97, 99
People's National Movement (PNM), 174, 178
pickney, 109, 114, 115
Pioneer Industries Act, 178
Piven, F.F., 191, 192
plantation, 2, 4, 34, 38, 41, 76; capitalism, viii, xiii, 33
Plantations-in-Aid Act, 28
plantocracy, viii, 15, 23, 31, 33, 34–5, 41–2, 51, 131–3, 197, 234
population clusters, ix
Puerto Rican model, 178; *see also* Quintero Rivera
Purseglove, J.W., 195

Quintero Rivera, A., 233

Rastafarianism, xvii
Redfield, R., 1
redlegs, 30, 31, 32
Regis, V., 223
resource allocation, xi, 43, 126, 146, 167, 236

Riviere, W.E., 60
Rockefeller, David, 180
rural development: x, xi, xii; integrated and integral, vii, x, xix; principal objective of, xii, xiii
rural-urban imbalance, x, xiii, xv, 75; — drift, x, 100–1
rural youth, 72–4

St Kitts, 4, 8, 17
St Lucia: 6, 34–59, 215, 219; Banana Growers Association, 43, 48; Community Property System, 39; Malone Commission, 45–7; Worker's Cooperative Union, 57
St Vincent, 6, 17, 20, 202
Self-Anchoring Scale Method, 89–91, 94–5

self-reliant development, 123, 125–8, 131, 135
share croppers, 37, 38; *see also métayage*
Shurland, Olga, 175
Simey, T., 177, 192
Sinha, D.P., 214
slave emancipation, 34; *see also* plantation
Smith, M.G., x
Special Works Programme, 183–4, 186, 189
squatting, 36–7, 65
State Lands farms, 84
status boundary maintenance, 30–2
Studley Park, 79
sugar industry: 4, 5, 13, 17, 35, 37, 129, 195; *centres agricoles,* 27–8; "central" factories of, 15, 19, 25, 27, 29; Commission of Lord Olivier, 42–3; economic practices of, 44–7; European beet, 16; in French Antilles, 26; licence for, 5; outmoded technology, 21; value of exports from, 21

task work, 53–7
Tate and Lyle, 16
technological creativity, 127–9
Tennessee Valley Land Authority, 198
Texaco, 180
Thomas, C.Y., viii, 123–9
Thompson, A.A., 181
tobacco, 161, 166, 171
Tobago: 6, 77–100; coconuts, 82, 87; Encumbered Estates Act, 81; Hurricane Flora, 84; sugar production, 79–80
tourism, 59, 136, 138
transnational corporations, xiv, 44, 48, 124, 128, 135, 145, 180
Trinidad and Tobago: 173–93, 222; Achong, Tito, 176; Better Village Programme, 180–1; Chase Manhattan Bank, 180; Coterie of Social Workers, 174, 177; ethnic relations, 187–9; Gomes, Albert, 176–7; Kumar, Ranjit, 176; Maharaj, Chanka, 176; Meet the People Tour, 178–80; Ottley, Carlton, 177; Pioneer Industries Act, 178; Second Five Year Plan, 178, 180; Solomon, Patrick, 176; Special Works Programme, 183–4, 186, 189
Trollope, Anthony, 18